YVES CONGAR

OUTSTANDING CHRISTIAN THINKERS

Series Editor: Brian Davies OP

The series offers a range of authoritative paperback studies on people who have made an outstanding contribution to Christian thought and understanding. The series will range across the full spectrum of Christian thought to include Catholic and Protestant thinkers, to cover East and West, historical and contemporary figures. By and large, each volume will focus on a single 'thinker', but occasionally the subject may be a movement or a school of thought.

Brian Davies OP, the Series Editor, is Vice-Regent of Studies at Blackfriars, Oxford, where he also teaches philosophy. He is a member of the Theology Faculty of the University of Oxford and tutor in theology at St Benet's Hall, Oxford. He has lectured regularly at the University of Bristol, Fordham University, New York, and the Beda College, Rome. He is Reviews Editor of *New Blackfriars*. His previous publications include: *An Introduction to the Philosophy of Religion* (OUP, 1982); *Thinking about God* (Geoffrey Chapman, 1982); and he was editor of *Language, Meaning and God* (Geoffrey Chapman, 1987).

Planned titles in the series include:

Anselm
G. R. Evans

Yves Congar
Aidan Nichols OP

Denys the Areopagite
Andrew Louth

The Apostolic Fathers
Simon Tugwell OP

Reinhold Niebuhr
Kenneth Durkin

Karl Rahner
William Dych SJ

Bede
Benedicta Ward

John Calvin
John Platt

Jonathan Edwards
John E. Smith

Aquinas
Brian Davies OP

George Berkeley
David Berman

Teresa of Avila
Rowan Williams

YVES CONGAR

Aidan Nichols OP

GEOFFREY
CHAPMAN

MOREHOUSE-BARLOW
78 DANBURY ROAD, WILTON, CT 06897

Published throughout the world except North America by
Geoffrey Chapman
An imprint of Cassell Publishers Limited
Artillery House, Artillery Row, London SW1P 1RT

Published in North America by
Morehouse-Barlow
78 Danbury Road, Wilton, CT 06897

First published 1989

ISBN 0 – 225 – 66569 – 7 (Geoffrey Chapman: paperback)
0 – 225 – 66537 – 9 (Geoffrey Chapman: hardback)
0 – 8192 – 1487 – 6 (Morehouse-Barlow: paperback)
0 – 8192 – 1488 – 4 (Morehouse-Barlow: hardback)

British Library Cataloguing in Publication Data
Nichols, Aidan
Yves Congar.—(Outstanding christian thinkers)
1. Theology. Congar, Yves
I. Title II. Series
209′.2′4

Typeset by Colset Private Limited, Singapore
Printed and bound in Great Britain by
Biddles Ltd., Guildford

Contents

To the brethren of the
Order of Preachers

Editorial foreword

St Anselm of Canterbury once described himself as someone with faith seeking understanding. In words addressed to God he says, 'I long to understand in some degree thy truth, which my heart believes and loves. For I do not seek to understand that I may believe, but I believe in order to understand.'

And this is what Christians have always inevitably said, either explicitly or implicitly. Christianity rests on faith, but it also has content. It teaches and proclaims a distinctive and challenging view of reality. It naturally encourages reflection. It is something to think about; something about which one might even have second thoughts.

But what have the greatest Christian thinkers said? And is it worth saying? Does it engage with modern problems? Does it provide us with a vision to live by? Does it make sense? Can it be preached? Is it believable?

This series originates with questions like these in mind. Written by experts, it aims to provide clear, authoritative and critical accounts of outstanding Christian thinkers from New Testament times to the present. It will range across the full spectrum of Christian thought to include Catholic and Protestant thinkers, thinkers from East and West, thinkers ancient, mediaeval and modern.

The series draws on the best scholarship currently available, so it will interest all with a professional concern for the history of Christian ideas. But contributors will also be writing for general readers who have little or no previous knowledge of the subjects to be dealt with. Volumes to appear should therefore prove helpful at a popular as well as an academic level. For the most part they will be devoted to a single thinker, but occasionally the subject will be a movement or a school of thought.

The subject of the present volume, Yves Congar, is one of the leading theologians of the present century, with a particularly strong sense of history and tradition. His influence was particularly notable at the Second Vatican Council, which he attended as a theological adviser. The Council's documents reflect many of his preoccupations and ideas. His writing output has been translated into many languages throughout the world. In writing as he does about Congar, Aidan Nichols provides the first general survey of his work since 1967.

Brian Davies OP

Preface

A Dominican cannot but be grateful for the inspiration of Père Yves Congar. His love of the divine truth, and of its vehicles, shines out from his writing. His activity as a member of the Order of Preachers has largely taken the form of theological scholarship, chiefly historical in bent. Yet the palpable aim of that scholarship is itself evangelical and pastoral: to encourage others to respond as he does to the Church, to the Scriptures, to Tradition; to the liturgy, the Fathers and the saints. As this book hopes to show, Congar is an 'outstanding Christian thinker' in that he has let the voices of the Christian past think aloud in him, and in so doing, with mind renewed, has found a word to say to the Church of the present.[1]

When Congar visited Oxford and Cambridge in 1974, a visit on which he already showed signs of that paraplegia which would later confine his body, but not his spirit, to a chair, he spoke on two subjects rarely brought together in the title, or the content, of a single lecture, 'St Thomas and the spirit of ecumenism'.[2] Though I understood that this was unusual and even *piquant*, I was too young in the Order or theology to see its further significance. Perhaps only in the pontificate of John Paul II did this emblematic statement of Congar's characteristic thinking take on its peculiar pertinence to the felt needs of the Church's today and tomorrow. The consolidation of the Catholic tradition combined with ecumenical generosity 'that all may be one': this twofold task calls for that marriage of affirmation and nuance which is such a feature of Congar's work. In preparing this text I am greatly indebted to my confrère Father

Brian Davies, who has dealt both patiently and efficiently with the deficiencies of an unlovely typescript.

I dedicate this modest study to our fellow Dominicans in the hope that they will be, as were the best among their spiritual ancestors, at once stalwart guardians of Christian doctrine, and imaginative prophets of Christian life.

Aidan Nichols OP
Pontifical University of St Thomas, Rome
Solemnity of the Annunciation of our Lord, 1988

Notes

1 Cf. my attempt to illuminate this concept of 'originality' in 'T.S. Eliot and Yves Congar on the nature of tradition', *Angelicum* 61 (1984), pp. 473–85.

2 Published in *New Blackfriars* 55.648 (May 1974), pp. 196–208.

Bibliography

PRIMARY LITERATURE

Books

Chrétiens désunis (Paris, 1937); Eng. trans.: *Divided Christendom* (London, 1939)

Esquisses du Mystère de l'Eglise (Paris, 1941; 2nd ed. 1953); *The Mystery of the Church* (London, 1960)

Vraie et fausse réforme dans l'Eglise (Paris, 1950; rev. ed. 1969)

Le Christ, Marie et l'Eglise (Paris, 1952); *Christ, Our Lady and the Church* (London, 1957)

Jalons pour une théologie du laïcat (Paris, 1953; rev. ed. 1964); *Lay People in the Church* (London, 1957; rev. ed. London, 1965, repr. London/Westminster, MD, 1985)

Le Mystère du Temple (Paris, 1958; 2nd ed. 1963); *The Mystery of the Temple* (London, 1962)

Vaste monde, ma paroisse (Paris, 1959); *The Wide World my Parish* (London, 1961)

La Tradition et les traditions (Paris, 1960–63); *Tradition and Traditions* (London, 1966)

Les Voies du Dieu vivant (Paris, 1962); *The Revelation of God* (London, 1968) and *Faith and Spiritual Life* (London, 1969)

La Foi et la théologie (Tournai, 1962)

Sacerdoce et laïcat (Paris, 1963); *Priest and Layman* (London, 1967)/*Christians Active in the World* (New York, 1968)

Sainte Eglise (Paris, 1963)

La Tradition et la vie de l'Eglise (Paris, 1963; 2nd ed. 1984); *Tradition and the Life of the Church* (London, 1964)
Pour une Eglise servante et pauvre (Paris, 1963); *Power and Poverty in the Church* (London, 1964)
Chrétiens en dialogue (Paris, 1964); *Dialogue between Christians* (London, 1966)
Jésus-Christ, notre Médiateur, notre Seigneur (Paris, 1965); *Jesus Christ* (London, 1966)
Situation et tâches présentes de la théologie (Paris, 1967)
L'Ecclésiologie du haut Moyen Age (Paris, 1968)
Cette Eglise que j'aime (Paris, 1968); *This Church that I Love* (Densville, NJ, 1969)
L'Eglise. De saint Augustin à l'époque moderne (Paris, 1970)
L'Eglise une, sainte, catholique, apostolique (Paris, 1970)
Ministères et communion ecclésiale (Paris, 1971)
Une Passion: l'unité. Réflexions et souvenirs 1929–1973 (Paris, 1974)
Un peuple messianique. Salut et libération (Paris, 1975)
La Crise dans l'Eglise et Mgr Lefebvre (Paris, 1976); *Challenge to the Church. The Case of Archbishop Lefebvre* (London, 1977)
Eglise catholique et France moderne (Paris, 1978)
Je crois en l'Esprit Saint (Paris, 1979–80); *I Believe in the Holy Spirit* (London/New York, 1983)
Droit ancien et structures ecclésiales (London, 1982)
Esprit de l'homme, Esprit de Dieu (Paris, 1983)
Etudes d'ecclésiologie médiévale (London, 1983)
Martin Luther. Sa vie, sa foi, sa réforme (Paris, 1983)
Diversité et communion (Paris, 1983); *Diversity and Communion* (London, 1984)
Essais oecuméniques (Paris, 1984)
La Parole et le Souffle (Paris, 1984); *The Word and the Spirit* (London/San Francisco, 1986)
Thomas d'Aquin. Sa vision de théologie et de l'Eglise (London, 1984)
Le Concile de Vatican II. Son Eglise: Peuple de Dieu et Corps du Christ (Paris, 1984); two chapters, 'Moving towards a pilgrim Church' and 'A last look at the Council' trans. in A. Stacpoole OSB (ed.), *Vatican II by Those Who Were There* (London, 1986)/ *Vatican II Revisited* (Minneapolis, 1986), pp. 129–52 and 337–58
Appelés à la vie (Paris, 1985); *Called to Life* (Middlegreen, 1987)

Entretiens d'automne (Paris, 1987); *Fifty Years of Catholic Theology* (London, 1988)

Articles

Here an attempt has been made to identify those articles that are both weighty and representative of Congar's thought; so far as possible, they exclude those collected and re-published in book form.

'Une conclusion théologique à l'enquête sur les raisons actuelles de l'incroyance', *La Vie intellectuelle* 37 (1935), pp. 214–49.

'La signification oecuménique de l'oeuvre de Moehler', *Irénikon* 15 (1938), pp. 113–30.

'Schisme', *Dictionnaire de théologie catholique* XIV, cols 1286–1312.

'Théologie', ibid., XV, cols 341–502; revised trans. *A History of Theology* (New York, 1968).

'Le purgatoire' in *Le Mystère de la mort et sa célébration* (= Lex Orandi 12; Paris, 1951), pp. 279–336.

'L'ecclésiologie de saint Bernard. Saint Bernard théologien' in *Analecta Sacri Ordinis Cisterciensis* (1953), pp. 136–90.

'Marie et l'Eglise dans la pensée patristique', *Revue des Sciences philosophiques et théologiques* 38 (1954), pp. 3–38.

'Neuf cents ans après. Notes sur le "Schisme Oriental", 1054–1954' in *L'Eglise et les églises. Neuf siècles de douloureuse séparation entre l'Orient et l'Occident. Etudes et travaux sur l'unité chrétienne offerts à Dom Lambert Beauduin* (Chevetogne, 1954) I, pp. 3–95; *After Nine Hundred Years* (New York, 1959).

'Conscience ecclésiologique en Orient et en Occident du VIe au XIe siècle', *Istina* (April 1959), pp. 187–236.

'The historical development of authority in the Church. Points for Christian reflection' in J. Todd (ed.), *Problems of Authority, An Anglo-French Symposium* (London, 1962), pp. 119–56.

'De la communion des églises à une ecclésiologie de l'Eglise universelle' in *L'Episcopat et l'Eglise universelle* (Paris, 1962), pp. 227–60.

'Les saints Pères, organes privilégiés de la tradition', *Irénikon* 35 (1962), pp. 479–98.

'Jalons d'une réflexion sur le mystère des pauvres' in P. Gauthier (ed.), *Consolez mon Peuple* (Paris, 1965), pp. 305–27.

'Le thème du Dieu créateur et les explications de l'Hexaméron dans la tradition chrétienne' in *L'homme devant Dieu. Mélanges offerts au P. Henri de Lubac* (Paris, 1964) I, pp. 189–222.

'Un témoignage de désaccord entre canonistes et théologiens' in *Etudes d'histoire du droit canonique dédiées à Gabriel le Bras* (Paris, 1965) II, pp. 861–84.

'Notes sur le destin de l'idée de collégialité épiscopale en Occident au Moyen Age (VII–XVI siècles)' in *La Collégialité épiscopale* (Paris, 1965), pp. 99–129.

'Le Christ dans l'économie salutaire et dans nos traités dogmatiques', *Concilium* 11 (1966), pp. 11–26; 'Christ in the economy of salvation and in our dogmatic tracts', *Concilium* (Eng. ed.) 11 (I.2; 1966), pp. 4–15.

'La recherche théologique', *Recherches et Débats* 54 (1966), pp. 89–102.

'Le moment "économique" et le moment "ontologique" dans la *sacra doctrina* (révélation, théologie, somme théologique)' in *Mélanges offerts à M.-D. Chenu* (Paris, 1967), pp. 135–87.

'Théologie de la prière pour l'unité', *Verbum Caro* 82 (1967), pp. 1–13.

'L'idée de sacrements majeurs ou principaux', *Concilium* 31 (1968), pp. 25–34; 'The idea of "major" or "principal" sacraments', *Concilium* (Eng. ed.) 31 (I.4; 1968), pp. 12–17.

'La relation entre culte ou sacrement et prédication de la Parole', *Concilium* 33 (1968), pp. 53–62; 'Sacramental worship and preaching', *Concilium* (Eng. ed.) 33 (III. 4; 1968), pp. 27–33.

'Les laïcs et l'ecclésiologie des *ordines* chez les théologiens des XIe et XIIe siècles' in *I laici nella 'societas christiana' dei secoli XI e XII. Atti della terza settimana internazionale di studio, Mendola, 21–27.8.1965* (Milan, 1968), pp. 83–117.

'Structures et régime de l'Eglise d'après Hincmar de Reims', *Communio* 1 (1968), pp. 5–18.

'The Council as an assembly and the Church as essentially Catholic' in H. Vorgrimler (ed.), *One, Holy, Catholic and Apostolic. Studies on the Nature and Role of the Church in the Modern World* (London, 1968), pp. 44–88.

'Spiritualité oecuménique', *Seminarium* 3 (1968), pp. 476–89.

'Quatre siècles de désunion et d'affrontement. Comment Grecs et Latins se sont appréciés réciproquement au point du vue ecclésiologique', *Istina* 13 (1968), pp. 131–52.

'Autorité et liberté dans l'Eglise' in J. Loew *et al.*, *A Temps et contretemps* (Paris, 1969), pp. 7–39.

'Le Père M.-D. Chenu' in R. Vander Gucht and H. Vorgrimler (eds),

Bilan de la théologie du XXe siècle (Tournai/Paris, 1970) II, pp. 772–90.

'L'histoire de l'Eglise "lieu théologique"', *Concilium* 57 (1970), pp. 75–94; 'Church history as a branch of theology', *Concilium* (Eng. ed.) 57 (VII.6; 1970), pp. 85–96.

'Souci du salut des païens et conscience missionnaire dans le christianisme postapostolique et préconstantinien' in P. Granfield and J.A. Jungmann (eds), *Kyriakon. Festschrift Johannes Quasten* (Münster, 1970), pp. 3–11.

'Pneumatologie et théologie de l'histoire' in *La Théologie de l'histoire. Herméneutique et eschatologie. Colloque Castelli 1971* (Rome, 1971), pp. 61–70.

'De potestate sacerdotali et de Ecclesia ut ecclesiarum communione saeculis VII, VIII et IX', *Communio* 13 (1972), pp. 961–81.

'La réception comme réalité ecclésiologique', *Revue des Sciences philosophiques et théologiques* 56 (1972–3), pp. 369–403.

'Tradition et ouverture' in *Fidélité et ouverture* (Paris, 1972), pp. 55–68.

'Histoire des dogmes et histoire de l' Église', *Seminarium* 25 (1973), pp. 75–88.

'Rudolf Sohm nous interroge encore', *Revue des Sciences philosophiques et théologiques* 57 (1973), pp. 263–94.

'On the *hierarchia veritatum', Orientalia christiana analecta* 195 (1973), pp. 409–20.

'Non-Christian religions and Christianity' in J. Pathrapankal (ed.), *Service and Salvation. The Nagpur Theological Conference on Evangelisation* (Bangalore, 1975), pp. 167–81.

'St Thomas Aquinas and the spirit of ecumenism', *New Blackfriars* 55.648 (1974), pp. 196–208.

'1274–1974. Structures ecclésiales et conciles dans les relations entre Orient et Occident', *Revue des Sciences philosophiques et théologiques* 58 (1974), pp. 355–90.

'Modèle monastique et modèle sacerdotal en Occident, de Grégoire VII (1073–1085) à Innocent III (1198)' in *Mélanges E.-R. Labande, Etudes de civilisation médiévale* (Poitiers, 1975), pp. 153–60.

'Pour une histoire du terme *magisterium*', *Revue des Sciences philosophiques et théologiques* 60 (1976), pp. 85–97.

'Bref historique des formes du "magistère" et de ses relations avec les docteurs', ibid., pp. 99–112.

'Regards sur la théologie française d'aujourd'hui' in *Savoir faire, espérer. Les limites de la raison. Hommage à Mgr H. van Camp* (Brussels, 1976) II, pp. 697–711.

'Le théologien dans l'Eglise d'aujourd'hui', *Les Quatres Fleuves* 12 (1980), pp. 7–27.

'Trials and promises of ecumenism' in *Voices of Unity. Essays in Honour of W. A. Visser't Hooft on the Occasion of his 80th Birthday* (Geneva, 1981), pp. 23–32.

'Intentionnalité de la foi et sacrement. Aperçu de S. Augustin au concile de Trente' in H. J. Auf der Maur *et al.* (eds), *Fides sacramenti, sacramentum fidei. Studies in Honour of Pieter Smulders* (Assen, 1981), pp. 177–91.

'Reflections on being a theologian', *New Blackfriars* 62.736 (1981), pp. 405–9.

'The sacramental value of the Word', *Dominican Ashram* II.3 (1981), pp. 134–42.

'Théologie historique' in *Initiation à la pratique de la théologie. Introduction* (Paris, 1982), pp. 233–62.

'Sur la trilogie Prophète–Roi–Prêtre', *Revue des Sciences philosophiques et théologiques* 67 (1983), pp. 97–116.

'Christ–Eucharistie–Eglise. Cohérence de leurs représentations. Sa validité et ses limites' in R. Stauffer (ed.), *In necessariis unitas. Mélanges J.-L. Leuba* (Paris, 1984), pp. 69–80.

'Le Pape comme patriarche de l'Occident. Approche à une réalité trop négligée', *Istina* 28 (1983), pp. 374–90.

'De Marburg (1529) à Leuenberg (1971). Luthériens et Réformés au temps de l'opposition et sur la voie de I'union', *Istina* 36 (1985), pp. 47–65.

'La place de Jean de Raguse dans l'histoire de l'ecclésiologie' in *Analecta Croatiae Christiana* (1986), pp. 259–90.

'Romanité et catholicité. Histoire de la conjonction changeante de deux dimensions de l'Eglise', *Revue des Sciences philosophiques et théologiques* 71 (1987), pp. 161–90.

Secondary literature

J. M. Connolly, 'Yves Congar. The Church and the churches' in *The Voices of France* (New York, 1961), pp. 98–117.

W. Henn OFMCap, *The Hierarchy of Truths according to Yves Congar OP* (Rome, 1987).

J.-P. Jossua OP, 'L'oeuvre oecuménique du Père Congar', *Etudes* 357 (1982), pp. 543–55.

J.-P. Jossua OP, *Le Père Congar. La théologie au service du peuple de Dieu* (Paris, 1967).

M. J. Le Guillou OP, 'Yves M. J. Congar' in R. Vander Gucht and H. Vorgrimler (eds), *Bilan de la théologie du XXe siècle* (Tournai/Paris, 1970) II, pp. 791–805.

C. MacDonald, *Church and World in the Plan of God. History and Eschatology according to Yves Congar* (Frankfurt/Bern, 1982).

T. I. MacDonald SA, *The Ecclesiology of Yves Congar. Foundational Themes* (Lanham, MD, 1983).

D. Ols OP, 'Diversité et communion. Réflexions à propos d'un ouvrage récent', *Angelicum* 60 (1983), pp. 122–50.

J. Prunières, 'L'Ecclésiologie du Père Congar, oeuvre témoin d'une crise', *Etudes franciscaines* 39 (1966), pp. 253–83.

J. Puyo, *Yves Congar. Une vie pour la vérité* (Paris, 1975).

S. P. Schilling, 'Yves Congar' in *Contemporary Continental Theologians* (London, 1966), pp. 185–205.

A. Stacpoole OSB, 'Early ecumenism, early Yves Congar, 1904–1940', *The Month,* CCIX.1441 (1988), pp. 502–10.

M. Winter, 'Masters in Israel: Yves Congar', *Clergy Review* 55 (1970), pp. 275–88.

A full listing of Congar's works may be found in:

P. Quattrocchi, 'Bibliographie générale du Père Yves Congar' in J.-P. Jossua OP, *Le Père Congar*, op. cit., pp. 213–72;

and for the subsequent period in:

A. Nichols OP, 'An Yves Congar bibliography 1967–1987', *Angelicum* 66 (1989).

Abbreviations

Where English translations are cited, page numbers refer to the translation, not the French original.

ANHY	*After Nine Hundred Years* ('Neuf cents ans après')
CC	*Challenge to the Church. The Case of Archbishop Lefebvre (La Crise dans l'Eglise et Mgr Lefebvre)*
CVII	*Le Concile de Vatican II. Son Eglise: Peuple de Dieu et Corps du Christ*
DBC	*Dialogue between Christians (Chrétiens en dialogue)*
DC	*Divided Christendom (Chrétiens désunis)*
DivComm	*Diversity and Communion (Diversité et communion)*
DS	H. Denzinger, rev. A. Schönmetzer, *Enchiridion Symbolorum*
ECFM	*Eglise catholique et France moderne*
EE	*L'Eglise et les églises. Etudes et travaux sur l'unité chrétienne offerts à Dom Lambert Beauduin*
EOe	*Essais oecuméniques*
ETLS	*Une Ecole de théologie. Le Saulchoir*
FT	*La Foi et la théologie*
FYCT	*Fifty Years of Catholic Theology (Entretiens d'automne)*
HT	*A History of Theology* (rev. trans. of 'Théologie')
IBHS	*I Believe in the Holy Spirit* (*Je crois en l'Esprit Saint*)
LPC	*Lay People in the Church* (*Jalons pour une théologie du laïcat)*

MCE	*Ministères et communion ecclésiale*
ML	*Martin Luther. Sa vie, sa foi, sa réforme*
MT	*The Mystery of the Temple* (*Le Mystère du Temple*)
PG	J.-P. Migne (ed.), *Patrologia Graeca*
PL	J.-P. Migne (ed.), *Patrologia Latina*
RSPhTh	*Revue des Sciences philosophiques et théologiques*
STPT	*Situation et tâches présentes de la théologie*
TCIL	*This Church that I Love* (*Cette Eglise que j'aime*)
TT	*Tradition and Traditions (La Tradition et les traditions)*
TVE²	*La Tradition et la vie de l'Eglise* (2nd ed.)
VFRE	*Vraie et fausse réforme dans l'Eglise*

1

The man and his work

Although this book is a study of Congar's thought, it cannot dispense with some attention to the biography of the human being whose thought this is. After the brief sketch of Congar's life here offered, there follows a survey of his work, which provides a bridge to the detailed exposition of Congar's theological activity found in the succeeding chapters.

A SKETCH OF CONGAR'S LIFE

Yves Congar was born on 13 May 1904 at Sedan in the French Ardennes.[1] His family belonged to the lower bourgeoisie. He is reported as being a self-willed child, who once, when his wishes were frustrated, sat down on the municipal tram-lines. His childhood friends were Jewish and Protestant, an unusual thing for the period of the Third French Republic. Tension between Church and State, which led via the expulsion of the religious orders in 1902 to the enforced abrogation of the Concordat in 1905, fed off the belief of many Catholics that the official establishment, at all levels of a '*république des camarades*', was dominated by Protestants, Jews and Masonic-connected agnostics in a manner out of all proportion to the real size of those constituencies. The exception was the Army, as the Dreyfus affair had recently demonstrated, unflatteringly. Congar later regarded his chosen companions of boyhood as the seeds of his ecumenical vocation. His parents, though smiling indulgently on his taste in friends, were by no means Voltairean or religiously lukewarm. On the contrary, they were devout and informed Catholics who took the boy regularly to Mass in the small chapel which, after the outbreak of the Great War and the consequent German investment of Sedan, the local Reformed pastor kindly lent to a now churchless parish priest.

Despite earlier attraction to medicine (his request at First Communion was for a microscope), Congar decided in 1921 to study for the priesthood. He entered the Parisian seminary known as 'of the Carmelites' where his spiritual director encouraged him to study Thomism, at the time the most sophisticated theological idiom available in the Catholic Church. He dallied briefly with the neo-conservative movement of cultural and monarchical restoration called the Action Française, but cut his ties when it suffered condemnation as a form of covert paganism by Pope Pius XI (1922–39) in 1926. (It seems likely that this painful experience of an incipient totalitarianism of the Right encouraged him to keep a safe distance from the totalitarianisms of the Left so fashionable among the Parisian intelligentsia in the later 1960s.)

His mind awakened, he attended the Thomistic courses of the rising philosophical star Jacques Maritain (1882–1973) at the 'University Seminary', and frequented retreats given by Maritain's theological mentor, the Dominican Réginald Garrigou-Lagrange (1877–1964). Garrigou, unlike most Dominicans, had received his philosophical formation within the State system. He was concerned with challenges to traditional Christian wisdom raised after the Middle Ages, notably by René Descartes (1596–1650) and Immanuel Kant (1724–1804). A firm 'Neo-Thomist', he was as much indebted to commentators on St Thomas Aquinas (*c.* 1226–74), such as Cajetan (1469–1534) or John of St Thomas (1589–1644) as he was to Thomas himself. The Neo-Thomist disdain of Maritain and Garrigou for the more historically-minded study of Aquinas emerging in the latter's Order, which they termed 'Palaeo-Thomism', accusing it of antiquarianism, foreshadowed certain conflicts in Congar's later career. Meanwhile, the young ordinand was frequenting the Benedictine abbey of Conques, whence he drew his lifetime love for the Catholic liturgy. He nearly joined the Benedictines, but decided instead for the Dominican noviciate of the Province of France at Amiens, which he entered in 1925.

Congar's serious studies were carried out at the Dominican study-house of Le Saulchoir, then at Kain-la-Tombe in Belgium where teachers and pupils had sought refuge from the anti-clerical legislation of the Third French Republic. Thanks to the high standards of its 'regent' or president, Ambroise Gardeil (1859–1931),[2] this institute had reached a level of academic attainment comparable with any university. Historical theology was a particular strength. The young friar read deeply in texts, whether classical, biblical, patristic or mediaeval. His concern to set Thomas within the context of the thirteenth century led to relations with the historian of mediaeval philosophy Etienne Gilson (1884–1979) but cooled the ardours of his friendship with the Neo-Thomists. The geographical and conventional isolation of Le Saulchoir deprived him of much human contact of a wider kind, save through correspondence with the missions of the Province. Norway attracted him, as did the 'Russian seminary' entrusted to the management of the Dominicans at Lille in French Flanders. It was no coincidence that most Norwegians were Lutherans, and most Russians Orthodox. Congar's master, Marie-Dominique Chenu (1894–), had communicated an enthusiasm for the infant ecumenical movement, now drawing Protestants and Orthodox together, notably at the Lausanne Faith and Order Conference of 1927. Chenu suggested that a suitable model for a sympathetic Catholic contribution to that movement might be the ecclesiologist of the nineteenth-century German Catholic revival, Johann Adam Möhler (1796–1838). Accordingly, Congar selected as the subject of his 'lectoral' thesis (an internal Dominican degree) in 1928 Möhler's favoured theme, the unity of the Church. On the eve of his ordination to the priesthood on 25 July 1930, he prepared himself by meditating on Jesus' high-priestly prayer for the unity of his disciples in John 17, with the help of the commentaries of Thomas and the contemporary biblical scholar Marie-Joseph Lagrange (1855–1938). This he recognized in retrospect as the true launching of his ecumenical vocation.

During two visits to Germany he discovered the 'High Church' movement in German Lutheranism and, on a tour of the places associated with the career of Luther (1483–1546), intuited in the latter 'depths . . . which demanded investigation and understanding'. Back in Paris, he was allowed to attend lecture courses by theologians of the Reformed Church of France, who were at the time rediscovering the classical dogmatic Protestantism of Calvin (1509–64) and thereby preparing the way for the French reception of the anti-liberal neo-orthodoxy of Karl Barth (1886–1968). In time, Congar would be deeply affected by Luther's stress on the primacy of grace, and of the Scriptures, though avoiding Luther's accompanying negations of the role of charity, and of tradition. He would also be influenced by Barth's massive emphasis on the sovereignty of the revealing, redeeming and reconciling *Word* of God, whilst regarding Barth's denial that God grants a saving co-causality to creatures as 'disastrous' (DBC, p. 12). Though, at this early stage, Protestantism still meant more to him than did Orthodoxy (a state of things which would later be reversed), he also participated in Catholic–Orthodox 'reunions of Franco-Russian friendship', as these were discreetly called, where he encountered the ideas of Möhler's Orthodox contemporary and counterpart, the lay theologian Alexis Stefanovič Khomiakov (1804–60). The Catholic expert on Orthodoxy Abbé Albert Gratieux (1874–1951)

> was not only my first Russian teacher, but also the 'last of the slavophils', as his nephews maliciously dubbed him. Since he had known the son of Alexis Stepanovich Khomiakov personally and had held numerous conversations with him, he constituted a link in the living tradition of slavophil thought. (DBC, p. 8)

Through Gratieux, Congar conceived a great admiration for the Catholic moving spirit behind the 'Malines Conversations', Abbé Fernand Portal (1855–1926), who had animated that early attempt to establish the conditions of possibility for a reunion between Rome and Canterbury. He sought out the last survivors of those Conversations, as well as other pioneers of Catholic ecumenism such as Dom Lambert Beauduin (1873–1960), then living in exile from his 'Monastery of Union', and Abbé Paul Couturier (1881–1953). Perfectly aware of the 'difficulties' these men had encountered in pursuing an unpopular course, Congar deliberately took care to gain credit for the cause of ecumenism by making himself respected simply as a theologian.

> I hoped, by means of studies of incontestable scientific and theological value, to gain the credit necessary to cover and support my views on ecumenism and thus convert whatever kudos and prestige might accrue to my humble reason to the profit of the cause I served. (DBC, p. 11)

So far as his own teaching was concerned, he was obliged by Chenu's absence in Canada—for the founding of the Institute of Mediaeval Studies at Toronto—to take responsibility for a course of theological propaedeutics, 'introduction to theology'. As part of his preparation he looked into the work of the Modernist exegetes and thinkers of the turn of the century. (The monumental autobiography of Alfred Loisy [1857–1940] had just appeared.) The idea came to him that his own generation should rescue for the Church whatever was of value in the approach of the Modernists. In his judgement this meant two things. First, it meant the application of the historical method to Christian data—though not a restrictively 'historical-critical' method where the dimension of faith was epistemologically blotted out. Secondly, it meant greater attention to the viewpoint of the experiencing subject, whose needs and concerns shift with the contours of history itself. In the course of this work he discovered the contribution of the highly original Catholic philosopher Maurice Blondel (1861–1949), whose reflections on the relation of history and dogma had tried to chart a course between the Scylla of Modernism and the Charybdis of what he dubbed 'Veterism': essentially, closed-mindedness to everything that historical study could offer to the better grasp of a revelation which, though supernatural and miraculous, was mediated by the texture of history. Blondel's concept of tradition struck him particularly forcibly.[3]

Congar's lectures on introducing theology, which were the origins of his interest in fundamental theology, were soon supplemented by far more numerous ones on ecclesiology. This was to remain, with ecumenism, the great passion of his life. It gave him the excuse to broaden his contacts, and so extend his sense of the Church. Just as this led him in 1932 to the bi-ritual Byzantine–Latin monastery of Amay and its ecumenical pioneer founder, Beauduin, it also took him in 1937 to England, where he made Anglican friends and began to acquire a thorough knowledge of the chequered theological history of the Anglican tradition. His host was Arthur Michael Ramsey (1904–88), then principal of Lincoln Theological College and later archbishop of Canterbury. Congar fell under the spell, as is not difficult, of the Anglican service of Evensong. This did not prevent him from divining ecclesiological 'weakness' in Anglicanism.

However, such visits, like his regular excursions to French cities for the preaching of the Christian Unity Octave, were simply punctuations of a domestic round of study and teaching, set within an austere monastic and liturgical framework. This conventual round continued until the outbreak of the Second World War when he found himself first mobilized as a military chaplain, and then immobilized, as a prisoner-of-war at Colditz. There he learned with dismay and stupefaction of the Roman condemnation of Chenu's academic manifesto entitled 'A School of Theology, Le Saulchoir', which had set out the shared theological vision and methods of that house.[4] The blow was felt not simply as hurtful to a friend, but as touching his own understanding of the theological task. As one student of his work has put it:

> One is struck, in reading *Une école*, by the many resonances with Congar's writing which it contains, such as its critique of a baroque scholasticism in the form of a closed system of acquired truths, its appreciation of Möhler, Newman and Gardeil, its advocacy of an historical method which looks into and values various philosophies and theologies in the light of their respective contexts, its emphasis on return to the sources, its insistence on the temporal conditioning of every human grasp of truth, and its desire to relate theology to the living concerns of contemporary human beings.[5]

As late as 1964 Congar confessed himself unable to comprehend the sense of this action, which he could only regard as based upon informational error. In fact, as later investigation has shown, the charge against Le Saulchoir was 'Semi-Modernism', a slippery concept indeed.[6] In Rome voices were raised, not least that of the Dominican 'master of the sacred palace', Mariano Cordovani (1883–1952), protesting that the emphasis of the Saulchoir men on historical context would end up by turning theology into cultural anthropology, deprived of any real hold on its divine subject-matter, revelation.[7]

Meanwhile, from the distinctly untheological vantage-point of a cell at Colditz, a new ecumenical realism was injected. In contact with ordinary Protestant and Anglican laity (and sometimes their padres), as distinct from theological students attracted by ecumenism, Congar felt disillusioned to discover that the dominant impression was 'one of distrust and repulsion with regard to "Rome" '(DBC, p. 30). However, as he noted confidentially, he did not propose to let these negative reactions deter him.

> I believe more than ever that the essential ecumenical activity of the Catholic Church should be to live its own life more fully and genuinely; to purify itself as far as possible, to grow in faithfulness, in good works, in depth of prayer and in union with God. In being fully herself, in the full strength of her vigour, she will develop her ecumenical power. (DBC, p. 31)

And this would involve, he went on in this scribbled memo, that Catholicism should take on a 'post-Reform' nature, that is, one in which the challenge of the Reformation has been faced in depth, any positive elements that the Reformation produced assimilated, and an answer to the questions it raised honestly supplied.

In the creative ferment which characterized the French Catholicism of the immediately post-war years, Congar made a major literary contribution which will be outlined in the next section. However, the hesitations of more conservative churchmen about his work were increasing. As early as 1947 he was refused permission to publish an article on the position of the Catholic Church *vis-à-vis* the ecumenical movement, which was entering a new phase with the preparation of the first assembly of the World Council of Churches. The Master of the Dominicans warned him against a 'false eirenicism' which might be construed as indifference to specifically Catholic doctrines. Further editions, and any translations, of one of his works were prohibited.

Despite these severe vexations, the forging of ecumenical links went on, especially among the Orthodox as a result of a lecture tour in the Near East during the winter of 1953–54. In early February of the latter year he returned to France, to hear the news that, following an article in the defence of the 'priest-worker' movement, to which a number of French Dominicans had lent their support, the Master of the Dominican Order, in the vacuum caused by the enforced resignation of all three French priors-provincial, proposed to remove him from his teaching work. At Congar's own suggestion he was assigned first to the Ecole Biblique in Jerusalem, where he managed to write a substantial essay on biblical theology, and then, in November 1954, to Blackfriars, Cambridge. There, in the Italianate house perched on the top of Mount Pleasant, and neighbour to Dr Ramsey's family home, Howfield, Congar found himself subjected, through the excessive zeal of the English prior-provincial, to 'odious restrictions on my ministrations and movements', obliged to restrict contact with Anglicans to a minimum and to remain silent on ecumenical questions. Only the kindness of Mgr Jean Weber, bishop of Strasbourg, enabled Congar, at the time of his return to France in December 1955, to resume a pastoral and theological ministry. In retrospect, Congar believed that these difficult years had called forth in him an 'active patience', especially fitted to the work of ecumenism, a 'long process of convergence' as this was, bound up with the inner renewal of each Christian communion (DBC, p. 45).

With the coming of Giuseppe Roncalli to the papal chair as John XXIII (1958–63) in 1958 all was changed. Shortly after the new Pope's announcement of the calling of a General Council, Congar was named as theological consultor to the preparatory commission. At the Second Vatican Council itself, he helped write the 'message to the World' at its opening, and worked on such major documents as *Dei Verbum* (the 'Dogmatic Constitution on Divine Revelation'), *Lumen Gentium* (the 'Dogmatic Constitution on the Church'), *Gaudium et Spes* (the 'Pastoral Constitution on the Church in the Modern World'), *Ad Gentes Divinitus* (the 'Decree on the Church's Missionary Activity'), *Unitatis Redintegratio* (the 'Decree on Ecumenism'), *Presbyterorum Ordinis* (the 'Decree on the Life and Ministry of Priests'), and *Dignitatis Humanae* (the 'Declaration on Religious Freedom').[8] Looking back on how so much of his pre-conciliar choice of theological subject had prepared him for these conciliar activities, he could only regard this as a providence active in his life:

> I was not to know—Another knew it on my behalf!—that this would pave the way for Vatican II. I was filled to overflowing. All the things to which I have given special attention issued in the Council: ecclesiology, ecumenism, reform of the Church, the lay state, mission, ministries, collegiality, return to the sources and Tradition.[9]

The second Pope of the Council, Paul VI (1963–78), and his successors did Congar no less honour. In 1965 he became a member of the official Catholic–Lutheran commission of dialogue, a recognition of his lifelong erudite interest in the Reformer of Wittenberg. And by way of testimony to his wider theological service, Paul VI added his name to the newly-founded Pontifical International Theological Commission, which had been brought into existence in order to lend a broader expertise and vision to the work of the Roman Congregation for the Doctrine of the Faith. John Paul II (1978–) invited him to attend the Extraordinary Synod of 1985, convened to consider the fruits of the Second Vatican Council, itself deeply indebted to Congar's master-ideas, but his health was by then too poor for him to accept. These post-conciliar years were serene for Congar, though he did not hesitate to speak of a 'crisis' in the Church beyond, where 'openness to novelty' had too often been traduced by a 'proposal of rupture' (TVE², p. 5).[10] He himself lived in the fraternal ambience of the Couvent Saint-Jacques at Paris, to which the library of the now defunct Saulchoir had been transferred. There he received a flow of visitors, enquirers, students and well-wishers, though their numbers were inevitably reduced by his move to the Hôtel des Invalides in 1984, when his paraplegia had become too advanced for the brethren to be able to nurse him at home. As a former Colditz internee who was also a luminary of French learning, he had a claim to be housed in the great military hospital, along with the marshals of France. It may be doubted whether he devoted much psychic energy to sentiments of *gloire*. As he himself had written:

> Each one has his place. It matters not a whit whether it be glorious or modest. . . . It is the plan which is grand. One is great only in occupying one's own place within it. The most modest place is quite incomparably great, provided only that it is inhabited with faithfulness.[11]

A SURVEY OF CONGAR'S WORK

The following summary survey of Congar's writing must be seen against the background of the history, and influences, charted above. It will emphasize what is most significant, and that in broadly chronological order.

Congar's literary activity first received wide attention with a controversial essay of 1934 on the pastoral mission of the Church in contemporary society.[12] He ascribed the alienation of French culture from the Church to the latter's 'disfigured visage', which made the Catholic community seem too juridically-minded and defensive, and thus a poor expression of the 'incarnation of grace' and the 'humanization of God' found in the person and work of Jesus Christ. In 1936 he launched a series of ecclesiological enquiries under the general title *Unam Sanctam*, a reference to the words of the Creed: 'one holy (Church)'. Their ecumenical inspiration was signalled by his decision to make the first volume his own *Divided Christendom*,[13] which sought, through reflection on the essential nature of the Church and its unity, to work out 'principles for Catholic ecumenism' in the light of the different conceptions of unity, and so of ecumenism, among liberal Protestants, Anglicans and the Orthodox.

In the war-time *The Mystery of the Church*[14] Congar countered the claim that, in his work so far, there was little of the traditional Dominican Thomism by outlining a distinctive approach to Thomas. This took the form of a two-fold concern: first, for Aquinas's continuity with the Fathers (something which had an obvious ecumenical import), and, secondly, for what Aquinas might offer by way of materials for the construction of a contemporary theology (highly pertinent to the needs of the 'Mission de France'). The truly breathtaking grasp of theological history he had acquired by the age of 40 was revealed in the article 'Theology' which he contributed to the *Dictionnaire de théologie catholique*, later published in English as an entire book under the title *A History of Theology*.[15]

After the war, he wrote his courageous but careful call for ecclesiastical reform, *Vraie et fausse réforme dans l'Eglise* (Paris, 1950). This, after distinguishing the senses in which the Church must be holy (thanks to her divine origination) but could be sinful (owing to her human composition), pleaded for a reform not of abuses (for there virtually were none) but of the structures of the Church, her concrete adaptation, or, as it too often seemed to be, inadaptation to the world to which she preaches. Such a reform should, he argued, proceed by way of 'return to the sources', a phrase he took from the poet and social critic Charles Péguy (1873–1914), as well as from the liturgical changes inaugurated by Pope Pius X (1903–14). Congar laid down the conditions on which the return could be 'true', that is, manageable without disrupting the continuity of the Church's history, or disturbing the peace and charity of the Church's members. In his *Lay People in the Church*[16] he devoted special attention to the making of a theology of the laity, who must mediate between the Church and the world. There he insisted that the laity are not simply the objects of the ministrations of the hierarchy, but are, on the basis of their baptism and confirmation, acting subjects in their own right of the threefold office of Christ as Priest, Prophet and King. They exercise this threefold office in their own distinctive sphere, which is at the 'suture' of Church and world. The laity are responsible for the interchange between the two great histories, sacred and profane. By relating the world to the Church, they provide the Kingdom of God with its earthly material. In so doing, they contribute to the *plērōma*, 'fullness', which Christ is destined to have in his total reality, which includes his Church-body.

Major Church anniversaries gave him the opportunity for further significant contributions. In 1952, for the fifteenth centenary of the Council of Chalcedon, celebrated the previous year, he produced *Christ, Our Lady and the Church*,[17] an exposé of the theological principles underlying and connecting orthodox Christology, ecclesiology and Mariology. In 1954, for the ninth centenary of the schism of Michael Kerullarios (d. 1058), he published the important study of Catholic–Orthodox relations *After Nine Hundred Years*,[18] thanks to the good offices of Beauduin's monastery, now transferred to Chevetogne, in Belgium. During his exile in Jerusalem he turned his hand to the wider issues of the God–world relationship as that unfolds in history. *The Mystery of the Temple*[19] outlined a theology of a developing divine–human relationship, whose stages are marked by an ever-increasing interiority of divine presence, whose climax is in Jesus Christ as the God–man, and whose goal as well as terminus is the eschatological 'temple' of the divine presence described in the Johannine Apocalypse.

In *Tradition and Traditions*,[20] written as the Second Vatican Council was proceeding, Congar's attention began to shift from a Christologically-oriented picture of the Church to one which, though by no means neglecting the dominical determination of the Church's life made by the Word Incarnate and Risen, gave greater weight to the mission of the Holy Spirit, by whose agency the gifts of Christ to the Church are concretely realized in the lives of believers. Manifesting the vast reading which the hidden years of Le Saulchoir had made possible, there followed two major chronicles of the history of ecclesiology, *L'Ecclésiologie du haut Moyen Age* (Paris, 1968) and *L'Eglise. De saint Augustin à l'époque moderne* (Paris, 1970). He also offered a more personal synthesis based on these traditional materials in *L'Eglise une, sainte, catholique, apostolique* (Paris, 1970), which was a contribution to the Franco-German handbook of salvation-historical theology, *Mysterium Salutis*. In the course of this research he learned that the two most important alternative perspectives in which ecclesiology can be approached are by starting from the local church (an 'ecclesiology of communion') or from the Church universal (a 'universalist ecclesiology').

In addition to numerous collections of essays on his favoured subjects, from Luther and the ecumenical movement to Church, ministry and the Second Vatican Council, he also produced in the years 1979–80 a full-scale pneumatology, the three-volume *I Believe in the Holy Spirit*.[21] Beginning from the witness to the Spirit in the Old and New Testaments and in various phases of Church history, Congar considered the role of the Spirit in the corporate life of the Church, as in the personal lives of Christians, with a sizeable section on the 'Charismatic Renewal'. In the last volume of the trilogy he looked at the theology of the Spirit found historically in East and West; attempted to resolve the delicate problem of the procession of the Spirit (from the Father only, or from the Father *and the Son*), which still divides Catholic and Orthodox, and concluded, after an exploration of the activity of the Spirit in Confirmation and Eucharist, with a portrait of the Church's life as a prolonged epiclesis, or prayer for the Spirit's advent. By his own account, as offered in what he assures his readers will be his final book, *Fifty*

Years of Catholic Theology,[22] his own sensibility and reflection have moved, in conformity with the inner movement of the Holy Trinity itself, from Father, through Son, to the Holy Spirit (FYCT, p. 61).

Notes

1 For Congar's life I have used chiefly J.-P. Jossua OP, *Le Père Congar. La théologie au service du peuple de Dieu* (Paris, 1967), along with Congar's own autobiographical remarks in *Chrétiens en dialogue. Contributions catholiques à l'oecuménisme* (Paris, 1964); Eng. trans. *Dialogue between Christians* (London, 1966), pp. 1–68. For the early period, see also A. Stacpoole OSB, 'Early ecumenism, early Yves Congar 1904–1940', *The Month* CCIX.1441 (1988), pp. 502–10.

2 For this figure, who deserves a theological revival, see H.-D. Gardeil OP, *L'Oeuvre théologique du Père Ambroise Gardeil* (Etiolles, 1954).

3 Congar's course of theological propaedeutics is substantially present in *La Foi et la théologie* (Tournai, 1968).

4 M.-D. Chenu, *Une Ecole de théologie. Le Saulchoir* (Tournai, 1937) outlines the school's programme. This book was reprinted by Editions du Cerf (Paris, 1985) with four supplementary essays on the controversy provoked by its first appearance. Congar expressed his debt to Chenu in both historical theology and a sense of the Church's contemporary mission in 'Le Père M.-D. Chenu' in R. Vander Gucht and H. Vorgrimler (eds), *Bilan de la théologie du XXe siècle* (Tournai/Paris, 1970) II, pp. 772–90. For Chenu's work see O. de la Brosse, *Le Père Chenu. La liberté dans la foi* (Paris, 1969).

5 W. Henn OFMCap, *The Hierarchy of Truths according to Yves Congar OP* (Rome, 1987), pp. 74–5.

6 E. Fouilloux, 'Le Saulchoir en procès 1937–1942' in ETLS, pp. 36–59.

7 See R. Spiazzi OP, *P. Mariano Cordovani dei Frati Predicatori* (Rome, 1954), with a preface by the future Paul VI praising Cordovani's gifts of theological understanding and Christian friendship.

8 For Congar's part in, and view of, the Second Vatican Council, the major source is the two-volume *Mon Journal du Concile*, typescripts deposited at Congar's request in the library of Le Saulchoir, itself now in the Rue des Tanneries, Paris, and at the University of Leuven (Louvain), Belgium, where they may be consulted after the year 2000. They are dated 1967, at Strasbourg. Meanwhile, the student has access to Congar's published comments in his *Vatican II. Le Concile au jour le jour* (Paris, 1963), Eng. trans. *Report from Rome. The First Session of the Vatican Council* (London, 1963); *Le Concile au jour le jour. 2e Session* (Paris, 1964), Eng. trans. *Report from Rome. The Second Ses-*

sion of the Vatican Council (London, 1964); *Le Concile au jour le jour. 3e Session* (Paris, 1965); *Le Concile au jour le jour. 4e Session* (Paris, 1966). See also, in longer retrospect, *Le Concile de Vatican II. Son Eglise: Peuple de Dieu et Corps du Christ* (Paris, 1984).

9 'Reflections on being a theologian', *New Blackfriars* 62.736 (1981), p. 409.

10 For the twentieth birthday of the theological journal *Concilium* (on whose editorial board he has served since its launch in 1967) Congar wrote: 'If the only Church we knew was a Church in movement, a theology parcelled out in questions, a world in a state of ferment, a shattered culture, where could we stand and from what soil could we draw our sap? *Concilium* must bear witness to the presence of enduring principles as well as following changes and challenges': 'Où en est l'expression de la foi?', *Concilium* 190 (1983), pp. 139–40; 'Where are we in the expression of the faith?', *Concilium* (Eng. ed.) 170 (1983), pp. 85–7.

11 *Une Passion: l'Unité. Réflexions et souvenirs 1929–1973* (Paris, 1974), p. 112.

12 'Une conclusion théologique à l'enquête sur les raisons actuelles de l'incroyance', *La Vie intellectuelle* 37 (1935), pp. 214–49.

13 Originally *Chrétiens désunis. Principes d'un oecuménisme catholique* (Paris, 1937; Eng. trans. 1939).

14 Originally *Esquisses du Mystère de l'Eglise* (Paris, 1941; 2nd ed. 1953; Eng. trans. 1960).

15 'Théologie', *Dictionnaire de théologie catholique* XV, cols 341–502; revised Eng. trans. *A History of Theology* (New York, 1968).

16 *Jalons pour une théologie du laïcat* (Paris, 1953; Eng. trans. 1957).

17 *Le Christ, Marie et l'Eglise* (Paris, 1952; Eng. trans. 1957).

18 'Neuf cents ans après. Notes sur le "Schisme Oriental" 1054–1854' in *L'Eglise et les églises* (Chevetogne, 1954) I, pp. 3–95; separate Eng. trans. 1959.

19 *Le Mystère du Temple* (Paris, 1958; Eng. trans. 1962).

20 *La Tradition et les traditions* (Paris, 1960–63; Eng. trans. 1966).

21 *Je crois en l'Esprit Saint*, I: *L'Esprit dans l'"économie": révélation et expérience de l'Esprit* (Paris, 1979), II: *'Il est Seigneur et Il donne la vie'* (Paris, 1979), III: *Le Fleuve de Vie coule en Orient et en Occident* (Paris, 1980). Eng. trans. *I Believe in the Holy Spirit* (London/New York, 1983), I: *The Holy Spirit in the 'Economy'*, II: *'He is Lord and Giver of Life'*, III: *The River of the Water of Life flows in the East and in the West*.

22 *Entretiens d'automne* (Paris, 1976); Eng. trans. 1988.

2

Congar's fundamental theology: (a) Revelation in history

Congar's understanding of revelation begins from the concept of the Word of God, a tribute at once to his own Dominican and Thomistic training; to the inter-war renaissance of biblical theology; and, more obliquely, to the influence of the great 'neo-orthodox' Protestant dogmatician, Karl Barth.[1] God's Word is the generative element in the history of salvation, the act by which he makes known to man his personal mystery and will in converting man to himself. Simultaneously, then, saving action and saving knowledge, the Word of God stimulates words and gestures with a revelatory sign-value among those to whom it is addressed. Through such language and motions, people are brought to understand and affirm a divine meaning by way of human means. Conformably to traditional Catholic and Thomist realism, Congar deems such 'thinking with assent' to be true with the truth of the Primal Truth itself. As this foretaste indicates, we must look here at how Congar treated three themes: *revelation, faith* and the '*sacred history*' in which the encounter of God and man is set.

REVELATION

Congar's account of man before the self-revealing God opens in a strikingly intellectualist way. Set within the ambience of nature is a creature capable of making certain true affirmations about God, the world, and all it contains.[2] But over and above this understanding which man can attain by his own (God-given) faculties, the Creator also communicates to man, in direct fashion, something of his *own* knowledge of himself and his will. For this purpose, he intervenes in a sacred history, charging select individuals to speak in his name. And to achieve this end, he arouses in the feeling mind, *l'esprit*, of such persons, and in their expressive capacities, what Congar calls 'formulae' valid with the validity of God's own self-understanding and bearers of the intention that he is pursuing in the history of salvation. Thus, as Congar explains:

> falling short of the perfect manifestation by which he has promised to disclose himself openly to us as he is open and manifest to himself, but going beyond what *we* could suspect of him as Creator of things in their natural regularities, God makes himself known to men in a word (*parole*) strictly so called—that is, in *signs* expressing the content of a thought. (FT, p. 5)

Such signs are aroused by God in the representational powers of those to whom he 'speaks', or, alternatively, should he find them already formed there, he assures their conformity to what he wishes to signify of himself and his plan. The gracious initiative by which God would raise us up to share in his own life has a delicate respect for our rationality, whose structures it will not contravene. Thus our new 'end' is proposed to us in human terms, in a communication of knowledge. That the knowledge is for the 'end' means, however, that whilst a doctrine of revelation—and so a theological epistemology, an account of what it is to *know* as a believer—must be crucial, it cannot be severed from a doctrine of salvation—a theological description of what it is like to *live* as a believer. As Congar puts it, the divine self-communication

> is not confined to knowledge alone; in actual fact, a new life-relation is in question, which requires on God's part a sharing with us of vitality and energy with a view to our achieving with him a fellowship which will be at once personal and collective. The new and definitive order brings, in this gesture of bestowal, wholly new gifts which render effectively possible the divinizing possession of God by his creatures. (TT, pp. 237–8)

The content of divine revelation is the Christian 'mysteries': a term which carries, in Congar's usage as in the preceding tradition, twofold meaning. Corresponding to the intimate interrelation of the act of revelation and the act of salvation it has at once a *noetic* sense—a sense concerned with knowing—and a *liturgical* sense—a sense connected with the celebration of salvation. What is common to both the liturgically celebrated sacraments and the object of revelation is that, in each case, a hidden reality acts and discloses itself, while yet remaining concealed—and thus establishes a tension towards a definitive or eschatological fulfilment.

> The mysteries are not a system of ideas, representations which we form for ourselves, but transcendent *realities* that become, by revelation, the object of knowing, and which, through God's power, work for our salvation, for our communion in the glory of God. (FT, p. 21)

In the noetic sense, the special *nuance* of the term 'mystery' is that of a hidden *truth*: a truth which shows itself whilst yet maintaining a certain reserve. Such a mystery is beyond the mastery of the mind, not simply owing to the limitations of our means of knowledge, but in virtue of the 'supereminence' of the reality concerned, which belongs to the order of absolute existence, the 'I am who am', of the book of Exodus (3:14). Congar stresses that a true theology will always be to some degree 'dialectical'. It will radically qualify its own assertions by the ways of 'negation' and 'eminence', saying ever that the truth is 'above this', 'beyond that'. He has gathered a remarkable florilegium of such 'apophatic' texts from the Fathers both Western and Eastern, and from the mediaevals.

Congar is concerned that this revelation, whose affirmations derive from the fourteen hundred years during which the Jewish-Christian Scriptures were written, and the nineteen centuries of the Church's tradition since, should be conceived by us as a profound unity. At first sight this mass of material is an impenetrable forest. However, it is capable of being subsumed under a single notion, that of a covenant whose centre is Jesus Christ and whose term is the God who would draw us to himself. This is how Congar understands the request of the First Vatican Council that revelation should be understood not simply by the explication of each individual mystery, but in terms of the 'connexion of the mysteries with each other, and with the final end of man' (DS 1976). And Congar points out that for Thomas, the articles of faith enjoy, from the viewpoint not of their motive—*why* we believe them—but of their content—*what* we believe—relative degrees of importance, depending on their closeness to the heart of the covenant relationship. Though God may reveal to us of himself and his ways whatever he wishes, including even truths that fall within the competence of our natural reasoning yet may be hard for everyone to grasp with security, the most proper concern of his revealing activity, and so of our theological faith, is 'that by which man is rendered blessed'. And this is the truth of that religious relationship which we call salvation. That relationship involves a set of differentiated yet integrated truths which, as Congar's mediaeval master puts it, 'we shall enjoy by seeing them in the life everlasting, and by which we are brought to share that life'.[3] In other words, they are the means and the term of the covenant God has made with man.

FAITH

When this revelation is received by man, it becomes *la connaissance de foi*, the 'knowing to which faith has access'. The structure of faith mirrors that of God's Word, the generator of revelation. Faith, as the human Amen to the divine utterance, shares the latter's structure as at once noetic and dynamic, knowledge and power of action.

> It is clear that its noetic aspect situates faith on the level of the Church's orthodoxy, the level of a collective reality, capable of being made an object and so communicated, whilst faith's existential aspect as the principle of conversion and salvation relates to personal living. (FT, p. 73)

But these two cannot be disassociated. They are united in the baptismal profession where the candidate presents himself to be catechized by the Church so that he can commit himself in the way of eternal life. Just as the living God simultaneously reveals and promises, so faith in the living God at one and the same time knows and acts in personal self-engagement.

In the context of fundamental theology Congar naturally places his primary emphasis on the first aspect: faith as knowing. He thus leaves in the shadow the existential dimension, whereby faith gives access to justification, and endures throughout the Christian life as that virtue whereby we are disposed to take the Gospel as the basis for our being. At this point, this is something of a pedagogic necessity. But in any case, Congar points out, while the contemporary rediscovery of faith as personal is good, it is not without its own temptation: namely, to neglect the dogmatic and contemplative aspect of believing. Consonant with his Thomist inheritance, Congar insists that faith is the total crediting of God as Truth itself, a resting on that Truth, and a 'renewal of one's judgement' (in the

Pauline phrase)[4] coming about through a new relation to the absolute Principle of everything that is true.

What, then, is the epistemological and psychological structure of the act of faith, as Congar understands it? Considered epistemologically, the believing mind is a mind secured in its grasp of its object, just as it is in simple apprehension or—after a suitable search—in 'scientific' demonstration, that is, in grasping conclusions which follow necessarily from what is already known. But in the case of faith, such security is assured by a movement of the *will* whereby the whole man, seeking his own good, perceives a bond between 'certain values of existence' and the option of believing.

> In faith, the adherence of the mind is decided by the engagement of the living human being, who seeks his total good and recognizes it in what the Word offers and promises. (FT, p. 77)

The same action can also be studied from the perspective of psychology, which Congar now proceeds to do. Fundamentally, he identifies four elements within the psychological process of coming to Christian faith. First of all, there must be proposed to the receiving subject not simply the object of faith *tout court* but, more precisely, that object under its specific and decisive aspect of being the promise of eternal life.

> What is proposed to men is essentially the good of communion with God, with Jesus Christ and with the saints: in brief, entry into the Covenant, the Kingdom. (FT, p. 77)

And Congar goes on to describe this as

> communion with the God who spoke to Abraham, who freed Israel and promised to free her from every 'pharaoh', internal or external, the God who punished his people and had mercy on them; the God to whom the saints prayed, and ultimately the God who, in Jesus Christ, made of himself the covenant of his people, the union of the created and the Uncreated. (FT, p. 77)

In communing with this God, faith enters into the assurance of his promises, entering into relationship thereby with what the writer to the Hebrews calls the 'cloud of witnesses' who, having lived out their faith, are for us its signs, with Jesus Christ, the pioneer and completer of our faith, at their head. Indeed, the Church herself, the *communio sanctorum*, in proposing to us these *credenda* or 'things to be believed', is simply a sign of saving communion with the God whose promises became entirely Yes (as Paul puts it in 2 Cor 1:20) in Jesus Christ.

Secondly, the process of arriving at faith presupposes a positive disposition on the part of the human subject. What is at stake here is an attitude Congar qualifies as 'filial', and which consists in 'openness, submission and receptivity'. He points out that some version of such a human stance is required by any entry upon the 'blessing of a grand quality of existence': the child knocking on the door of adulthood, wishing to enter the communion of the grown-up, or the student wanting to learn, to be received into the communion of those who know, and putting himself to school, accordingly, with some acknowledged master. (Nor does Congar fail to add, as a lover of France, *le petit Français* who wills to share in French culture and its greatness: the destiny of his country.) Now in the case of the spiritual good of communion with God, Jesus Christ and his saints we are presented with something which has equal, or greater, attracting power but is (even) less self-evidencing. It follows, then, that, in the case of faith, the role of freedom, and of quite complex moral dispositions, is all the more important. And here Congar has recourse to the *Pensées* of Blaise Pascal (1623–62), and notably fragment 430, in which the seventeenth-century philosopher–scientist speaks of the divine Word appearing amongst men in such a manner that he would be perfectly knowable to those who seek him sincerely, with all their heart, but hidden to those who, inversely, flee him with all their heart. As Pascal had put it:

> He tempers the knowledge of himself, in such a way that he gives visible signs of himself to those who seek him, but not to those who do not seek. There is enough light . . .[5]

Il y a assez de lumière, or as Congar himself explains the matter: the truth draws near to us, and displays for us its own desirable and authoritative quality, in the measure that we ourselves move close to it and welcome it in our lives.

But thirdly, the human freedom which, in the way just outlined, scans the horizon for a meaning for life and so is taken up into dialogue with the Word of God, is not alone. Within it (and not just outside it) God's grace is at work. To the clear affirmations of the Bible on this point have been added, since the Pelagian crisis in the Western Church of the patristic period, those of the conciliar tradition: Orange II (529), Trent (1545–63) and Vatican I (1869–70). Right from its genesis, when the psychological and moral 'preformations' of faith begin to take shape, faith has divine grace as its necessary condition. These are the 'aids' called by Thomas an 'interior calling', 'instinct' or 'movement' and Congar aligns himself with those interpreters of the thirteenth-century Dominican who describe them as intrinsically supernatural—and not supernatural from the viewpoint, simply, of their goal—since the process which they stir into life continues into the choice of faith itself, and, indeed, into that supreme mode of adhesion to God which is charity.

Finally, this interior call is accompanied by exterior signs which render a witness to the self-revealing God that is credible to the reasonable human being—and not simply desirable to those who seek their own meaning and good. At first, these signs are registered by reason alone; but, as the choice of faith 'incubates', reason becomes further aroused by the dispositions of the will and aided by grace. Finally, in the act of faith itself, the perception which the believer has of the object of faith through reason is powerfully reinforced, and rendered luminous, uplifted, joyful, by those attitudes, and that mind, proper to a child of God living the life of divine sonship.[6] Though after this point there may be many unanswered questions and many unresolved difficulties, 'ten thousand difficulties'—in the words of John Henry Newman (1801–90)—'do not make one doubt'.[7]

What, then, are the 'signs' which constitute the first stage of this process? At the time of Christ himself, they were: Jesus' own person, his teaching and his miracles, above all the Easter miracle of his resurrection. For the men and women of today they are, in addition to these, insofar as they can be critically established and admitted, the People of the Covenant itself: namely, the Church, which accompanies the witness she transmits by an *ensemble* of miracles, both moral and physical, and above all by the sign of holiness which Congar describes as 'the most easily read, the most difficult to reject, the most effective in leading to faith' (FT, p. 82). Thus if faith is, first and foremost, spoken of in *audial* terms (as a knowing which comes about through assent to a message heard), it has also, for Congar, a vital *visual* dimension. 'Faith has its eyes', as Augustine (354–430) remarks in Letter 120, eyes which focus on the signs that accredit the witness to revealed truth.[8]

Congar does not leave off the 'analysis of faith' without contributing to a solution of the problem, much discussed since the fourteenth century in theology, as to what faith's 'formal motive'—that which makes faith faith—can be. The interior attraction of grace; the reasons for believing which the signs of revelation suggest—these things are not so much what constitutes the act of faith as what prepares and authorizes it. Faith itself, as Congar presents it, is

> a spiritual novelty, consisting in a passage to an unconditional adhesion [to God]. It is motivated by the authority of God revealing, by the intervention in the feeling mind, of the First Truth in his own self-manifestation. (FT, p. 83)

In this formulation, Congar uses the theological work of Thomas to throw light on an issue unconsidered by Thomas because raised after his time. He is faithful to the ethos of Aquinas in his effort to integrate into his account the valuable elements to be found in those of his predecessors. Each of those accounts stressed one factor: that associated with the late mediaeval Thomists and Cardinal Francis Suarez (1548–1617) insisted that the motive of faith must be known in a supernatural light; that of the majority of Jesuit theologians, Suarez excepted, held, somewhat rationalistically, that, from the point of view of its status as knowledge, the motive of faith must be the same at the end of the rational preamble to believing as it is in the act of faith itself; lastly, for a somewhat heterogeneous variety of modern writers, with anticipations in such earlier figures as Ulrich of Strassburg (d. 1278?), the motive of faith is the divine authority taken in itself, as distinct from the knowledge that we have of it. In a decisive passage aimed at reconciling these positions (but above all at determining what is the case!) Congar writes:

> The act of faith proceeds from an interior communication of the First Truth making itself, in the human spirit, a principle of assent. This it does at once through a created effect of itself [Congar means here the 'light' of faith] and by manifesting itself exteriorly, in Scripture and the Church's teaching, by a created similitude of itself. (FT, p. 89)

Faith represents in this way a 'joining-together' of the spirit of man with that of God. It is the form which God's communication to us of his own knowledge takes in our situation of exile and journeying. In faith we leave 'what is ours', *quae nostra sunt*, for 'what is God's', *quae Dei sunt*. Faith is a passing over to a hitherto unknown level of existence for the spirit. It is a painful new birth. Faith's existentially necessary purifications form a conceptually necessary part of its theology. Reintroducing, then, the uniquely personal element in faith, Congar brings together the experience of the Christian mystics with that of the great figures of Scripture, from Abraham to the Blessed Virgin Mary.

> The life of spiritual men follows this law [of purification and rebirth] as it was followed alike by all the heroes of the history of salvation. (FT, p. 90)

And this brings us to a further aspect of Congar's fundamental theology: theological reflection on the saving history.

THE SACRED HISTORY

Although for Congar, as a Thomist, mind is intrinsically open to divine truth, he also acknowledges, with thinkers from the time at least of the Neapolitan jurist and philosopher Gianbattista Vico (1668–1744) onwards, that mind is, in addition, embedded in history.

> Each human being, and humanity as a whole, has a history and neither the angels above us, nor the animals below us in the scale of creation share this feature with us. For to have a history it is necessary to be in time and, at the same time, to go beyond it, to rise above it. (TT, p. 256)

That means: man is able not only to survive time (which animals also do in replicating their kind) but also to transcend time in the sense that he can communicate the 'acquisitions' of his generation to be integrated into the fulfilment of a meaningful destiny. The Church, as a community continually re-created by the gracious initiatives of God, also has an historical time of her own, with her own acquisitions, unity and destiny. This Congar calls the 'sacred history'. It is a divine history, in that, by it, the living God establishes his covenant relationship, or relation of reciprocal knowledge and shared life, with humankind, and, having established it, ushers human beings into that covenant in the particular historical moment when they are themselves alive. The sacred history is also a human history in that to it belong all the responses whereby men and women in their freedom have answered the call of God. Because it is both a history of divine initative and a history of human response, it is necessarily a history of salvation (TT, pp. 257–64).

The drama of God's self-communication is worked out, then, through a protracted saving history, but its climax is Jesus Christ. He it is who unveils the total design of the covenant relationship between God and man, as that relationship's unconditional realization, its 'Absolute'.

> The mystery, the Father's plan, has as its centre Jesus Christ, but includes also all that depends on him. Jesus, in his lordship over time, sums up in his own consciousness all those 'Christian' values which his Mystical Body is called upon to live out and know through the passage of the centuries, thereby attaining its full stature. . . . We ourselves cannot try to understand the 'mystery' by starting at its luminous heart; on the contrary, we can only arrive at this heart through the communion of the faithful, and chiefly through communion with the apostles, the first believers, Jesus' companions and witnesses. (TT, p. 268)

But this is not to say, of course, that the God of revelation leaves our receptive powers unaided before the figure of Jesus or, even more darkly, his 'consciousness'. As the divine plan unfolds, the noetic conditions for its perception are progressively created. The Son acts as our 'interior teacher' (a phrase borrowed from Augustine) and the Spirit (in the language of the first letter of John) as our 'unction', the gracing of our sensibility. The Word of God requires, and thus can receive, its co-responding word from us. The unseen Father is manifested and communicated in the missions of the Son, incarnate in Jesus Christ, and the Spirit, poured out into the world from the Paschal mystery at Pentecost. Of those missions the modifications of our mind and feeling are the internal echoes. In the time between the Resurrection and the Parousia, God continues to restore human persons to himself, and thereby to disclose his own being as the Trinity, and this he does by means of a community, the Church, living in communion with the ceaseless consubstantial exchange of the divine persons (FT, pp. 41–53).

As Congar presents it, the plan of God for the world takes the form of a continuous process of development, whose crucial stages depend upon a series of divine interventions. He draws, most notably, on the biblical theme of the 'temple' to express this cumulatively formed divine indwelling among men. As the preface to *The Mystery of the Temple* puts it:

> We intended to develop this great . . . theme by following the stages of its revelation and realization, the stages in fact of the economy of salvation; this of course by means of a study of Scripture which, inspired as it is and guaranteed by God, provides the evidence of the economy of grace he has freely willed. This economy develops along a line which embraces the whole of history and the world itself. It had a beginning and it

> will have an end, it began as a seed and it will reach a fullness of growth, and the whole process is dominated by the Person of Jesus Christ. Hence the story of God's relations with his creation and especially with man is none other than the story of his ever more generous, ever deeper Presence among his creatures. (MT, p. ix)

It is in this context that the importance of ecclesiology to Congar must be situated. The Church is the definitive stage in the evolving plan of God, and will yield only to the eschatological fulfilment of his purposes. With the Old Testament, the Church shares the hope of a future fulfilment; with the Kingdom, she has in common the very presence of the Cause of all salvation (VFRE, p. 136).

This eschatological movement of history has its origin in protology, man's creation to God's image and likeness. To express the twin poles of protology and eschatology Congar uses mythopoeic language: the 'temple of Paradise' (MT, p. 245) and the 'temple of the world to come'. From Genesis to Apocalypse, from promise to fulfilment, protology and eschatology form the two co-ordinates of the divine plan, and it is in the movement from the first to the second that the Church is to be understood. The foundations of this movement can be seen in terms of either the mission of the Son, or of that of the Holy Spirit, or of both. In Congar's earlier work, the tendency is to articulate the continuing saving history by reference to Christology.

> Christ is the Alpha and Omega of the whole relation of man with God, which has to be a relation of fellowship. . . . But he is its Alpha only through all his *acta et passa in carne*, for us . . ., whilst he is its Omega *with* us, not only in the body of flesh that was born of Mary and was crucified, but in his fellowship-body which we compose with him and in him—and he in us. He is its Alpha as principle and root, and his powers of hallowing, ruling and revealing consequently endure in the state of abasement. . . . He will be Omega as effect and fruit, in a state of fulness, of blossoming and unfolding, of 'apocalypse', of all the powers of the Shoot. (LPC, p. 163)

But with the writing of *Tradition and Traditions* a more pneumatological emphasis comes to the fore.[9] The Spirit gives life to the forms instituted by Christ, interiorizing his gifts in human hearts throughout all subsequent time. Whereas Tradition as a once-for-all 'deposit' is the work of the Son, the same Tradition, as interiorized and actualized in the lives of faithful in the course of history, is the work of the Spirit (TT, pp. 342–3). Naturally, these statements should not be seen as contradictory. If there are within the single mystery of Christ, two 'moments'—Christ in his Paschal and in his Parousial condition, the Christ of the Resurrection and of the Second Coming—in both cases he is Lord of the Church because of the working of the Holy Spirit in and through his glorified humanity. Pentecost is thus the central event of the apostolic age, the turning point of the *histoire sainte* in which we live. It is to Congar's notion of Tradition that we must now turn.

Notes

1 For Congar's testimony to Barth, see his 'Karl Barth: un homme qui aimait Jésus Christ', *Signes du Temps* (January 1969), pp. 13–14; the polyvalent senses of 'the Word' in European theology are discussed in R. Morgan, 'The Word', *Theology* 74 (1971), pp. 213–22.

2 A valuable discussion of where Congar fits in on the spectrum of Thomist accounts of truth is provided by W. Henn OFMCap, in his *The Hierarchy of Truths according to Yves Congar OP* (Rome, 1987), pp. 29–72. Henn shows that Congar implicitly rejects the twentieth-century 'Transcendental' school of Thomism, for which knowledge of reality is ultimately grounded in a non-noetic factor, namely the desire for, or dynamism towards, being. As Henn writes, 'Either our knowledge of reality is known to us from within those very means by which anything is known to us (i.e. image or *species*, concept or idea, judgement) or it is not known to us at all' (p. 66).

3 A great number of references to Thomas's work may be adduced here: from the *Summa Theologiae* one may cite Ia IIae, q. 106, a. 4 ad 2; IIa IIae, q. 1, a. 6 ad 1; a. 8; q. 2, a. 5 ad 7.

4 Cf. Rom 12:2; Eph 4:23.

5 B. Pascal, *Pensées*, fragment 430; ed. Brunschvicg, pp. 526–7.

6 Here Congar is indebted to P. Rousselot, *Les Yeux de la foi*, originally published by the young Jesuit killed in the First World War in *Recherches des Sciences religieuses* 1 (1910), pp. 241–59; 444–76; ibid., 4 (1913), pp. 1–36; ibid., 5 (1914), pp. 57–69.

7 J.H. Newman, *Apologia pro Vita Sua* (London, 1865; 1934), p. 239.

8 Augustine, *Epistolae* 120, 2, 8 (PL 33, 456).

9 Cf. C. MacDonald, *Church and World in the Plan of God. Aspects of History and Eschatology in the Thought of Père Yves Congar OP* (Frankfurt/Bern, 1982), pp. 124–6.

3

Congar's fundamental theology: (b) Tradition in the Church

For Congar, the origin of Tradition lies in the central moment of the sacred history: the Father's handing over of the Son to the world in the Incarnation, and the Son's subsequent acceptance of betrayal (in Latin, *traditio*, another 'handing over') at the hands of sinful men. But this twofold 'productive act', linked to a *masculine* divine symbolism, is received and transmitted in the Church's Tradition—whose ultimate subject is the Holy Spirit and which Congar conceives in essentially *feminine* terms (TVE², pp. 16–17, 25–6). The entire Church, lay and clerical together, is the mediate subject of Tradition which she passes on not just as a teaching but as a reality, the reality of Christianity itself. And in terms drawn from Blondel's *History and Dogma* Congar insists that Tradition constitutes 'the permanence of a past in a present in whose heart the future is being prepared' (TVE², p. 86)—thus transcending the limitations of a fixist conservatism or a falsely radical disregard for continuity.[1] In each age, the Church of Tradition puts forth expressive monuments, ranging from a liturgical text to an artwork, from a theological classic to a saint.

This rich variety of cues for grasping the meaning of Tradition cannot dispense, however, with the need for doctrine, which is the raising into propositional intelligibility of the original Christian 'given'. Yet doctrine, like Tradition, is not without its history: through her Spirit-guided *magisterium* or teaching authority the whole Church is able to verify the continuity between the origins and such 'development' of doctrine. What is transmitted is the revelation given once and for all.

THE IDEA OF TRADITION

Congar does not venture to set forth his own idea of Tradition, however, until he has made a thorough investigation of the problem of Tradition in the Christian sources. Here we shall not follow him in detail, but simply note the results he obtained in their broadest outline. In his historical survey, Congar seeks to show two things: first, that the concept of Tradition has a firm foothold in Scripture; and secondly, that it is wider and deeper than that version of it sometimes entertained in the heat of polemics, by both Protestant and Catholic authors alike.

The crucial importance of the concept of Tradition in Congar's eyes is that it is, in effect, the idea of the Church's life itself, a life lived

> in the communion of faith and worship, as the setting in which the Catholic sense is fostered and finds expression. (TT, p. 235)

Tradition is the river of which the Gospel is the source. If God were simply in direct and personal contact with each mind, it would suffice to speak in this context only of revelation. In fact, however:

> God's plan is that the *doctrina salutaris* should be brought to many from its source in a small number of witnesses for whom it is a direct revelation; and in such a way that all men who benefit from this teaching and welcome it in faith should form spiritually one people, one body—in short, a Church. And not all at once, or in a short space of time, but throughout a long succession of generations and centuries. (TT, p. 239)

Thus, if mission is the transmission of a task, Tradition is the communication of an object: both are necessary in the plan of God. As Tradition, that plan involves the taking up into the divine action of a general law of human interdependence and brotherly mediation. Just as, in the vast web of the biosphere, creatures live on and by each other, and human beings need their fellows for their own fulfilment, so too, in the supernatural order, we receive our faith from another: we cannot baptize ourselves. In our sharing in the divine life through the mediation of others in this way, Congar sees a reflection of the divine life itself, which is the self-giving of the triune Persons to each other.

Such relations of giving and receiving, dependence and exchange, hold true, moreover, not only of individuals but also of communities, of groups. For what is transmitted brings about an incorporation into a communion, and the act whereby others are united to the historic apostolic preaching found in Tradition is *baptism*. Congar describes the faith professed in baptism as

> essentially one transmitted and delivered, an object of *paradōsis* or *traditio*. (TT, p. 244)

This is something symbolized in the ceremony of 'handing over' the Creed in the course of the neophyte's instructions, spread out as these are through the liturgical celebration of Lent. The patristic and liturgical texts reviewed by Congar express, in his view:

> a fundamental unity and continuity between faith conceived in the heart, then progressively nurtured in the maternal bosom of the Church, professed in baptism where a man commits and consecrates himself, ratified by the physical action of baptism (immersion in Christ's paschal mystery through both water and the profession of faith), and lastly, faith professed in praise. (TT, p. 248)

Right faith is initiation and sharing in the doctrine and worship of the Church as the fellowship of those who live in Christ—which explains why Cyril of Alexandria (d. 444) could describe the Christological heretic Nestorius (d. *c*. 451) as one who had despised 'the tradition of the mystagogues of the *oikoumenē*'.[2] For the Creed given in baptism is a summary of the faith contained in Scripture, and thus of the apostolic faith.

That faith must be *received*, in correspondence with the structure of God's relations with humanity, not least in Scripture, which take the form of dialogue. Here Congar draws his readers' attentions to the last of Newman's *University Sermons*, where the Blessed Virgin Mary is presented as 'our pattern of Faith, both in the reception and in the study of Divine Truth':[3] not merely accepting the truth, but dwelling on it, developing, reasoning upon it. Such dialogue with the Word can and must take place in each Christian life, but it is only what God wishes it to be when it is corporately realized within the whole body. And, in Teilhardian language, Congar speaks of the Christian's faith as ever surrounded and penetrated by an 'ecclesiosphere', the living, concrete reality of the Church.

In relating Tradition, thus understood, to the divine missions, Congar distinguishes between the role of the Son and of the Spirit. From the viewpoint of the role of the Son, we can say that Tradition is not in dependence on time; rather, it triumphs over time, or even discounts it altogether. For the Incarnate Son, reigning as Lord above time, in giving the Church her life also assures the continuing identity of the truth she possesses: 'Jesus Christ is the same yesterday, today and for ever', as the letter to the Hebrews puts it (13:8). On the other hand, in relation to the Holy Spirit, we can say that Tradition is not simply the permanence of a structure: it is continual renewal and creativity within that structure. The Spirit gives it the 'inner movement of its life' (TT, p. 265). As the Johannine Christ has it, 'When the Spirit of truth comes, he will guide you into all truth' (Jn 16:13). The origins are the seed and the first-fruits, the promise of fulfilment, yet biblical ontology is 'radically eschatological': truth is found at the end of things where the gracious plan of God brings things to that condition for which they were always intended. So Tradition is development as well as transmission. It is not only a sacred deposit, but also the explication of that deposit as, over the years, it is lived and defended by the People of God.

> What we receive in the twentieth century is always the 'faith which was once for all delivered to the saints' (Jude 3), but we cannot detach this deposit from the fellowship of the saints who have received it, preserved and lived it from the time of the first 'saints' until our own times. We ourselves communicate with the apostles through and with the whole Church which sprang originally from them and has been the dwelling place of the Spirit since Pentecost. Finally, by them and through them we are in communion with the consciousness Jesus Christ himself had in his created human soul of the Father's plan, in short of the whole of the 'mystery'. (TT, p. 268)

From this vantage point Congar is able to consider four vital topics: the 'subject' of Tradition; the Gospel as the source of Tradition; the relation between Scripture and Tradition; and the relation of Tradition to its own forms of self-expression, its 'monuments'.

THE SUBJECT OF TRADITION

First, then, who or what is the 'subject' of tradition? The ultimate subject (or agent) of Tradition is always the Father, from whom the entire saving economy takes its rise. The Incarnation and the subsequent ministry of Jesus are the mission of the Word, the divine Son, in time. The apostles as messengers of Christ, his *shaliachim*, form one 'person', one subject of rights and activities, with him who sends them. The Church too is dedicated to a mission in prolonging that of Christ and the apostles. But if, in this way, mission is the 'external' cause of the unity between these agents, their *inner* principle of unity in the communication of Tradition is identified by Congar as the Holy Spirit.

> The unity of the subjects of Tradition has for its inner principle the Holy Spirit who accompanies each phase of the mission, giving it that reality demanded by God's part in the activity, according to its particular nature and degree. Thus the mission is, in its divinely instituted structures, a kind of sacrament of the Spirit who 'spoke through the prophets', who was the interior principle of Christ's mission from the start of his public ministry, and is also the interior principle of the apostles' and of the whole Church's ministry. . . . The Spirit does not cease to inhabit and animate the Church, concelebrating with it in the testimony which it gives. (TT, p. 313)

Drawing on the Fathers, the Tridentine doctors and the nineteenth-century Tübingen school, above all Möhler, Congar presents the Spirit as—in dependence on the Father—the transcendent subject of Tradition. The Spirit creates from within the Church's unity, and with that unity, the organs or expressions of its genius—its Tradition. It is characteristic of the Spirit, in Congar's presentation, that he acts within persons without in any way constraining them: so Congar interprets the references of Scripture to a divine inspiration scarcely distinguishable from the normal workings of human minds. The Spirit's goal in this inner working is the bringing about of unity and unanimity. 'He disposes each, according to his nature, vocation and place, to seek and promote the communion of all' (TT, p. 342).

So far this account of the Holy Spirit as the transcendent subject of the Church has been bereft of any Christological reference. But this Congar now deftly adds:

> As the 'Spirit *of Christ*', he does only Christ's work, neither actualizing nor personalizing anything other than the Gospel pattern of saving truth and life brought to men by Christ, who also ceaselessly watches over their accomplishment. (TT, p. 343)

Throughout the course of the historic succession of Tradition's witnesses, Christ the invisible, heavenly Head of the visible, temporal Church's body acts through the Spirit to make his Gospel ever new, in continuity with the form he gave it for once and for all. The Christ-given *institution* thus fructifies in *events*, thanks to the Spirit's work: thus Congar overcomes the antinomy in some Protestant writing on the Church where we are asked to choose between 'institution', a negative value, and 'event', a positive one. However, he stresses that the Spirit's rendering fruitful the founding activity of the Son does not mean that absolutely everything in the Church's historical life is guaranteed by the Spirit. On the contrary: the Spirit's inspirational role encourages us, among other things, to refer back to the original deposit, there to find the criteria which will enable us to evaluate what is happening here and now. And, using language he had already adopted in his celebration of Chalcedon, *Christ, Our Lady and the Church* (pp. 43ff.), he insists that we must avoid with equal care the Scylla of 'ecclesiological monophysitism'—a too unilaterally divine view of the Church—and the Charybdis of 'ecclesiological nestorianism'—a too unilaterally human one. The Church sees more in the deposit than does the historian; yet she must study that deposit with all the help available, including that of the historian himself.

> It [the Church] is truly indwelt, animated and assisted by the Spirit of Christ, and this will render any purely historicist conception of Tradition insufficient, to say the least. No truth or foundation can be found for the Catholic doctrine on Tradition if we deprive it of the support it claims to find in the New Testament theology of the Holy Spirit. But this Church in which the Spirit dwells, which is animated and assisted by him, is only assured of his presence if it remains within the framework of the covenant and in order that it may faithfully preserve the structure of the covenant. (TT, p. 344)

That Church is the immanent subject of Tradition, just as the Spirit is the transcendent subject. Faith, that is, has an essentially ecclesial character. Faith is a conviction to which we commit ourselves; but we do not manufacture its content. Here Congar cites his beloved Möhler:

> Without tradition, there would be no Christian doctrine, no Church, only isolated Christians; no community, only individuals; no certitude, only doubt and opinion.[4]

The Church is the 'supra-personal and sole ultimately adequate subject of faith' (TT, p. 319). Not only Möhler, but also Newman, and other writers of the last hundred years and more, have spoken of the Church's corporate sense of faith, her *sensus fidei*, in terms of 'consciousness'. Congar accepts this vocabulary, while noting, however, that this consciousness is not just (corporate) *self*-consciousness. The Church has more than self-awareness; it preserves the living memory of the revelation it has received, whose 'presence and freshness' are continually renewed by Christ and the Spirit. Of course, consciousness belongs to persons, and persons cannot be fused into some higher unity. The unity of persons in the Church is, rather,

> a 'communion': a large number of persons possess in common the same realities . . . as the content of their inner life, their memory and thus of their consciousness. Thus they are conscious not of their *personal* opinions but of the teaching *of the Church* that derives from the apostles. (TT, p. 320)

This is the basis of the Church's conciliarity, itself a *sobriquet* for the Church as communion, as simultaneously one and Catholic.

This reference to the roots from which the phenomenon of Church Councils draws life necessarily brings Congar to ask how this 'consciousness' is distributed among the Church's members. Are all equally and without distinction the bearers of the *sensus fidei*? What are the respective roles of the faithful laity and the ordained ministry in the work of traditioning the Gospel?

It must be said at once that *all* the members of the Body of Christ are active and responsible where Tradition is concerned. But there are two possible ways of exercising such responsibility. All of us have received the Christian life, and with that life the duty to 'share, bear witness and serve'. But alongside that mode of responsibility is a second, which consists in special commissioning to public office in the Church, a task accompanied by the resources of grace and spiritual authority necessary for its fulfilment. This was the situation of the apostles at the Church's beginnings; of the ministers commissioned by them to preside over the early communities; and of the ordained ministry in the Church today. To show the bearing of this for the idea of Tradition, Congar draws upon another nineteenth-century German theologian, the Cologne priest Matthias Joseph Scheeben (1835–88). Scheeben distinguished between, on the one hand, preserving and transmitting a tradition, and, on the other, defining that teaching.[5] The whole body of the faithful preserves Tradition, by living out its fidelity to the Christian covenant. Within this body there are some, such as lay theologians, who enjoy a teaching function which comes to them through particular circumstances and gifts. The task of the apostolic ministry, of the bishops, on the other hand—a task sacramentally conferred—is to define this same Tradition, either by the promulgation of its meaning in their day-to-day teaching or by its fixing in 'dogmas' properly so-called: rules for belief which are at the same time canonical criteria for shared communion. Congar does not intend to fall into the trap of Khomiakov who, as some of his Orthodox brethren have pointed out, in denying the authority of a *magisterium* in favour of the faith-preserving role of the people in their 'togetherness' or *sobornost'*, failed to distinguish between the 'defender' of the truth, *hyperastitēs*, and its 'judge', *kritēs*. The first is the layman and laywoman preserving the truth, the second the bishop, formulating it in authoritative canons.[6]

TRADITION AND THE GOSPEL

The *source* of this ecclesial Tradition is described by Congar, in a way consonant with the teaching of the Council of Trent, as *the Gospel itself*. Placing the decree of Trent in the context of contemporary sixteenth-century theology, he shows how, for the conciliar fathers, the Gospel is the source of all the Christianity which came from the apostles, its life-giving waters transmitted through the distributaries of Scripture and the traditions. Congar stresses the rich symbolism of the 'source', and also the way in which that symbolism carries the meanings of both saving knowledge (the 'noetic' dimension of the Gospel) and saving power (its 'dynamic' aspect).

The early Fathers, struck by the cry of Jesus in the Temple court as described in John 7:37—'Whoever is thirsty let him come to me and drink'—together with the Evangelist's comment on the 'streams of living water' that shall flow from the Messiah, were quick to produce a Christian symbolism of the source and its waters. Hippolytus of Rome (*c.* 170–*c.* 236), in his commentary on Daniel, describes the Church as a new Paradise with, at its centre, the true tree of life. From that garden flow four rivers, which water the whole earth. 'Christ, who is the river, is announced throughout the world by the fourfold Gospel.'[7] Congar considers that, for St John's gospel, the promise of a river of living water, sprung from the body of Christ, is fulfilled typologically on the Cross, when the lance-thrust opened in the Lord's side a stream of water and of blood. At the same time, Paul's application to Christ of the description in

Exodus of the rock from which Moses made a stream gush forth secured an honoured place for such symbolism. As Irenaeus of Lyons (*c.* 130–*c.* 200) has it

> The rock is Christ; and it has produced twelve streams, that is, the doctrine of the twelve apostles.[8]

In terms of iconography the theme receives frequent visual representations in the baptisteries of the age of Constantine (d. 337) and afterwards. In the baptismal mystery the believer is immersed not only in water, but in the Spirit, and in the faith transmitted to him, which is the Lord's law and Gospel. Outside of the baptisteries, the symbolism of the rivers recurs and Congar sums up its drift as follows:

> Christ is *fons*: source and font. He is simultaneously the source of Scripture, or of the Gospel, and of baptism, of saving knowledge, and of salvation, or life. (TT, p. 279)

This being so, Congar finds himself obliged to expand somewhat the concept of Tradition as normally understood. It is not so exclusively intellectual as has been supposed:

> *Traditio* came to its completion in (*re*)*generatio*. Its communication as knowledge and law was completed in a gift of life. . . . Tradition is not only noetic but real. It is a handing over of salvation, of the Christian life, of the reality of the covenant. (TT, pp. 279–80)

The Word, as investigation of the equivalent term *dabar* in the Hebrew Bible would show, both gives knowledge and produces an effect. Drawing on the 'actualism' (the equating of the divine utterance with the divine act) in the theology of the Swiss Protestant Karl Barth but also, and by preference, on the patristic witness, Congar holds that Scripture, sacraments and traditions are simply means whereby God's Word reveals and acts: *loci*, 'places', into which the Word has come, and still comes, as a living Person. Though the Word had not come as incarnate in the Old Testament, Congar nevertheless brings that Testament under his general account by insisting that the Old Testament is only life-giving for Christians when Jesus Christ comes and reads the Scriptures to us: a notion he has taken from the homilies of the Alexandrian doctor, Origen (*c.* 185–*c.* 254).[9] He concludes from his survey of Fathers, baptismal liturgy and early Christian art that the 'Gospel' is the source of the whole Christian life: knowledge, rebirth, ethics, holiness.

When transmitted, the 'Tradition' whose content it forms will be that of Christianity itself.

But Congar still has to consider the various modes of transmission of the single Gospel, and what is original or specific to each. First of all, Congar distinguishes, in the words of the title of his great book, between 'traditions' and 'Tradition'. The traditions are

> determinations, normative in conditions which we shall have to examine and not contained formally, in the canon of Scripture. They may originate with Jesus, the apostles, or the Church, and thus may be respectively divine, apostolic or ecclesiastical. They may be permanent or temporary in character. We may infer that, without prejudice to their dogmatic implications, their principal concern is worship and discipline. (TT, p. 287)

Congar notes here that, for a tradition to be termed 'divine' by the Fathers and great Scholastics, its formulation might well be ecclesiastical yet it was nonetheless understood to have come substantially from the apostles. For Leo the Great (d. 461) this was true of fasts, and of charitable collections; for Thomas Aquinas of the Creed; for Bonaventure (*c.* 1217–74) of such sacraments as Confirmation and the Anointing of the Sick; for authors too many to enumerate, of the institution of the Roman primacy. The identity involved, between the present practice and the origin,

> is less one of exterior form than of inspiration or general direction, maintained throughout later history by the Holy Spirit who guides the faithful so that they should preserve the deposit, and understand its meaning. (TT, p. 289)

Tradition, by contrast, is a far more comprehensive term. As Congar presents it, it comprises *three* main meanings. First, and fundamentally, it signifies the transmission of the whole Gospel—the whole Christian mystery—in whatever form. This will cover, then, the Bible and the preached word, confessions of faith, the sacraments and other liturgical actions, customs and prescriptions for conduct: these, together with the reality they 'convey or produce'. Such transmission of the Gospel, in its variety of modes, may itself be understood either in an *objective* sense, as the content thus transmitted; or in a *subjective* sense, as the act of transmitting this same content: a frequent meaning, the latter, in the Fathers of the ante-Nicene age. With regard to the ways in which Tradition in this aboriginal, primordial and all-encompassing sense is given to us, Congar, in keeping with the classical position of Catholic theology, stresses the unique place of Scripture. Not only does Scripture have an absolute dignity and value derived from the fact that God willed that this collection of texts should exist and enabled its authors to produce it by a special grace. More, we can set forth the 'advantages' of this dispensation. Scripture, like any text or series of texts, has a public character; it is permanent, solid, for the 'written letter abides'; it enables verification or 'indisputable reference' for the oral proclamation of the Gospel. Congar, it is true, accepts Newman's point, made in the *Apologia pro Vita Sua*, that

> the sacred text was never intended to teach doctrine, but only to prove it, and if we would learn doctrine, we must have recourse to the formularies of the Church.[10]

Yet with the mediaeval Byzantine mystic, Symeon the New Theologian (949–1022), he points out that, for the Fathers, Scripture was much more than a means to combat heresy. It was a source of saving knowledge. Symeon wrote of his own reading of the Bible:

> Each time that I found myself at the well, you took my head and plunged it into the stream, letting me see the brilliance of your Light.[11]

However, and this brings us to the second reference for the term 'Tradition' which Congar discerns in the historic documents, we may distinguish here between the *objects* into which, in Tradition, the Gospel has crystallized—above all, then, the Bible—and the meaning, or right interpretation, of those objects. Here Tradition becomes the meaning found in those objects by the community to and within which they have come down. With reference to the Bible in particular, Tradition is 'a certain usage and reading . . . made from the viewpoint of the Christian mystery', an interpretation which has multiple dimensions—at once Christological, ecclesiological and eschatological—all held together by the 'analogy of faith', the principle which permits an understanding of one part of the Scripture in terms of some or all of the rest, since all have a primordial unity in the divine act of self-revelation in Christ and his Spirit.

TRADITION AS INTERPRETATION

Congar lays especial stress on this second sense of the term 'Tradition'. And here he is particularly indebted to Blondel. In Blondel's lifetime, the brilliant—and eventually apostate—Scripture scholar Loisy had presented the problem of exegesis, of understanding the Bible, as a choice between, on the one hand, traditional dogmatic affirmations in their unadorned rigour and, on the other, the treatment of the texts by the very same historical-critical methods that one would use in any secular historical enquiry. In his 'History and Dogma'[12] Blondel had sought to avoid both this 'historicism' of Loisy and its spuriously traditional alternative, the rational-apologetic approach to Scripture favoured by the orthodox of the period, stigmatized by Blondel as 'extrinsicism'. Congar follows Blondel in regarding both positions as vitiated by the same mistake. Their supporters failed to grasp the true pattern of religious understanding, the mode of subject–object relations proper to the reading of Scripture by the eye of faith. For both neglected the Christian experience of an ever-present reality, the economy of salvation, to which the documents bear witness at their own level and in their own way. As Congar cites Blondel:

> Some part of the Church is beyond the power of science to check; and it is this which, without dispensing with or neglecting the data of exegesis and history, yet at the same time checks them all, since it has, in the very same Tradition that constitutes it, other means of knowing its author, sharing in his life, relating facts to dogmas, and justifying ecclesiastical teaching root-and-branch.[13]

While gratefully agreeing with this viewpoint, Congar nevertheless enters certain caveats in connexion with Blondel's discussion as a whole.

First, while the Church's faith can penetrate the meaning of texts and events, it is not, strictly speaking, creative. Faith, and declarations about the faith by the *magisterium*, do depend on evidence, 'at least in a mediate way'. The value of this evidence is determined in part by its historicity, and in part by those considerations which classical apologetics has introduced. Congar feels that Blondel minimized both the need to refer back to documentary data, and the intrinsic 'possibilities of history'—perhaps because the dominant school of historiography which he faced was an historicist first-cousin to scientism. Today, Congar thinks, when this positivist strait-jacket has been shaken off by historians, or at least by many of their fellowship, a more 'complete' history

> less bookish and critical, and more open to human realities, can offer better resources to the believer who wishes to dis-

> cover what support his religious experience can find in the relevant evidence. (TT, p. 367)

Furthermore, though Blondel was right to see Tradition as something implicit in the lives of the faithful, this should not be taken to exclude reference to the apostolic witness as already containing and communicating a theological interpretation of facts. The Church is in contact with revelation not just as a reality to be lived, but also as a precious intellectual 'deposit' with a dogmatic character from the start.

Nevertheless, Congar's account of Tradition, although better informed exegetically and theologically than Blondel's, fundamentally re-creates his. To it Congar adds from his own reading of the 'great pedagogues' the *nuance* that Tradition is, above all, an educative *milieu* for faith. Education is only secondarily instruction; primarily, it is an 'infectious contact with living models'.[14] In the fashioning of this unique environment, Congar ascribes a special role to *women*, and notably to wives and mothers. Just as the novel celebrates woman as warm and faithful maker and guardian of the home, in, for example, Sigrid Undset's *Kristin Lavransdatter*, or, at a different level of achievement, in A. J. Cronin's *The Citadel*, so have Catholic poets and theologians celebrated Mother Church in the same language: lyrically, in the 'hymns' of Gertrud von le Fort (1876–1971), with erudition and conceptual power in the Jesuits Hugo Rahner (1900–68) and Henri de Lubac (1896–   ), and the Dominican Humbert Clérissac (1864–1914).

THE MONUMENTS OF TRADITION

But thirdly and lastly, this interpretation of Scripture which is Tradition in one of the senses of that word is itself expressed in a range of expressions or 'monuments'. These are referred to *en bloc* in the manuals of the period from the mid-eighteenth century to the Second Vatican Council (the time of Congar's writing) in the famous phrase *probatur ex Traditione*, 'to be proved from Tradition'. Congar explains:

> A certain spirit or living understanding in the Christian community . . . may be recognized as the origin of such monuments, just as one argues that there exists a certain spirit behind the cultural manifestations of a people, or a certain ethos in a family. Tradition is thus that Catholic sense which the Church

> possesses as the supra-individual and living subject of a series of testimonies in which is expressed its interpretation of what it transmits and what it lives by. (TT, p. 288)

The identification of such 'monuments' and their relation to Tradition will be one of Congar's main preoccupations. No movement of theological and ecclesial *ressourcement* such as that of which his work forms part could do without a closer look at what *are* the sources. And here Congar proposes to distinguish between those sources which *constitute* Tradition—the apostolic heritage—and those which simply *declare* it. In the first case, what actually constitutes Tradition is the twofold reality described at the Council of Trent: Scripture and the unwritten traditions. However, and in the second place, whereas Scripture is immediately available to us in the highly material form of a physical book, the Bible, that other constitutive source, the unwritten traditions, only becomes available through a range of mediations which 'declare' its content. These declarative sources Congar calls the 'monuments of Tradition'. He lists them as: the teaching of the *magisterium*; the liturgy, and, to a lesser degree, iconography and Christian archaeology, even down to such things as epigraphy—theologically relevant inscriptions left behind by the Christian generations of the past; the Fathers and Doctors of the Church; the sacred canons (which he expands to include other 'facts of the Church's life and customs'); and, lastly, the witness of theologians.

In practice, however, Congar concentrates on three kinds of monument: the liturgy, the Fathers, and what he calls 'ordinary expressions of the Christian life'. Congar holds a high doctrine of the liturgy as a monument of Tradition. As the active celebration of the Christian mystery, the liturgy contains that mystery in its fullness and transmits all its essential elements.

> The Church has invested the whole of its faith in its prayer, and though fervour does not *create* truth, yet the liturgy contains, offers, and expresses in its own way all of the mysteries, only certain aspects of which have been formulated by our theological understanding and in dogmas. (TT, p. 355)

With an eye on Protestant sensibilities, Congar describes the liturgy as presenting us continually with the most basic Scriptural truths, thus enabling us to respond fittingly to the Word it proclaims. However, he also warns against a didactic exploitation of the liturgy, which would be to misconceive its proper mode of working. The liturgy's manner of teaching in its confession of faith takes the form of praise. It is doxological tuition that

> simply goes ahead, calmly confident, with the affirmation of what it does and affirming the content of what it hands on in its celebration. (TT, p. 356)

Though there are limited portions of the liturgy which have particular heresies in view (Pelagianism in a number of the collects of the Roman rite, Arianism in the *Gloria Patri*), by and large the liturgy is directed against no one. It simply portrays salvation, whence its serene and joyful character. It is essentially conservative, preserving intact 'something entrusted to the faithful and withdrawn from profanation'. It is an act of the whole body, congregational and hierarchical at one and the same time. It is 'mysteric', in the term preferred by the theologian of the liturgy and monk of Maria Laach Dom Odo Casel (1886–1948). That is, it is a holy thing, presupposing prayer, fasting and openness to the Spirit. Its only weakness, as a monument of Tradition, lies in the relative imprecision of its language, notes Congar, confessing in the same breath, however, that to it he owes at least half of what he has understood in theology.

Congar stresses that the liturgy is centred on Christ, in his Paschal mystery, but not without his holy ones, the saints. Into the natural time of the world, and the course of human life, it inserts the fact of Christ:

> making him present there so that he may become the source of salvation and holiness for men and for the world, and the source of glory for God. (TT, p. 430)

This it does through the unique reality of the sacramental order, in which the hidden reality of Christ becomes revealed and active, as the crucified and risen Lord brings to perfection in mankind that new creation which he founded in his passing over to the Father. The liturgy is *Paschal*, created in the light of Easter and Pentecost: it is, furthermore, an active sharing in the passing over of the Lord, and not simply its retelling. Its content is, therefore, the truth of the divine–human covenant relationship, a relationship finally confirmed in the death and resurrection of Christ, the definitive point of encounter between God and man. The liturgy shows Christ more specifically, as in the act of joining to himself a holy people: it celebrates with Christ the mystery of the saints and their communion. Congar insists that we must not allow distortions and abuses to cloud for us the meaning of this sanctoral cycle, and its necessary accompaniment, the cult of images and of relics. Among the ruins of a North African basilica (Belezma, in Numidia), so Congar reports, a broken reliquary vase bears the inscription: *in isto vaso sancto congregabuntur membra Christi*, 'in this sacred vessel, Christ's members are gathered together'.

> The liturgy has understood, and will help us too to realize, that if the whole of Scripture unfolds before us man's true relation with God, it does not speak only about Christ, but about us as well, it does not sunder Jesus Christ from his saints: in it he appears as *clothed* with them, as with his visible body. (TT, p. 432)[15]

All this is summed up in what the liturgy has to say about Mary, when, using the analogy of faith, it applies to her themes, images and texts taken from the whole body of Scripture, thus becoming Tradition's most vital source for Marian doctrine. This is possible, Congar writes, only because

> Mary, as the Mother of Jesus, is together with him at the centre of God's saving plan: she is thus seen in a christological light and at the same time as the centre of the mystery of the Church, which is itself at the heart of the redeemed world. (TT, p. 433)

Congar concludes by echoing Dom Prosper Guéranger (1805–75) of Solesmes, to the effect that the liturgy *is* Tradition, 'at its highest degree of power and solemnity'.[16]

Congar deals more briefly with the Fathers, whom he presents in such a way as to justify the description of his own work as that of a 'neo-patristic' theologian. It is a commonplace of Catholic theology that the 'Fathers' are those who satisfy certain dogmatic requirements, namely: orthodoxy of doctrine; antiquity; sanctity; the approval of the Church, and especially of the Roman church in whose communion they must have lived and died. Whilst not disputing the validity of such a list of qualities, Congar finds it somewhat external and even imprecise: how ancient, for example, must 'antiquity' be? He prefers to speak of the Fathers as those who have contributed a decisive element to the Church's life: either to its faith, its worship, its discipline or its 'general attitude'. The Fathers were able to give a permanent form to the life of the entire subsequent Church because they were, as the mediaevals loved to call them, the '*holy* Fathers', men raised up, enlightened and strengthened by the Holy Spirit.

> Indeed, when one reflects on the part played by St Athanasius or St Hilary on behalf of faith in the Trinity, by St Basil in establishing belief in the divine person of the Holy Spirit, by St Jerome in giving the Latins a better Bible text, by St Augustine in the doctrine on grace, by St Cyril and St Leo on the Incarnation, together with the councils which correspond to these stages in doctrinal development . . . one realizes only too well how none but men and assemblies of men raised up by God and sustained by his Spirit were able to wield such a decisive influence upon the life of the people of God. (TT, p. 439–40)

And Congar calls the patristic effort of clarifying revelation a true, though secondary, continuation of the part originally played in the divine self-communication by Scripture.

Not that Congar is unaware of the *lacunae* in patristic theology. Naturally their teaching, overwhelmingly exegetical as it was, lacked the sense of historical perspective, the philosophical resources and understanding of literary genre which later scholars possessed. It suffered too from its excessive recourse to the rhetorical procedures of the time; from the philosophical weaknesses of the Platonist tradition which was the Fathers' predominant intellectual background; and from the restricting effects of the pressing pastoral need to combat the pullulating heresies of the early Church. Their work was historically conditioned and should not be appealed to as a final conclusion that would disallow other historical movements, analogous to their own, in the bosom of the Church. Nevertheless, and here is where the primary emphasis of Congar's account falls, the Church of the Fathers was possessed of 'something quite special and privileged'. They brought about the fundamental determinations of the Church's character and structure at a time when its past 'consisted only of the apostles, their disciples and the martyrs'.

> This definite historical phase belonged to the Church's youth; it was the period not of birth, nor of the very first years, but the time when there first come to light the themes and images, convictions and deep reactions, first orientations and experiences, and rejections, too, which define the bases of a character and will continue to have an influence throughout the rest of life. (TT, p. 446)

In the Fathers we see the Christian religion crystallizing into that form which, in its historic mainstream, it has preserved ever since: confessionally, in the Creeds and conciliar definitions, liturgically, in the great rites, Western and Eastern; canonically, in its first rules of common life, filled as these are with an implicit ecclesiology.

Congar does not leave the subject of the Fathers without offering a character-sketch of their theology, and that sketch is something of a mirror of his *own* portrait of what theology should be. He lauds patristic theology for three features: concentration on fundamentals; pastoral fruitfulness; and a symbiosis of theology with spirituality. Because their theology focuses on the principal Christian dogmas of God, Christ the Spirit and the Church, and reflects a sense of the faith as an interconnected whole, the Fathers are effective witnesses of tradition. With the help of Dom Odo Casel, another pioneer of the twentieth-century patristic revival, Congar describes this concentration on fundamentals as 'theocentric', 'Christocentric', 'ecclesiocentric' and 'mysteriocentric'.[17]

It is *theocentric*, presenting God as the primary reality. All else is seen in relation to him. The creature issues from God and moves back to God by tending through the Holy Spirit to the perfection God has willed for it. But this Spirit is the Spirit of Christ: hence *Christocentricity*. Furthermore, Christ gives the Spirit as 'head' or source of the Church: hence *ecclesiocentricity*. The Church's life is, however, fully realized only through the celebration of her sacraments or mysteries: hence *mysteriocentricity*.

Patristic theology was also, Congar tells us, a pastorally useful theology. Most of the Fathers were pastors, often bishops, and they wrote to serve the needs of the Church of their day. Though making them more time-bound, perhaps, to the accidents of history, such a pastoral finality corresponds well to the intrinsic purpose of theology itself: the building up of God's people in wisdom and understanding.

Finally, we find in patristic theology, a union of what today might be regarded as purely theological with strictly spiritual elements. The Fathers, many of whom were monks, committed Christian ascetics, did not regard the life of prayer—conscious striving for union with God in Christ and his Spirit—as irrelevant to theological practice. Theology and spirituality in them had not yet gone their separate ways.

Congar's last chosen monument of Tradition is 'ordinary expressions of the Christian life'. In the first place, this means those actions and customs expressive of the Christian spirit in the normal settings of human life: birth and death, childhood and old age, love and the family, sickness and festivity, work, consideration for the poor. The witness to Tradition here is located in the social effects produced by faith in the Gospel. But secondly, the most striking and theologically richly laden of such effects are what we call the 'saints'. Although the saints are frequently enough humble folk, whose faces are scarcely registered by public history, in and through them the Church 'lives in a special manner'. Their lives help us to understand Scripture, since both are under the inspiration of the same Holy Spirit.

DOGMA

Though all such monuments embody insights into revelation, yet faith cannot for that reason do without dogma proper, presented by Congar as at once a truth and a value: a *religous* truth, filled with helpful significance for the believer's life and destiny. The essential meaning of dogmas is that which the Church's profound intention gives them, 'ever the same', independently of the movement of human ideas. Yet of the formulae in which such dogmas are expressed Congar can only say with Galileo (1564–1642), 'And yet it moves', for they are ever-changing, and the Church's pastors and theologians are duty-bound to seek out those that are most effectively 'catholic', universal, in terms *both* of the many different cultures to which her mission takes her, *and* of the ecumenical demands of the re-construction of her integral unity (FT, p. 69). But it should not be thought that these *desiderata* of Congar's amount to a plea for the deliberate obfuscation of dogma in any sense that the plain Catholic could recognize. He insists that the value of dogma presupposes three things which the history of the centuries since the Protestant Reformation has called into question. And these are: first, the existence of a *magisterium* in the Church; secondly, the validity of conceptual affirmations concerning what lies beyond the empirical realm; and thirdly, the continuity of that bond which links together in a single chain: the historic, revelation-charged facts; the testimony to these facts; the meaning given to these testimonies once the generation of eyewitnesses had passed away; and finally, the formulation of this meaning in the dogmas which the Church proffers to the faithful for their assent.

Congar's discussion of the nature of dogma takes as its most significant background the Modernist crisis of the turn of this century. He describes the origins of Modernism as a 'conjunction between a problem and a philosophico-religious climate' (FT, p. 56). The *problem* was the tremendous historical and critical achievement of nineteenth-century scholars, which necessarily confronted Churchmen with the difference between, on the one hand, the primitive Christian 'given', and, on the other, the dogmatic and institutional expressions of that 'given' which Christianity made its own in later centuries. How should the relationship between these two be conceived? The *climate*, philosophically speaking, was a subtle blend of evolutionism and the doctrines of Kant. Evolutionism, the tendency to construe reality in terms of the biological model offered for the life sciences by Charles Darwin (1809–82), naturally took development to be 'transformism': a sloughing off the old, rather than its continued being in a fresh guise. Kantianism criticized all claims to a conceptual knowledge of meta-empirical realities, for which it desired to substitute an ethical affirmation of the values implicit in existence. This same climate, considered religiously, was dominated by a 'desire to rejoin the modern world': in other words, to mediate between the Church's tradition and contemporary culture by some appropriate explanation of the former to the latter.

> In these conditions, the Modernists properly so-called proposed a theory not only of dogma and dogmatic formulations, but of revelation itself. To keep religion free of those intellectual categories they deemed to be changing, relative, even outworn, they disengaged religion from intellectuality itself. They unburdened it of the claim, which they judged ruinous, to be a revelation, that is: a divine supply of ideas, of *truths*, conceptual in kind. (FT, p. 57)

Congar finds that the thought of Loisy and George Tyrrell (1861–1909) corresponds adequately to this summary, though he partially removes from the company of the French exegete and English spiritual theologian his fellow-countryman the philosopher Edouard Le Roy (1870–1954): for while Le Roy believed the positive sense of doctrine to be essentially *practical*—an imperative for conduct—he did not deny that the divine reality must be such as to justify the behaviour thus imposed, and so its later dogmatic representation. However, the Church's *magisterium* insisted that this is not enough: there is in the dogma concerned a true conceptual articulation, itself the measure and rationale of the religious practice. Yet as this account suggests, this does not prevent dogma from being simultaneously truth *and* value: if pragmatism forgets the first, a 'wholly juridical orthodoxy of the mere letter' forgets the second. Though the Church's doctors and saints have attached the highest importance to certain formulae in which the meaning of the apostolic faith becomes transparent (the *homoousion* of the Arian crisis, the *transubstantiatio* of mediaeval Eucharistic controversy and the Council of Trent), nevertheless, at the end of the day, since faith is a 'power for life and contemplation' it terminates not in its own formulae but in God himself. Or, as Congar puts it, in a characteristic recasting of Thomas's own statement to this effect, faith finds its end in the covenant relationship which is 'God for us and we ourselves for God' (FT, p. 71).[18]

THE DEVELOPMENT OF DOGMA

Congar addressed himself to a recurrent problem of Catholic fundamental theology since Newman: the development of doctrine. After scanning the evidence up to the crisis of interpretation of that idea known as Modernism, Congar concludes that the Fathers, notably Gregory Nazianzen (329–389), Augustine and Vincent of Lérins (d. *c.* 450), are not without some recognition of development, and that, moreover, the Middle Ages 'remained in their line'.

> On the one hand, it was convinced that all truth lies in Scripture, and all dogma in the articles of the Creed, which comes from the apostles. On the other hand, it admitted with equal tranquillity that God himself does not cease to 'reveal' to the Fathers and the Councils elements of liturgy, discipline and doctrine. (FT, pp. 94–5)

However, what dominated was the idea of the unity of faith, and the 'perfect' knowledge of revelation in the apostolic heads of the Church. In the wake of the great Scholastics and their commentators, little interested in history as these were, theologians became absorbed in disengaging what was (merely) logically implicit in revelation. While the First Vatican Council admitted 'soberly, yet clearly' the existence of such a thing as doctrinal development, it took the Modernist crisis to shake people out of their ahistorical dogmatic slumbers into reflecting on the conditions of such development. Since then, Congar continues, we have distinguished more successfully between the possibilities of understanding opened up by historical science as such, and those—much richer, from the theological viewpoint—which belong to the 'properly ecclesial and Christian tradition' in the matter of discerning whether and how some truth is included in the apostolic deposit. And Congar proposes as a guiding star the following proposition:

> The fact of a progress in the understanding of the faith finds its foundation in the very nature of revelation as in the proper character of the 'time of the Church', the latter being a community of human beings *en marche*. (FT, p. 99)

Like the Neo-Scholastics of the earlier part of the century, above all the Spanish Dominican Neo-Thomist Francisco Marin-Sola (1873–1932), Congar initially describes such doctrinal development as an explicitation of what is still implicit in the normative *donné* or 'given' of the apostolic teaching. As he points out, a reality or a truth can either be perceived in itself, 'in its own contours, or forms', or as enveloped in the gift of another reality or truth. With the Neo-Scholastics, Congar holds that the process of separating out one truth from the original reality may be thoroughly intellectual, and even strictly logical in character: an implicit truth, formally contained in another explicit truth, can be teased out by (deductive) 'explicitative' reasoning. If, by contrast, the implicit truth concerned is only *virtually* contained in the truth established earlier, the reasoning process involved will require more *finesse*, what Newman called, in relation to the act of assent, the 'illative sense'. However, Congar, with his more acute feeling for history than the Neo-Thomists, proposes that, in addition, this kind of relationship of implicit to explicit also exists in the *practical* order. The dogmatically implicit can be enveloped in, for example, a liturgical practice. Thus, the doctrine of the sacramentality of the episcopate may be said to have been so 'contained' in the Roman liturgical practice of ordaining the 'archdeacon'—the senior deacon—of the local church to the episcopal order without an intermediate promotion to the presbyterate. Yet Congar is sufficiently Thomist in his fundamental allegiance to add that what is thus implicit in action only becomes consciously explicit through the work of intelligence, of mind in act.

He insists that this business of the implicit element in revelation is not a regrettable necessity due to human stupidity, but fits in well with revelation's own nature as the 'unveiling of a free and gracious design'. How does he understand this *convenientia*, or 'fittingness' of doctrinal development? He maintains that the Word of the revealing God is not a pure act of God which can function without engaging human co-operation. While classical Protestant theology characteristically fails to recognize the significance of our *agi*, 'acting', conceiving the Church's faith as, rather, a simple mirroring of the

Word, and her history as a series of returns to that Word in the face of temptations to syncretism, Catholicism can echo the philosopher Henri Bergson and say, 'God has created creators'. The immanence of God in his creature means that the truth is not simply given to us but also lived out or acted upon—even though everything that is thus lived out is indeed graciously given. Congar finds the enduring value of Newman's essay to lie in its author's abilities to combine the qualities of historian and psychologist, for

> the living reception of the faithful and the Church follows the conditions proper to the spirit of man. (FT, p. 104)

And here Congar notes, again, in Bergsonian language, that the Church has her own *durée*, her proper mode of temporal existence.

> This *durée* is characterized at once by a permanence or identity of the work of Christ . . . and by the ceaseless visitations of God, appropriated to the Holy Spirit, which theology analyses in its discussion of the 'divine missions'. The Holy Spirit, who is Christ's Spirit, first interiorizes the work of Christ, but also, secondly, accomplishes it in never ceasing to 'take from him', our Alpha, to bear him to his plenitude, as our Omega. (FT, pp. 105–6)

These being the fundamental conditions which mark the 'time of the Church', that time may be described as

> filled by, in the first place, the free response of men to the word of the prophets, of Christ himself and of the apostles, a word given once for all, a Word itself normative and situating.

This response is conditioned in large part, Congar explains, by the changing circumstances of history. In the *second* place, however, the time of the Church is *also* made up of

> divine initiatives or 'missions', given to men to arouse and fulfil a response of faithfulness and holiness. (FT, p .106)

The development of the original *donné* in this way marries 'purity' with 'plenitude'.

How, in the concrete, does this development work? Congar does not speak of a single, unilateral way, but of ways in the plural. Fundamentally, they may be reduced to two.

First, there is the way of 'faithful life', for between faith and the Christian life there is a 'constant coming and going'. Congar is careful to distinguish this position from that of Tyrrell, for whom devotional life enjoyed complete autonomy *vis-à-vis* dogma, and preceded belief. On the contrary, he says, history often shows the Church intervening to prune back a devotion or even to suppress it altogether.

Secondly, there is the way of theological precision: here we find faith in its rational mood, thinking out the sense of its own affirmations. Yet, he warns, dogmatization by reference to this way of 'theological conclusions' alone is rare. In both 'ways', Congar stresses, development may take place through response to pressures, or currents, in the circumambient secular sphere wherein the Church's life and thought are set.

> Any fact of civilization can be the starting-point for a movement of thought in the Church. This is only normal, because the Church lives in the world, in time, and she receives assistance so that she may, precisely, offer divine testimony in time, through responding to the questions which history poses. (FT, p. 111)

Finally, Congar must consider how we can make our judgement that some putative development really is a case of authentic development, one where a relationship of homogeneity unites a new expression to the primordial 'fact' or 'given'. To some degree, Congar holds, such a judgement is made by way of teasing out what is logically implicit in an earlier stage of doctrinal truth. However, this factor plays a much smaller rôle for Congar than for earlier Dominican theorists of doctrinal development. What is implicit in revelation is above all the relation of things to the covenant design of the living God; and, in any case, unless some truth is formally attested by the Word of God, it can hardly be proposed to people for their *assent of faith*, though, should it be a logical entailment of truths that are so attested, it may well be presented to them for their *theological agreement*.

From this logical or quasi-logical approach, characteristic of Scholasticism both mediaeval and modern, Congar passes on to the more historical manner of proceeding which relies on *documentation* for establishing the homogeneity of development. For Congar, such interrogation of the written witnesses of Tradition is necessary, but only partially effective. Apart from the possible loss or corruption of such evidence in the course of time, an implicit knowledge of later explicit truths is extremely difficult, if not impossible, for a student of the relevant documents to establish. And Congar frankly admits that not all of the early Christian evidence is likely to point towards the later positions of the Church: it is only on the basis of Catholic faith that the historian of doctrine lays aside divergent witnesses as constituting a minority report. This leaves only one other possibility: we must make our judgement by reference to the Church's awareness and to her *magisterium*.

As a Thomist and an historian, Congar is, however, careful to say that in judging on this basis, we must incorporate and use to their full limits the other two 'methods', those of logic and of appeal to documents. His appeal to the faith-awareness of the Church, and the judgement of her *magisterium*, is not, of course, as our investigation of his concept of Tradition should indicate, a counsel of despair. Theologically, the Church is the only subject capable of grasping adequately the internal homogeneity of the revealed 'given' in its self-expression through time. With the assistance of the Holy Spirit, perception of the homogeneity between the apostolic deposit and its later explicitation can be found in the 'sense of the Church', the judges of which are the bearers of the apostolic ministry.

> If the final criterion of the homogeneity of developments is the Church's awareness of the self-identity of her life, and of the conformity of some 'novelty' arising in that life's duration with the form given once for all, then this awareness only receives its definitive character and its value as a criterion in and by the teaching of the episcopal body in communion with the successor of Peter. (FT, pp. 116–17)

Thus the judgement of the hierarchy is the formal element which constitutes Tradition in its dogmatic value.

The revelation given once for all, then, is conserved and proposed to all mankind by the Church Christ founded. Though the Church's mediation of revelation issues in objective determinations of its content, namely dogmas, Congar insists that public doctrine must be contextualized within a wider whole. The Church is not only a teacher; she is also 'Mother Church', and her total membership provides, over and above the specific doctrinal contribution of the apostolic ministry with its teaching office, 'the nourishing and educative milieu of faith' (FT, p. 51). It is to Congar's reflections on the being of the Church as such that we must now turn.

Notes

1 One might usefully compare Congar's concern with *ressourcement* in supernatural society to that of his French contemporary Simone Weil

in natural society. As she writes, 'due to this continuity, a collectivity has its roots in the past. It constitutes the sole agency for preserving the spiritual treasures accumulated by the dead, the sole transmitting agency by which the dead can speak to the living': *L'Enracinement* (Paris, 1943); Eng. trans. *The Need for Roots* (London, 1952; 1978), p. 8.

2 Cyril of Alexandria, *Quod unus sit Christus* (PG 75, 1257 B–C).

3 J. H. Newman, *University Sermons* XV. 3.

4 J. A. Möhler, *Symbolik* XXXIX; ed. J. Geiselmann (Cologne, 1958), pp. 421–2; quoted in TT, p. 315.

5 M. J. Scheeben, *Dogmatik* XIII. 170; XV. 200, 206; cited in TT, p. 322.

6 For critical comments by Orthodox writers on A. S. Khomiakov's interpretation of the 1848 letter of the Eastern patriarchs, see S. Bulgakov, *The Orthodox Church* (London, 1935), p. 92; Metropolitan Germanos of Thyateira, preface to S. Bolshakoff, *The Doctrine of the Unity of the Church in the Works of Khomyakov and Moehler* (London, 1946), p. lx.

7 Hippolytus, *In Danielem* I, 17 (*Sources chrétiennes* 14 [Paris, 1942], p. 86).

8 Irenaeus, *Proof of the Apostolic Preaching* 46 (*Ancient Christian Writers* 16 [Westminster, MD/London, 1952], pp. 77–8).

9 Origen, *In Jesum Nave Homilia* 9.8 (PG 12, 876A–877A).

10 J. H. Newman, *Apologia pro Vita Sua* (London, 1865; 1934), p. 9.

11 Symeon the New Theologian, *Discourses* 91; as cited by M. Lot-Borodine in *La Vie spirituelle* 27 (June 1931), pp. 305–6.

12 M. Blondel, 'Histoire et dogme. Les lacunes philosophiques de l'exégèse moderne', *La Quinzaine* 56 (1904), pp. 145–67; 349–73; 433–58; repr. in *Les Premiers Ecrits de Maurice Blondel* (Paris, 1956), pp. 149–245.

13 Ibid., pp. 205–6; cited in TT, p. 362.

14 Congar is thinking here of M. Scheler's *Vorbilder und Führer* of which a French translation had recently appeared as *Le Saint, le Génie, le Héros* (Lyons/Paris, 1958), p. 36.

15 The reliquary vase was described in J. Gage, '*Membra Christi* et la disposition des reliques sous l'autel', *Revue archéologique* (1929), pp. 137–53.

16 P. Guéranger, *Institutions liturgiques*, quoted in TT, p. 435.

17 O. Casel, 'Neue Zeugnisse für das Kultmysterium', *Jahrbuch für Liturgiewissenschaft* 13 (1933), pp. 99–171.

18 St Thomas's statement that *actus credentis non terminatur ad enuntiabile sed ad rem* may be found at *Quaestiones disputatae de Veritate*, q. 14, a. 8 ad 5; a. 12; and also at *Summa Theologiae* IIa IIae, q. 1, a. 2 ad 2.

4

Congar's ecclesiology: (a) The Church at large

As we saw (Ch. 1), Congar's interest in ecclesiology can hardly be separated from his concern with a Church reform that will 'return to the sources'. He discerned a crying need, both in missionary outreach and in ecumenical endeavour, for 'a concept of the Church which is broad, rich, living, and full of biblical and traditional sap'. To foster such a notion, the theology of the Church must live by 'an intimate and organic contact with its own data, its "given" '.[1] It is this desire to restore to the contemporary community its own historic heritage which explains the copious documentation in which Congar's ecclesiological essays seem positively to exult. The chronicling of successive ecclesiologies in Congar's strictly historical works provides the treasury of theological concepts on which he draws for his attempts to reproduce the pattern of this many-faceted reality.

UNITY AND PLURALITY

There is no one Congarian ecclesiology. In *Divided Christendom*, however, he shows a characteristic concern to illuminate the rationale of the Church's unity by disengaging the basic principles of her life. First and foremost she is 'the Church of the Trinity', the extension of the divine life, itself a unity in plurality. Echoing Cyprian of Carthage (d. 258), Congar remarks that

> the unity of the holy and undivided Trinity which is the perfect unity in plurality is the model and principle of the unity of the Church. (DC, p. 58)

In more Augustinian mood, he stresses particularly the role of the Holy Spirit as unifier for us as for the divine Trinity, since the Spirit is the gracious source of all the supernatural gifts and virtues which orient us towards God's own inner-Trinitarian oneness.

The Church is also, secondly, 'the Church in Christ', the Body of the Mediator of the divine self-communication. If she is to be divinizing, she must be a 'Christic' reality,

> bound up with the life of him who alone can return to the Father from whom he came. (DC, p. 63)

We enter the Body of Christ, and partake of the life it brings, by the sacraments in which faith is expressed and rendered vital. As Congar describes them, the sacraments of faith are not, strictly speaking,

> new acts, but, under the spiritual mode of a symbolic-real celebration, the true substantial presence . . . or the sanctifying power . . . of the redeeming mystery of Christ. (DC, p. 62)

Lastly, the Church is 'the Church taken from amongst men', since God's relations with mankind must take a social form and face, man being a *polis*-dwelling animal. The law of incarnation, adopted by God in the work of our redemption by Christ, from the Flesh-taking through Passion to Resurrection, also governs the work of our deification, from Pentecost to the Parousia. It follows that the life of the Church-Body must be served by an institution, for the earthly Church must assume the human and social form of any community of people bound together in pursuit of common ends. Drawing on the principles of Chalcedonian Christology, identified as the key to theological evaluation in all realms of a Christianity 'recentred' on Christ, Congar proposes that, like Christ's two natures, the Church's mystery and her institutional existence are united inseparably but without confusion. Or again, on the analogy of Aristotle's doctrine of man, he suggests that, as the body is the instrument and manifestation of the soul, so the visible Church is the instrument and manifestation of Christ's invisible life (DC, pp. 59–110).[2] He insists that:

> There is not, on the one hand, an invisible disembodied, purely 'mystical' Body, and, on the other, a lifeless corpse consisting of the external ecclesiastical organization. For that which is thus organized is precisely the human fellowship of the friends of God, and the mystical Body *is* the ecclesiastical *societas* itself. (DC, p. 80)

In a way crucial for both reform and ecumenism, Congar describes the Church's catholicity as the 'dynamic universality of her unity'. It is the capacity of her principles of unity to unite with God all human beings and every human value. Trinitarian and Christological in its foundations, that catholicity expresses the relation between the unity of God and the manifold of the creature. It is defined simultaneously in terms of unity and diversity. Though it demands on the visible plane a unity and uniqueness in the measure in which interior unity must have institutional and organic expression (and here the 'organs of oneness' for faith, grace and the common life are given with the apostolic ministry, in its threefold office of teaching, sanctifying and governing), it also demands, for the vital increase of that unity, appropriate adaptation to the multiform humanity in which the Church's unity is expressed. Variety of language, culture and custom, manifesting itself in variety of religious temperament and style of theological thought, is a human value, a reflection of the divine image in man. Catholic communion is capable of incorporating all that is true, good and lovely, though, Congar admonishes, the diversity of values must be integrated into the unity of régime of the Holy Spirit.

> The precise measure in which diversities can be asserted in the Church is fixed by the effective hegemony of the unity of the Spirit. . . . Values and cultures . . . which have been engrafted into Catholic unity, cannot claim to assume control of it, still less to subordinate Christianity itself. (DC, pp. 111–12)

Despite such warning-shots across the bows of what will later be called movements for theological *pluralism* and cultural *indigenization*, for even in these good things the unity of God and man requires us to set a *ne plus ultra*, Congar's basic tone is optimistic. Here, for the first time, through the concept of 'integrable value', Congar has laid out his ideal of a Catholicism maximally polychrome in culture, and enriched by the 'reconciled diversity' of separated Christian churches, whose spiritual, liturgical and intellectual flourishing witnesses to the evangelical values they have taken with them into schism (DC, pp. 115–48).

STRUCTURE AND LIFE

In his meritorious attempt to bring lucidity into reflection on the Church, Congar, in his post-war writing, introduced a distinction, which some found over-schematic, between 'structure' and 'life'. The institutional elements of the Church, given directly by Christ and sharing in his changeless holiness, provide her structure: the deposit of faith, the sacraments and the historic threefold ministry. The Church's members, on the other hand, determine her communitarian *life*, the quality of operation of her God-given structure. If the first is bound up with the founding activity of the Son, and his continued activity in his signs and offices, the second depends more closely on the Spirit, as Pentecostal distributor of charisms for the life which the work of the Son has structured. Insisting as he did that the charisms of the community can only be fully integrated into the Church of the Incarnate by the action of the ecclesiastical hierarchy, Congar left himself open to the charge that none save the ordained ministry are truly active in the Church, all else being a reflection, as in many mirrors, of an image projected by the successors of the apostles.[3] Subsequently, he would prefer to say that in the original Twelve, both hierarchy *and* Church were co-founded, so that, within a community itself prophetic, priestly and regal, the ordained ministry acts in the service of what all the Church is called to do and be (MCE, pp. 9–30).

MODELS AND IMAGES

Where models and images of the Church are concerned, Congar's essays exemplify his belief in the simultaneous employment of many, and his hand can be discerned in the acceptance of such multiplicity in the Dogmatic Constitution of the Second Vatican Council on the Church.[4] The Church is, for Congar, at once the People of God and the Body of Christ, the temple of the Holy Spirit and a communion, a society and an extended sacrament. In his writings during the conciliar period and its aftermath, two of these particularly exercised him: 'People of God' and 'sacrament of salvation'.

Of the expression 'People of God', Congar remarks that it

> carries in itself such a depth, such a strength, that it is impossible to use it in describing this reality which is the Church, without our minds failing to open to certain perspectives. (TCIL, p. 10)

Resuming the history of the recovery of this biblical *motif*, Congar points out that it is essentially a rediscovery of the years immediately before and after the outbreak of the Second World War. In this period, the German Dominican M. D. Koster (1901–81) proposed that an adequate definition of the Church could only be made in terms of a divine people whose number individuals entered through Baptism and within which they were 'ordained' (as either lay people or clerics) by Confirmation and Orders.[5] Again, the French exegete Lucien Cerfaux (1883–1968) showed at just the same time that for the Pauline corpus the concept of People of God was crucial: Paul set out from the Jewish concept of an elect people, the guardian of the testament and the promises, of the knowledge, worship and presence of the true God.[6] Congar's account includes a small niche in the hall of fame for the abbot of Buckfast, Dom Anscar Vonier (1875–1938), whose brief *The People of God* appeared in 1937.[7]

The advantages of the 'people of God' motif are many. It expresses the continuity of the Church with Israel and thus her place in a divine plan working itself out through history in view of the world's end. Through the renaissance of this partially forgotten theme, Catholic Christians, Congar remarks, may regain an awareness of the Church's messianic character: of how she is

> the carrier of the hope of the completion of the world in Jesus Christ. (TCIL, p. 18)

By token of the same idea, we are better able to affirm at one and the same time the equality of all the faithful in their Christian dignity, and the functional *in*equality of the distribution of their tasks as members of the Church. For in Israel the sacerdotal and regal character of the people called by God was understood as calling for the existence of priestly leaders instituted for, and devoted to, the service of public worship.

Lastly, this 'model' of the Church enables the theologian to speak eloquently of the local community gathered for the Eucharistic celebration, the people of God in miniature, and of the many particular churches as representing, within the one Church, a diversity of human peoples and cultures, all brought into divine unity as the people *of God*.

On the other hand, the same ecclesiological theme is not without certain attendant disadvantages, a point which Congar introduces by noting that the enthusiasm of Protestant theology in its regard is perhaps something of a warning sign. In that theology, he writes

> There is a tendency to bring the Church back to the conditions of the People of God under the Old Testament. In the dialectics of the 'already' and the 'not yet', which is characteristic of the

> Church in her state of itinerancy, it seems that, according to Protestant thought, the 'not yet' destroys or darkens the truth of the 'already'.[8]

Congar concludes that the concept of the People of God, however rich and true, is by itself

> insufficient to define adequately the mystery of the present Church. (TCIL, p. 29)

As he explains, that concept is not sufficiently Christologically determined, nor is it adequately placed to do justice to the role of the Spirit of Pentecost in the Church's fashioning. That Jesus is not merely the Messiah but the very Son or Word of God made flesh obliges us to transpose the idea of the People of God into a new key: that of the Body of Christ. Incorporated into Christ, we are able

> as his co-heirs, to share the joy, not of a land of this creation any more, but of the patrimonial blessings of God himself. (TCIL, p. 30)[9]

Again, in the New Testament, the Spirit is revealed for the first time as a Person. The gift of the Spirit as personal principle of the life of the Church obliges us, analogously, to introduce a distinction between the weak and sinful congregations of Christians, of whom we may speak, with Vonier, as the 'People of God', and the Church as a

> definitive superpersonal reality united to Christ with the bonds of an indestructible covenant. (TCIL, p. 34)

The Church, in other words, is Christ's own Bride.

For this reason, Congar prefers to highlight another image, that of the Church as 'universal sacrament of salvation'. Here, Congar finds, the Christological and pneumatological aspects of the Church are better expressed. Putting together the various references of *Lumen Gentium* to the Church as sacrament, we find Christ presented as the 'principle' that pre-contains all that his Church-Body will be, and the Holy Spirit as the 'agent' who co-operates with that 'apostolic organism', so to accomplish in the world the salutary blessings of the mystery of Christ. The salvation which this *motif* speaks of is, indeed, not

> a mere rescue of individual souls in the way some survivors are saved from a shipwreck, where the rest of the passengers are lost. (TCIL, p. 44)

Salvation is, rather:

> the consummation in God of all his visible creation, together with man who is the crowning and immanent goal. (TCIL, p. 45)

The union between man and the cosmos is such that, through man the cosmos reaches its own purpose. This union Congar terms a 'union of destiny', founded at once on God's unity of plan in his own communications *ad extra*, 'beyond himself', and on that unity of the universe in itself perception of which Congar regards as the valid element in the thought of the priest–scientist Pierre Teilhard de Chardin (1881–1955). In salvation, the world as it exists in and through man is supernaturalized by receiving a new and gratuitous communication of life, and with it a new relationship to God who is its goal. Derived from the perfect filial love of Christ on the Cross, as accepted by the Father in the resurrection, such salvation is, when we make it ours, our 'absolute realization'. By it, human existence becomes complete on the level of *value*; it attains its *purpose*; it acquires the sense of its own *meaning*. And of all of this the Church is the sacrament, that is to say, the effective sign.

> The Church is the visible or corporal form which receives God's grace when grace is understood not as individually applied but according to the totality and universality of the divine plan of salvation, as it is realized in dependence on the Incarnation of the Son of God. (TCIL, p. 47)[10]

Of this universal sacrament, the seven 'classical' sacraments are, in their different ways, particularizations.

Congar applies the concept of sacrament of salvation to the two main senses in which he has consistently understood the reality of the Church: the Church as, first, the institution of salvation, the ensemble of the objective means of grace, and, secondly, the Church as the community of those who live by these means of grace. (This is the distinction earlier adumbrated as that between 'structure' and 'life'.) In the first sense, it is through the Church's treasure—the deposit of the Word of God, the sacraments, the apostolic ministry—that the gift of grace made irrevocably in Jesus Christ flows out to the world. In the second, Congar points out that

> only a public revelation, only a public sacrament of salvation, within universal reach, can gather a visible People of God and answer to God's design [of unity]. (TCIL, p. 55)

In this context of the gracious unification of humankind Congar increasingly came to prefer the term 'messianic People', which *Lumen Gentium*, moreover, had itself used.[11] Man has not only a natural desire to see God, his Father; he also has an irrepressible need for union with other men, his brothers. Modern philosophies of history, he writes (thinking notably of Marxism) are largely secularizations of Judaeo-Christian eschatology, so it is not surprising that there are secular analogues for the hope for universal communion, even as, at the same time, the Christian sense of an ending includes dimensions undreamt of in those philosophies. These missing dimensions are not only the doxological aspect of adoring worship of the Father who makes all brothers, but also the Christian assertion of

> the incapability of nature to realize itself in its profound desires, and even in its limitations as nature, without a new infusion, entirely gratuitous, by God. (TCIL, pp. 71–3)

Through the missions of the Son and the Spirit, and the missionary activity of the Church which prolongs them, a new people of God is established which, simply by being itself, but *fully* itself, can contribute to the unity, integrity and peace of the world. And citing some words of the future Pope Pius XII, Congar insists that the Church 'civilizes at the same time that she evangelizes' (TCIL, p. 72).

> Christianity, from the beginning, has been building schools and hospitals, taking care of bodies and teaching man the dignity of labour, respect of things and persons, and the value of life. The Church has constantly started enterprises for the promotion of man, until the time when she could be relieved from this activity by the temporal society, and moved farther to start all over again. (TCIL, p. 79)

For grace does not only raise up nature to share the life of God; it also works to heal the wounds of the common humanity so elevated.

Congar's interpretation of the sacramentality of the Church is, then, that the Church is the sign of the appearing of God's grace in Jesus Christ. The attributes of the Church—one, holy, Catholic, apostolic—are 'notes', notifiers, which indicate this appearing or epiphany in the world.

> Unity, catholicity and apostolicity attest that the unique event of Christ has an absolute and universal value for salvation.

> Unity and sanctity reveal her nature and content, namely a principle of communion with God [holiness] and among men [unity]. (TCIL, p. 49)

This will be the theme of Congar's contribution to *Mysterium Salutis*, that multi-volume theological manual, designed on the basis of the notion of salvation history, which was one of the many collaborative enterprises to issue from the fertile mind of Karl Rahner (1904–84).[12] It was, perhaps, the closest thing to a systematic ecclesiology that he ever produced, though its 'system' lies primarily in gathering together material which otherwise lies scattered through a variety of writings. The notes of unity and catholicity draw in much of his reflections on ecumenism; the note of holiness his work on the idea of the Church's self-reform; the note of apostolicity his investigations of the apostolic ministry, itself placed, in Congar's vision, at the service of the apostolic faith.[13] We shall be investigating his consideration of these areas in the chapters to come. If *L'Eglise une, sainte, catholique, apostolique* is distinguished from his earlier work by a quality peculiarly its own, that quality is surely the emphasis now placed on eschatology, a theme which had announced itself ever more forcefully since the investigations of the biblical view of time in *The Mystery of the Temple*. What remained steady was his conviction of the irreducible multiplicity of images and notions with which, following the cue of Scripture, the ecclesiologist must work. Fundamentally, this linguistic generosity of Congar's does not derive from theological indecisiveness, but from the legitimate desire to keep in equilibrium the institutional aspect of the Church, linked chiefly with the mission of the Son, and its charismatic side, connected mainly to that of the Spirit. There can no more be ultimate incompatibility between these two dimensions than there can be dissonance between the two divine missions. The humanity of the Word Incarnate is Spirit-filled, just as the Spirit himself is always the Spirit of the Son. The two are, in a phrase of Irenaeus of Lyons beloved of Congar, the 'two hands' of the Father. 'No Christology without pneumatology, no pneumatology without Christology' (*The Word and the Spirit*, p. 1).

PNEUMATIC ECCLESIOLOGY

Congar's ecclesiology in its last phase does indeed find his own earlier distinction between structure and life too rigorous. The role of the Spirit is found not only in the raising up of prophetic individuals or groups, from Catherine of Siena (?1347–80) to Alexander Solzhenitsyn (1918–), from human rights movements to the Charismatic Renewal. The Spirit enters into the very texture of the hierarchical society fashioned by the Son, and this on a threefold path of conciliarity, collegiality and reception, whereby the dominical authority of the Roman Pope (for the universal Church) and of the individual bishop (for his particular church) is conditioned by the free play of Christian minds and hearts among the wider episcopate and people. The impulses of the Spirit spread through the Church's whole conciliar being, her *sobornost'*, are manifested in Councils; the episcopate co-witnesses to them as a college around the Pope who, even when acting 'alone', acts as collegial head; and the determinations of bishops, including the chief bishop, cannot bear fruit in the Spirit save through reception by the whole *laos*.[14]

Thus Congar's ecclesiology, in sharp contrast to that of his original inspiration, Möhler, became less Christological and more pneumatic as he grew older. Convinced as he was that Western Catholics have not done justice in recent centuries to the person and work of the Holy Spirit—here his early dialogue with the exiles of the Russian Orthodox diaspora had left a permanent mark—it was understandable that Congar should end his theological career by, at least in appearance, turning away from his great love, ecclesiology, to what was, in fact, its own deepest basis, the doctrine of the Spirit. Before examining Congar's pneumatology, however, we must look at his theology of the Church's two great 'orders': laity and clergy, and at an aspect of ecclesiology which he made peculiarly his own: ecumenism.

Notes

1 Cited from the prospectus to *Unam Sanctam*, included as a separate sheet in *Chrétiens désunis* (not in DC).

2 These analogies Congar drew from Leo XIII's encyclical of 1886, *Satis cognitum*.

3 See J. Prunières, 'L'ecclésiologie du P. Congar: oeuvre témoin d'une crise', *Etudes franciscaines* 39 (1966), pp. 253–83.

4 J.-P. Jossua, *Le Père Congar. La théologie au service du Peuple de Dieu* (Paris, 1967), pp. 99–111.

5 M. D. Koster OP, *Ekklesiologie im Werden* (Paderborn, 1940).

6 L. Cerfaux, *La Théologie de l'Eglise suivant saint Paul* (Paris, 1942); Eng. trans. *The Church in the Theology of St Paul* (New York/Edinburgh and London, 1959).

7 A. Vonier, *The People of God* (London, 1937).

8 See further 'Richesse et vérité d'une vision de l'Eglise comme "peuple de Dieu" ', CVII, pp. 109–22.

9 Cf., on the 'body of Christ' motif, '*Lumen Gentium* No. 7, "L'Eglise, Corps mystique du Christ", vu au terme de huit siècles d'histoire de la théologie du Corps mystique', CVII, pp. 137–62.

10 Cf. 'L'Eglise, sacrement de salut' in *Un peuple messianique. Salut et libération* (Paris, 1975), pp. 13–98.

11 *Lumen Gentium*, 9.

12 *L'Eglise une, sainte, catholique, apostolique* (Paris, 1970).

13 Ibid., pp. 13–122; 149–80; 123–48; 181–254, respectively.

14 On conciliarity, see 'Structure ou régime conciliaire de l'Eglise', CVII, pp. 33–43; on collegiality, 'Synode épiscopal, primauté et collégialité épiscopal', MCE, pp. 187–227; on reception, 'La réception comme réalité ecclésiologique', *RSPhTh* 56 (1972), pp. 369–483. And, in general, for an attempt to integrate these themes into Congar's ecclesiology as a whole using the key concept of *communio*, see T. I. MacDonald SA, *The Ecclesiology of Yves Congar. Foundational Themes* (Lanham, MD, 1984), pp. 207–75.

5

Congar's ecclesiology: (b) A theology of the laity

Having thus traced the grand lines of Congar's multi-faceted ecclesiological vision, we must now turn to consider the two more particular themes which he has perforce attended to within ecclesiology as a whole: *perforce*, since they reflect the two fundamental 'orders' of which the Church is composed. These are the 'order' of the laity, entered by the sacraments of initiation, and that of the apostolic ministry, a threefold or tripartite order which is entered by that sacrament which we call, quite simply, 'Order' or 'ordination'.

Congar's account of the various factors which help to explain how writing a theology of the laity was a supreme concern of the hour showed that, though an observant and highly studious friar with a primarily historical bent, he had not, in the words of a metaphysician made archbishop of Dublin, 'lived in a teapot'. He reviews an entire series of pastorally significant developments (LPC, pp. xi–xiii). The much-maligned nineteenth century had seen the beginnings of what would later be called 'Catholic Action': the active engagement of lay people, in the name of the Gospel, in the transformation of the spirit of society. He evidently had in mind such figures as Antoine Frédéric Ozanam (1813–53), founder of the Society of St Vincent de Paul. Then there was the liturgical movement, and Catholic Action proper, which together would reawaken the sense of the laity as the 'holy people of God', their fully ecclesial character within the mystery of the Church. In this connexion he laid especial weight on the recovery of the idea of the married couple, and their family, as the fundamental cell of the Church. Finally, Congar offered an inventory of other miscellaneous factors, ranging from the renewal of mystical studies, and the re-evaluation of a life of holiness lived within the world, to the contemporary flourishing of the religious book, especially studies of that original library of Judaeo-Christianity, the Bible, and, not least, the purification of the minds of the clergy from clericalist attitudes.

Congar approaches his subject in a well-planned way. First he sketches a preliminary portrait of the layperson. Then he considers the position of the laity in the divine plan. Finally, he considers the laity in the exercise of its activities in the Church's life.

PORTRAYING THE LAITY: PAST AND PRESENT

Pursuing the first of these self-set tasks, Congar points out that in the Septuagint (the Greek version of the Old Testament), what we encounter is not the individual *laikos*, but rather the corporate *laos*. It follows that our word 'lay'

> is connected with a word that for Jew, and then for Christians, properly meant the sacred people in opposition to the peoples who were not consecrated. (LPC, p. 3)

When we reach the Christian use of the word in Clement of Rome, *laikos* designates the non-priestly element among the holy people: one of the People of God who is not a cleric. Congar considers that this meaning, which is our own today, is conveyed in the New Testament itself by such phrases as 'the brethren' or (1 Cor 6:1) 'the others'. Yet, to do justice to the vision of the Church handed down from the Fathers, Congar thinks we should bring into the picture a third factor, namely, the monastic institution. Although Congar has a high view of monasticism, whose flourishing is a sure sign of a local church's awareness of the nearness of the Kingdom, this is not why he mentions it in this context. Here such reference has, rather, a heuristic purpose: it is meant to help us disengage, by contrast, what is specific in the life of the laity. Although the distinction between the Church's lay and ordained members is vital both for her essential 'structure' as laid down by the Lord Jesus himself during his ministry, and for her 'life', given by the breath of the Holy Spirit at Pentecost, laity and clergy do not exhaustively constitute the Church's 'permanent pattern', which entails a distinction between *three* conditions: the lay, the clerical and the monastic. The significance of this is that the definition of a layman as a Christian who is not a cleric will not suffice, even for the minimal purposes of distinguishing groups within the Church. For the monk need not be a cleric, and in the earliest times was rarely so. The monk's condition (by contrast with which Congar will make more precise his account of the layman's) is

> that he shall not live for the world and in the world's way but rather so much as possible for God and in God's way, [and] this consists in living apart from the world, leading so far as may be a heavenly or angelic life, the life of the Kingdom that is not of this world. (LPC, p. 7)

By contrast, layfolk are Christians who are 'working out their salvation in the everyday life of the world'. Nevertheless, in the course of the history of the Latin Church, by a process of assimilation of clerics to monks and monks to clerics, there emerged, for instance in the great Bolognese canonist Gratian (d. *c.* 1159), a double division into men of religion and men of the world. Bearing in mind the older, and richer, division of ecclesial labour, Congar proceeds to offer an account, somewhat skeletal in character, of the idea of the layman in the 'Christian centuries' of mediaeval Europe.

In relation to the monastic condition, Congar tells us, the lay state was held to be that of one living among earthly things. Although it was always accepted, even by upholders of the eremitical life, that there were among the laity holy individuals and true contemplatives, the dominant mediaeval tendency was to present the secular context of lay life as a concession to human weakness, and one that could not but be, in the words of the twelfth-century Stephen of Tournai, 'fleshly'. In the iconography of the Middle Ages, and notably in such illuminated texts as the *Exsultet* rolls of the British Museum and the Barberini MSS of the Vatican Library, we find a scheme whereby the Church exists as two peoples. One, behind the Pope, is made up of bishops, priests and monks; the other, behind the Emperor, of princes, knights and peasants. For Congar, the early and high Middle Ages adopted this scheme to express unity, as can be seen from the writings of, for instance, Hugh of Saint-Victor (d. 1142) and Pope Boniface VIII (1294–1303).[1] After all, the Church could also be looked at as a *respublica christiana*, with the Emperor the Church's most important member. Unfortunately, the 'diagram of the two sides' suffered a different fate.

> In the critical and antihierarchical currents of the fourteenth and fifteenth centuries, which prepared the way for state

laicism and the ecclesiology of the Reformers, it lent itself to quite another interpretation. Instead of two sides, a figure of unity, the fourteenth-century critics spoke of two bodies, each with its own head, of one side the emperor or king, of the other the pope. (LPC, p. 14)

It became possible to turn ecclesiology into hierarchology, to conceive of the Church theologically as consisting in the clergy alone.

In relation to the clerical condition equally negative elements can be discerned. Bonaventure's commentary on that ubiquitous mediaeval textbook, the *Sentences* of Peter Lombard (*c*. 1100–60), shows the beginnings of a closer approximation to *post*-mediaeval attitudes to the clergy–laity distinction. The point of view is no longer that of what Congar terms 'clericature': a form of life in which clergy are, effectively, monks. Rather, Bonaventure understands the clerical life as a matter of active duties, tasks and competence.[2] But the trouble is that, following this shift of emphasis, the laity's position becomes defined theologically in terms of receiving, being objects of, such clerical action. In the canon law, which is primarily a law of the sacraments, the laity are described in terms of their right to receive spiritual goods from the clergy. Once again, they are in danger of being conceived of as 'negative creatures' (LPC, p. 18).

To counteract these grievous omissions of the mediaevals (and Congar's documentation is not meant to provide a complete overview of the mediaeval understanding of the laity, which would have to include a host of monuments other than strictly theological texts, consideration of which might well produce a much less bleak picture[3]), what preliminary portrait of the laity does he sketch for his readers? His first move is to transfer to his easel the valid features of the mediaeval scheme. It is true that lay people do not live exclusively for heavenly things, as do contemplative monks. It is true that while layfolk are Christians in the fullest extent as touching the life in Christ, they have only a limited competence as touching the properly ecclesial means to that life in the Church—the deposit of faith, the sacraments, Church discipline—which means belong to the competence of clerics. But, in the second place, such an essentially negative characterization cannot suffice. Congar paints in the positive colours in this way:

> Lay people are called to the same end as clergy or monks—to the enjoyment of our inheritance as sons of God; but they have

> to pursue and attain this end without cutting down their involvement in the activities of the world, in the realities of the primal creation, in the disappointments, the achievements, the stuff of history. (LPC, p. 18)

The laity are Christians in the world, 'there to do God's work in so far as it must be done in and through the work of the world'. The Church needs to have some members whose lives are directly and exclusively dedicated to the coming Kingdom, and are, therefore, dispensed from the world's work. But her total mission, corresponding as it does to the design of God, requires that

> the Lord's reign be prepared in and through that creation in the perfecting of which man must co-operate. (LPC, p. 19)

In other words, there must be a lay faithful who will glorify God without lessening its engagement in the work of the world if the creation is to be saved.

Furthermore, such lay relationship to God's world is not only necessary for a fallen creation's faithful transformation. It is also an essential counter-balance to the tendency of monk and cleric simply to use the world for the attainment of supernatural goals in a way that does less than justice to the inwardness of things as God has made them. The danger is one of withholding full respect for earthly human things on the ground that they are being given a transcendent reference, and Congar considers that those indebted to the thirteenth-century 'Albertino-Thomist revolution', whereby the consistency of the created order was first given whole-hearted recognition in Christian theology, should be the first to reaffirm the specific glory of the lay vision in this sense. Distinguishing between an anti-Christian and falsely secularizing 'laicism' (*laïcisme*), and a 'laicity' (*laïcité*) concerned simply to protect the due autonomy of the created order from a premature and ill-conceived spiritualization, Congar regards it as tragic that the true meaning of lay 'revolt' was misunderstood by Church authority. For that meaning was simply that

> the various priesthoods of secondary causes rose against the alienation of their domain into the hands of the priesthood of the First Cause. (LPC, p. 22)

In this perspective, Congar calls Thomas 'authentically lay, even though a cleric' (LPC, p. 24).

THE LAITY IN THE PLAN OF GOD

How does Congar approach his second principal question in *Lay People in the Church*, namely the place of a theology of the laity within the body of Christian thought as a whole? He refuses to consider it save in strait connexion with ecclesiology proper. A theology of the laity is a reflection on the richness of the traditional term *fidelis*, 'one of the faithful'. Living as we do, Congar suggests, in a world that is desacralized, individualistic and academic, where ideas are easily separated from their sensuous embodiments, we tend to think of one of the faithful as simply a 'believer'—someone who holds certain religious convictions. But in the Christian tradition at its finest, and especially up until the thirteenth century:

> a *fidelis* was someone sacramentally incorporated in the ecclesial reality. Not only was the faith he professed essentially the trinitarian faith of the Symbol, it was the reality in him of baptism and his being part of the Church which, after having brought him to birth, formed him, nourished his life, governed all his actions, consecrated and united every moment of his existence to Christ. (LPC, p. 36)

The sixteenth-century Reformers kept the term, but altered its meaning when they placed the *fidelis* in individual and non-mediate association with an act of God, whether in terms of the Word as in Luther, or of God's predestining and saving work as in Ulrich Zwingli (1454–1531) and Calvin. Moreover, this exaggeration of the sense in which the Church is made by her members, rather than making them, had not been unknown inside the Catholic tradition, for instance in the anti-hierarchical movements of the high Middle Ages and even in Conciliarism, which, though largely an affair of clerics, so stressed the community of the faithful as to leave in shadow the Church's other dimension as the 'institution' or 'order' of the means to salvation. Such Conciliarism, Congar finds, was corrupted by a 'radical nominalism' or, again, a 'representative individualism'. In reaction to these challenges, Catholic apologists came to stress the institution, moulded by the dominically ordered *structure* of the apostolic ministry, at the expense of the community with its God-given *life*.

> Thus it was that of the Church's two aspects which Catholic tradition requires to be held together—that in which the Church is an institution that precedes and makes its members,

> and that in which she is the community made by its members—the theological treatises practically ignored that one according to which a role of the laity could be *a priori* conceivable. (LPC, p. 47)

Congar hastens to add, however, that such one-sidedness in a clerical direction has been more in theoretical ecclesiology than in the lived reality of Catholicism, pointing to such phenomena as lay people taking their part in parish life, meeting in societies and confraternities, responding to that post-Tridentine *invasion mystique* of which the French historian of spirituality Henri Bremond (1865–1933) wrote, and the contemporaneous rise of lay apostleship. Nevertheless, too often, and in too many places, the Catholic laity have got into the habit of receiving without actively co-operating, like citizens who leave the making of their country to civil servants, and its defence to the military. What theology can remedy this situation by recovering for the laity, at the level of ecclesiology, their full dignity and rights?

It turns out to be a meditation on the interrelation of three crucial terms: Kingdom, Church and world. Congar points out that, for the New Testament, Christ is head of the Church but he is also head of the whole creation.

> He is the supreme head of the body of the saved who will be glorified, he is the principle of salvation, of fellowship with God; but he has also a cosmic sovereignty, which extends to the whole of creation, seen and unseen; the 'powers' are subject to him; he is king of all the ages, now and hereafter, he is Pantokrator. If, then, we think of the great divisions of all that is created—things visible and invisible, things heavenly and things earthly, the order of creation and the order of the purpose of grace, or, if you will, the 'natural' and the 'supernatural'—Christ's kingly power is seen to be precisely dominion over them all. This is of capital importance for our subject. (LPC, p. 64)

To demonstrate the importance of this twofold headship, Congar is obliged to bring into play another 'twofoldness' in the work of Christ, namely the twofold manner in which it is displayed in time. There is a time during which the 'principle' constituted by the Incarnation of the Word and his Paschal victory is active, but does not exert the fullness of its power. There is also a time when this fullness will be manifested in all its completeness, and the

Kingdom—the order of things in which man and creation are conformed to the will of God—definitively established. Before Christ's kingly, priestly and prophetical power comes to its 'rightful and complete fruition', the twofold headship holds good. In the in-between time separating the Resurrection and Pentecost from the Parousia, there is a duality of Church and world, two realities each of which has its own relationship to the single final Kingdom.

> It is not sufficiently understood that during the anteparousial era, Christ's kingship is shared and ought to be honoured, not only in a Church which is his body, but also in a world which has its own proper needs. (LPC, p. 83)

And, with considerable realism, he adds that such a duality of orders will inevitably create problems and entail hardship, but that this must be endured, as part of the tense and suffering-filled time which precedes the final coming of the Kingdom.

In God's unitary design, then, Church and world are both ordered to the Kingdom, but in different ways. Naturally, Congar is obliged to be more specific about what these ways are. It is in the nature of the *Church* that

> she already has within herself, and as the very things that make her Church, the self-same and decisive causes of that renewal of which the Kingdom will be the consummation: the kingly, priestly and prophetical power of Christ, and the Holy Spirit. Therefore the Church co-operates *directly* in the constitution of the Kingdom, through the exercise of energies that are her own and constitute her reality as Church. (LPC, p. 95)

The Church is the seed or germ of the Kingdom, whose powers are already active within her. Being the direct preparation for that Kingdom, she cannot but strive to transform the world to the utmost. But she should do so, aiming to reduce the world's evil and to rebuild it in goodness, only through influence and service—not through authority and power.

What, then, of the world itself? Through its history, the world strives to attain a 'state of reconciliation' wherein the various oppositions from which human beings suffer will be overcome. Congar has in mind such contrasts or alienations as those between spirit and nature, between the person and social authority, between classes, or between nations. Without knowing it, the world seeks the Kingdom—but in its 'cosmic' not its 'spiritual' or 'religious' aspect. However, the world's implicit tending towards the Kingdom is ambivalent and defective. First of all, as Congar's confrère Dominique Dubarle (1909–87) had been stressing in the contemporary dispute among French theologians between 'incarnational' and 'eschatological' humanists,[4] a redeemed universe and a sinful universe are being produced simultaneously. There is virtually as much reason for pessimism as for optimism when looking at the world. The history of modern culture, remarks Congar in spelling out this point,

> is dominated by various forms of immanentism, rationalism, the spirit of Faust; and eventually there is Marxism, the most consistent endeavour that has ever been made to give the world a purely immanent meaning, excluding all transcendence; an endeavour to overcome all contradictions and to attain integrity without any reference whatever to God. Even things that are in themselves good and true, authentic earthly values, are susceptible of becoming idols and a 'home-ground' for the Prince of this world. Think what can happen to country, production, progress, class, race, the body and sport, domestic comfort; and how many names can be given today to Egypt, Canaan or Babylon. (LPC, pp. 99–100)

However, Congar cautions that we are not to know with anything like total security which of the forces in history may not *in the end* work for the Kingdom.

But secondly, the world in its instinctive movement towards the fullness of life is not aware that God's Wisdom is the Wisdom of the Cross. There can be no higher life, in a post-lapsarian world, save by way of renunciation and a kind of death. And thirdly and lastly, the nature of the cosmos, man included, is such that its integral 'programme' cannot be fulfilled unless it is taken up into the gracious order given in Christian redemption. Yet the *gift* of consummation should not be wholly severed from the *effort* of the world's striving. Attempting to reconcile two schools of thought in the French Church of the period, Congar writes:

> Is not the gift . . . the issue, given from on high, towards which the effort tended, an effort already directed by him who would give all, but an issue which the effort would never have been able to attain by itself? If this be so, does it not suggest a certain conciliation, even a *rapprochement*, of the eschatological and

evolutionist-incarnationist theses which would be disadvantageous to neither? (LPC, p. 103)

And, in fundamental agreement with Maritain's call for a 'new Christendom' of a non-hierocratic kind, Congar argues that 'a *certain* Christendom', namely, an influence of the spiritual over the secular order, is needful in the world's quest for integrity and unity.

> The Christian has to energize in the earthly city in accordance with what he is, as a Christian; he cannot do otherwise than make use of the Christian powers that are in him and direct what he does towards the Christian end. (LPC, p. 106)

We are now within sight of our goal: an evocation of the place of the Christian laity in the divine plan. The messianic energies associated with Christ's offices as priest, king and prophet persist in the members of the Church in two ways. In the Church as a communion, they exist as a 'dignity' or 'form of life', qualifying all her members without exception. In the Church as institution, equipped with the means of grace needful for that institution's purposes, they qualify certain members only, giving them a ministry for the benefit of the rest. Here they exist as what Congar calls 'powers', that is, active means for promoting the life of the Body. By applying this to the interrelation of Kingdom, Church and world, the signal place of the laity in the divine scheme becomes clear. As Congar writes:

> According to God's design the one supreme mediation of Jesus Christ is exerted through a twofold mediation by men, corresponding to the double participation in Christ's messianic energies, as powers and as form of life. From the time that Heaven received him until the day when all will be restored anew, Christ's kingly, priestly and prophetical mediation is at work in two ways: through the apostolic hierarchy, for the formation of a faithful people; through the whole body, *in respect of the world*. The hierarchy exercises the mediation of the means of grace between Christ and the faithful; the latter *a mediation of life between the Body of Christ and the world*, and this also is a means of grace in its order. (LPC, p. 118; italics added)

The world is drawn to Christ in and through the laity—its human aspect to be transformed in him, its cosmic aspect to find its goal in him. Congar considers this an appropriate 'allotting' of respective parts to hierarchy and laity, so that together they may form one Church and carry out that Church's mission to the full.

THE THREEFOLD OFFICE OF THE LAITY

The idea of describing the activity of the laity in terms of just such a share in the threefold priestly, royal and prophetic office of Christ, analogous to that of the ordained ministry, entered into the conciliar statement on the laity in *Lumen Gentium* from Congar. This trilogy is, in its Christological form, supported in the texts of the Fathers, the liturgies and the Scholastic divines, but, as Congar admits, its ecclesiological use is no earlier than the sixteenth century.[5] How is it worked out in his scheme?

(i) The priestly office

Congar begins with the laity and the Church's *priestly* function. In the New Testament, the priesthood of the faithful is the offering of a holy life: prayer, charity, compassion. The offering and priesthood of the faithful are spiritual—in the biblical sense of 'spiritual-real', rather than simply metaphorical or moral. Though both Bible and the Apostolic Fathers of the age immediately after the New Testament bear witness to the uniqueness of Christ's priesthood and of his sacrifice, they apply priestly terms to Christians too. Congar comments:

> There is of course nothing contradictory about that: there is only one Christ, there are many Christians. It is precisely God's purpose that many should have part in Christ and that, being persons, they should freely and really co-operate in such participation. (LPC, p. 129)

In the terms worked out by Augustine in *De Civitate Dei*, the priesthood of the faithful consists in self-offering to God—whence it is not surprising that the supreme self-offering made by the martyrs has often received special emphasis as a Christian priestly act.

More precisely, Congar distinguishes between a *moral* priesthood of the faithful, which consists in 'living and doing with a priestly soul, in a spirit of religion'; an inward *spiritual* priesthood, that of prayer and the ascetic life; and lastly, a priesthood with a *sacramental* reference and import, connected not only with holy living but also with that baptismal consecration whose supreme activity is a sharing in the offering of the Eucharist. It was Thomas's understanding that the layman has two titles to priesthood: not simply the offering of spiritual sacrifices, recognized by the patristic tradition, but also his baptismal 'character', which, for Aquinas, is a mode of participation in the priesthood of Christ himself. As Congar interprets Aquinas, the *reditus* or 'return' to God of human beings can be considered in two ways. In the *Secunda Pars* of the *Summa Theologiae*, it is the moral life which itself is spiritual worship. Thomas was sufficiently Augustinian to accept that our 'sacrifice' may be 'everything done in order to realize our communion with God'. But this is not the whole story. In the *Tertia Pars*, after considering the person and life of Christ, who, through all he did and suffered, is the way by which we return to God, the one who renders our moral existence 'justified' and holy, Thomas turns to contemplate the specifically Christian aspect and reality of this return. And here he remarks that Jesus Christ

> has ushered in the worship or rite of the Christian religion by offering himself up as an oblation and sacrifice to God.[6]

As Congar points out, this does not mean that Christ has put an end to all positive religions in favour of a purely personal inwardness of worship. He has 'ushered in' a worshipping and sacrificial order—public, social, institutional—with himself, its sole true priest, as its *auctor*, the person who is

> rightly and ultimately responsible, on whose efficacious will these things depend. (LPC, p. 144)

In the measure that Christ communicates to men the power to celebrate his priestly worship with him—and the letter to the Hebrews shows that this is, in fact, the economy of God's grace—he dedicates them to share in his priesthood. Thus in the sacraments of Christian initiation, Baptism and Confirmation, as in the sacrament of Order, a 'character' is conferred on human beings, which renders them consecrated, priestly, so that the continuance of Christ's own worship may be ensured in the Church. Here, then, with the help of St Thomas, Congar has disengaged the three subjects of priesthood: Christ, the Christian people, and the Christian ordained ministry, and he expresses their interrelation in this way:

> There is only one high priest, Christ, priest in Heaven for evermore; . . . all the faithful have a real priestly quality, being incorporated in Christ by the sacramental consecration of baptism and by a living faith, . . . for the Church's benefit bishops and presbyters (and deacons) have a ministry of Christ's priestly actions, most particularly of the eucharistic

> memorial, whereby they receive a third participation in the priesthood of Christ. (LPC, pp. 150–1)

Given that priesthood may be analogously predicated of Christ, his people, and his ordained ministers, is it possible to come to a clearer understanding of what priesthood, *per se*, is? To find the answer to this question will be of obvious value in Congar's teasing out the sense of the priestly office of the laity.

Congar considers three possible definitions of priesthood: in terms of 'mediation' (Augustine and Pope Pius XII); 'consecration' (the French School of the seventeenth and eighteenth centuries) and sacrifice. It is for the latter that he plumps, while not disallowing an element of truth to the other two.

> In our opinion, faithfulness to Holy Scripture and sound theology requires that priesthood be defined as the quality which enables a man to come before God to gain his grace, and therefore fellowship with him, by offering up a sacrifice acceptable to him. (LPC, pp. 154–5)

In the concrete order of sin and grace which is our situation, the 'fellowship' concerned here must mean, Congar adds, reuniting, reconciling, or in the admirably serviceable English word he prefers, atoning ('at-one-ing').

What, then, of the laity's part in the Church's essentially 'sacrificial' priestly function? The laity offer to God through Christ a twofold cultus, interior and exterior. Their interior worship consists of acts of faith, hope and charity, the 'theological' virtues, those which bind us to God in the supernatural order as his friends; of inward acts of the virtue of religion, namely, devotion and prayer; and, furthermore, of the entire moral life inasmuch as it is a holy life, offered to God as a sweet savour in his presence. The exterior worship of the laity includes outward acts of virtue related to God—notably of the virtue of religion in public prayer, or sacrifice; the public confession of the faith, with its supreme form in martyrdom; and finally, participation in the Church's liturgical worship, above all in her sacraments, with the Eucharist at their heart.

If this account be something of a bald inventory, Congar offers a more humanly vivid and scripturally eloquent evocation of what it entails. The holy life offered by the laity in spiritual sacrifice is a life whose concrete content is found in the New Testament itself. We need have no vagueness about the manner of such a life. It is

> on the one hand, love and mercy towards our neighbour, the humble service of love, for the mystery of Christ is there present in our neighbour; on the other, thanksgiving to God, loving movement towards him, confession of faith by both praise and witness. (LPC, p. 195)

Congar reminds us of the importance accorded by Paul to the worship of the *body* in all this. For the body is that in which man lives and acts. Reflection on the Pauline theology of the body leads Congar to see the priestly service of the faithful in two other respects that implicate the body at the deepest level: death, and sexuality. After all offering of self comes death. We are not able, Congar writes with a touch of psychological innocence, to want death or to be glad to die. Yet we are able

> intensely to desire one day to offer God this definitive and total worship, this 'pasch'. Only man can thus offer it, for he alone is a spiritual person freely disposing of a mortal life; the angels cannot do it. And when he took on our flesh, Jesus gave himself the ability freely to offer death. (LPC, p. 197)

Here and there, Congar points out, Paul also connects the offering of the body to chastity. Our attitude to our own body, and to the bodies of others, cannot but raise the question of sexuality. By purity we are made royally free; we dominate instinctive selfishness; we treat the other as end, not as means. Such right ordering of sexuality is the vocation of all; but Congar notes in this connexion the high Pauline esteem for virginity. Consecration of the body is supremely realized in the giving of one's virginity to God, as a temple of the Holy Spirit for his worship, an apostle for his service.

From here Congar moves on to consider how the 'spiritual-real' priesthood of all the faithful is something exercised not simply in the sacrifice of self, of the bodily self, *in general*, but in highly particular situations of life. Congar develops this thought in two ways. First, we offer God our particular gifts: Christopher his strength, Dante his poetic power, the *jongleur de Notre Dame* his acrobatic skill. This is especially true of gifts which can be brought directly to God's service: notably those of sensibility, intelligence and artistic ability. Each's spiritual worship has its distinctive matter. But secondly, we offer with ourselves to God those particular human solidarities of which we are part. Congar instances the Mass offered by young workers for their comrades; or by students for their fellows; and the way in which, when the soldier and literary man Ernest Psichari (1883–1914) was converted, he at once started praying for the Army. Just so do parents offer and entrust their children to God. In each of these highly distinct solidarities, the laity act, like Israel of old, as a 'part standing for the whole', and are the Gospel leaven raising the entire dough. Congar pleads that the faithful should not neglect this intercessory duty, in which they are united with Christ and his saints.He reminds his readers how Catherine of Siena divided her *Dialogue* into three supplications: mercy for Catherine, mercy for the Church, mercy for the world. In such ways, Congar fleshes out his earlier teaching about the place of the laity in the divine scheme: the ambit of their activity as those living a priestly *form of life* is so much wider than that of the ordained ministry with its priestly *powers*. Christian priestly intercession goes beyond strictly sacramental celebration to embrace the whole world: all space, time and even inanimate nature itself. Here Congar is inspired by the poet Paul Claudel's (1868–1955) lyrical celebration of a cosmic liturgy in *L'offrande du temps*. All is summed up in a sermon of Jacques-Bénigne Bossuet (1627–1704), bishop of Meaux and counsellor of Louis XIV, on the Annunciation:

> Man is the contemplator and mysterious epitome of visible nature only in order that, through a holy love, he may be its priest and worshipper before unseeable spiritual nature.[7]

Having spoken of the priestly service of virginity, Congar naturally must say something of the lay priesthood's possible expression in marriage, and this he does at some length. There is, he writes, such a thing as a priesthood of the fathers and mothers of families, and it is among the finest and best things that the Christian life can offer. Marriage is, Congar points out:

> the sole example in the Christian economy of a natural institution, in itself and as such, being taken into the order of grace and made sacred. (LPC, p. 202)

The consequences of this are several. From the side of mission, apostolic responsibility and natural authority here coincide. Through Christian parents, the substance of the human world, in the very process of its increase, becomes the Body of Christ, the Church. A family is, in the phrase of John Chrysostom (*c*. 347–407), a 'micro-church', the Church in miniature. Or, in Congar's words, it is a living cell wherein

> the life and mystery of the whole Body exists in an elementary way. (LPC, p. 202)

And he points out how, for such Latin doctors as Augustine and Bede (*c.* 673–735), the father is regarded as a kind of bishop in his own home. One obvious corollary of this is the importance of family worship, the 'liturgy of the home'—grace before and after meals; evening prayers (here Congar mentions especially Compline); Bible reading; teaching the children to pray and to offer up their own lives to God. The married couple are well suited to preside over such a liturgy, since their own state is the priestly one of sacrifice, whose death to self is built into marriage's very structure.

And this takes Congar into the area of the 'external' acts of the priestly office of the laity: their role in the Church's sacramental worship. An understanding of Congar's position here requires some reference to his theology of worship. That worship has two aspects, one deriving 'from below', the other 'from above'. The Church, on her journey towards the eschatological Omega, is nourished from two sources: the first, Adam, and the Second, Christ.

> What at the end will be God's community-temple is mankind created in God's image, the increased and multiplied substance of Adam; but as a body of sonship in Christ it is a body that is spiritually renewed, with a new head, and derives from the incarnate Son. (LPC, p. 208)

The human aspect provides a 'source of increase'; the divine a 'source of animation and quality' whose principle is Christ, and that chiefly in the mystery of his 'passover' to the Father. The Church's worship reflects this twofold reality, at once deriving from 'above' and coming from 'below'. From above, the Church receives Christ's own worship, above all his sacrifice, and this she celebrates sacramentally, that is:

> under the form of a spiritual reality of eternal worth made present and applied under earthly veils. (LPC, p. 208)

The Church carries out this action *in persona Christi*, as forming one celebrant with him, something possible because first, the apostolic institution in providing *shaliachim*, 'those sent', enables the ordained priest to exercise a *ministerium* in regard to Christ as author of the sacraments; and because secondly, there is only one power at work: that of Christ and his Spirit. From *below*, the ordained priest acts rather as representative of the community, the president of its worshipping assembly. From this vantage point the Church is not so much the body of Christ as his bride. Her worship, considered strictly as her own, is worship as bride.

What is the role of the laity in all this? It is to participate in sacramental worship by 'consenting thereto, receiving, and uniting themselves therewith'. In connexion with the Eucharist, Congar declares in a formula that he will make more precise by subsequent discussion:

> The people's part is to offer the matter of the holy gifts and to unite themselves spiritually with the sacrifice, which includes the offering of Christ's members and finds its full significance in thus being the sacrifice both of the Church and of her Head. (LPC, p. 213)

The historic prayers of the Roman rite make it indisputably plain that the offering of the Eucharistic sacrifice pertains to the whole Church. Though only the ordained can carry out the sacramental celebration, the entire *plebs sancta Dei* co-operates and, in the words of Pope Benedict XIV (1740–58), 'co-oblates' with them. Admittedly, as the sacrifice of *Christ*, the holy sacrifice is the work of the ordained minister alone, who has been rendered its instrument, by the Holy Spirit, for this purpose. Here Congar cites with approval Pope Pius XII's words in his encyclical on the Church's worship, *Mediator Dei*:

> The bloodless immolation by which, after the words of consecration have been said, Christ is made present on the altar in the state of victim, is done by the priest alone, and by him as acting in the name of Christ, not as representing the faithful.[8]

However, the Mass is also the *Church*'s sacrifice, and that in two ways. It is her sacrifice inasmuch as Christ's sacrifice is offered by the Church; it is her sacrifice, too, in that she also has a sacrifice of her own to offer, which she offers in and through Christ's. In both of these aspects, the laity exercise their priestly office in the Eucharistic action.

(ii) The kingly office

What of the laity and the Church's *kingly* function? Here Congar distinguishes between the regal 'form of life' of Christians, and the issue of power in the Church. Through the divine life in him, the Christian 'reigns': he triumphs over sin, controls the enticements of the flesh, rules body and soul. Calling Augustine to witness, Congar declares that, in the life of grace, the body 'lives by the soul, and the soul by God'. Travelling on the *via regia*, the 'royal highway', as the Fathers termed the Christian life, the baptized find themselves at once engaged in the world, and yet transcending it. Both are aspects of their kingly status. Committed to the work of the world, for reasons beyond the world, the Christian exercises his spiritual kingship by using influence for the service of others, imitating the *diakonia* of the Son of Man himself (Mk 10:42–45). Congar understands such kingship in a remarkably realistic way as an anticipation of the eschatological reign of the saints. Commenting on Paul's statement to the Corinthian Christians that 'All things are yours', he remarks that

> sometimes God intervenes to show forth this subjection in some extraordinary and tangible way: it may be the spiritual man's dominion over space (movement through space, levitation), over time (prophecy), over ignorance (knowledge of secrets, gift of tongues, of counsel), over matter (multiplication of food), over sickness and even death (healings, raisings); or more simply still, over the elements (tempests stilled), over animals (St Francis of Assisi), over the most stubborn thing of all, man himself (sudden conversions). (LPC, p. 240)

And Congar acclaims St Francis (*c*. 1184–1226) as the 'most finished example' of spiritual kingship thus anticipating eschatology—and hints that this was made possible by his being also a stigmatic, because there is no realization of man's final destiny without the Cross. For, while the integrity of our spiritual kingship requires engagement in the world by way of preparation for the Kingdom, it also imposes a refusal of the world, and even a contempt for the world, inasmuch as the latter is the realm of an evil Prince. Not only by resisting sin, but also by withstanding worldly power, notably in martyrdom, the Christian says 'No' to the way of the world. The most radical form of this refusal, in Congar's eyes, is monasticism, a contracting out of the common law that involves us in the world's work. Such a withdrawal, for the sake of total engagement in the Kingdom of God, is, he writes, 'a sacred right of Christians'. Rightly, the tradition has applied the royal psalms of the Bible to the monastic life, and seen the tonsure as an emblem of spiritual kingship. In hagiography, holy monks and hermits are frequently described as exercising dominion over nature, the animals and brutish human individuals, while historically the Church has sometimes found in the monks the most doughty supporters of her freedom *vis-à-vis* worldly power—especially in the Byzantine East, but also occasionally in the West, as with, in Congar's own example, the English Carthusians who stood out against Henry VIII's claims to supremacy over the *ecclesia anglicana*.

From discussion of the kingly lifestyle of Christians, Congar moves on to the share of the laity in Christ's kingship as power properly so-called: as governing authority in the spiritual society of the Church. Reviewing the primitive evidence for the role of the laity in the selection of the Church's ministers, Congar distinguishes firmly between control and consent.

> There is not, there never has been, any *power* of ecclesiastical rule among the laity, nothing that determines or conditions the hierarchical and sacramental structure of the Church. It is infinitely regrettable that false claims in this sense, made at the dawn of the modern era, should have compromised a different and important principle, one found in the oldest, purest and most constant tradition: the principle, namely, of consent, as a principle not of structure but of life. (LPC, pp. 246–7)

Thus the North African councils of the age of Cyprian brought in members of the laity for advice and information on, for instance, the question of the *lapsi*: what to do about Christians who had temporarily apostatized under State pressure. Again, in the papal synods held in Rome, France and the German lands by Gregory VII (1073–85), that Pope required a numerous attendance of layfolk, the better to ensure wide approval and co-operation in his proposed reforms. At some councils the laity were called on to pronounce their consensual Amen, just as they did at worship, in the liturgy. Congar devotes particular attention to the phenomenon of the Christian prince. He reports on the widespread mediaeval notion that where ecclesiastical authoriy was failing in its duty, the prince, being, as a layman, a member of the same body as the hierarchs, could act to supply their deficiencies.[9] Congar finds this unobjectionable so long as, side by side with the idea of the Church as people of God, the complementary concept of the Church as the 'order of the means of grace' was preserved. For only where the second thought was vividly alive could the prince's intervention be seen for what it was, an emergency measure justified by *epikeia* or appeal to the fundamental intention of the Church's divine founder.

These remarks constitute a partial apologia for an institution that has almost wholly vanished from the face of the earth. Of continuing importance, however, is Congar's account of the role of the laity in the making of customary law. Taking his cue from Gratian's definition of custom as a 'kind of law established by what is done', Congar writes:

> Custom . . . is a law from below, which those who use it, namely the laity, also make. (LPC, p. 256)[10]

Consideration of custom leads Congar to speak more widely of the taking of initiative by layfolk. Though the bishop has the charism of judging, *what* he judges will often enough be the endeavours and proposals of the Church's ordinary members, by which the latter shape the Church's historic embodiment. But can lay people properly have a part in the Church's *executive* rather than (as so far discussed) her *legislative* function? Church history indicates that, at various times and places, *seniores laici*, elder statesmen among the laity, helped in the management of the Church's property, and in the administration of justice. The *Codex Iuris Canonici* of 1917, in force at the time of Congar's discussion of these matters, continued to give lay people administrative powers in regard to specific institutions, but the precedents for placing the entire temporal administration of parishes in lay hands were discouraging. The *Eigenkirchen* or 'private churches' of early mediaeval Germany, and the American trustee system of the eighteenth and early nineteenth centuries, served to make clear by contrast the close link there must be between the Church's temporal economy and the spiritual ends of its ordained ministry. In regard to the administration of justice, the Code allowed laymen to be advocates in matrimonial cases; since then, the new Code of the Latin Church enables them to be judges also.

Though the lay share in Christ's kingship is overwhelmingly exercised within his Church-body 'by way of energy and dignity', rather than over it 'by way of power and authority', that very energy and dignity requires that the ecclesiastical hierarchy govern non-despotically, in a spirit of partnership. Lay people must be consulted, and that not as a mere matter of form. Apart from any other consideration, this way of setting about things 'always gets results, and no other way does' (LPC, p. 269).

(iii) The prophetic office

Finally, Congar must consider the laity's part in the Church's *prophetical* function. The word 'prophetical' in this phrase denotes not simply teaching but Christian knowledge of all kinds.

> In its widest extension the prophetical function of the Church includes all the work of the Holy Spirit in her whereby, in her present state of pilgrimage, she knows God and his purpose of grace, and makes them known to others. (LPC, p. 271)

And while only some Christians receive a task of *magisterium*, of teaching doctrine with authority, all 'receive light and are active'. Just as, at the garden tomb, it was lay people, lay*women* indeed, who first saw the risen Lord and advised the apostolic college accordingly; just as, too, in the Arian crisis it was, by and large, the faithful people who resisted a 'heresy of intellectuals' swallowed by most of the bishops themselves; so, in the modern period, the belief of the laity was the main basis on which the Catholic Church dogmatized her faith in Mary's original righteousness (the 'Immaculate Conception') and her achieved share in her Son's resurrection (the 'Assumption'). Naturally, history also records widespread failures of faith among the Christian people: in the seventh-century East before the onslaught of Islam, in England and the Scandinavian countries in face of the Reformation; at various times and places in devotional excesses and distorted enthusiasms. It is the *total* body of the faithful which is infallible in professing its faith, and that not in a particular act or judgement, but in the living profession of the faith *at large*.

> The hierarchical pastorate alone teaches with authority, but the whole Church transmits the tradition; nor does that tradition consist solely in statements, but, more widely and deeply, in the very reality of Christianity. (LPC, p. 293)

The episcopate, with the Pope as its head, must teach, yet the laity must 'receive' their teaching—not in the sense of conferring on it a retrospective validity by their assent, but of rendering it fruitful in the Christian life of the entire body.

However, though the laity do not teach doctrine with authority, this is not to say that they do not teach at all. Most certainly they teach—in virtue of their own faith by which a Christian mind is born and grows within them. The laity may have spiritual gifts of knowledge and understanding, like Teresa of Avila (1515–82) or Blaise Pascal. They may preach, either by moral and spiritual exhortation as in the lay brotherhoods of the *Humiliati* whom Innocent III (1198–1216) reconciled with the Church in 1201, or by 'apologetic exposition'; as in the cases of François René de Chateaubriand (1768–1848) or G. K. Chesterton (1874–1936). They also mediate the faith to others by the indirectly didactic vehicle of symbolic expression in literature, art and other cultural forms. Moreover, they instruct society by the sometimes hazardous means of sturdily maintaining the public commitment to the obligations which faith brings with it. And, finally, there is nothing to prevent their being lay theologians: it is only an accident of history, the over-running of the Western Roman empire by barbarians, which led in the Western Church to the reservation of a high religious culture to the clergy. The exceptions, like the twelfth-century Tuscan Hugh Etherianus, became more numerous under the impact of Renaissance humanism in its more Christian mood, and, in the circumstances of modern society, the trickle, Congar confidently felt, would become a flood. However, on the whole Congar preferred to see the academic exercise of the lay prophetic function in mediating between the Christian faith and contemporary affairs. In dogmatic theology proper they were, he thought, less suited than the ordained man who:

> having the priestly charisms, celebrating the mysteries, . . . has to a greater degree living contact with the tradition. (LPC, p. 310)[11]

How, then, did Congar see the *alter pars* of the Church, its 'apostolic ministry'?

Notes

1 Hugh of Saint-Victor, *De Sacramentis* II, 2, 3; Boniface VIII, *Unam Sanctam* (DS 469).

2 Bonaventure, *In Sent*. IV, d. 6, p. 1, art. unicus, q. 4.

3 See, for example, the account of pre-Reformation English lay confraternities in J. J. Scarisbrick, *The Reformation and the English People* (Oxford, 1984), pp. 19–39.

4 For that debate, see B. Besret SOCist, *Incarnation ou eschatologie? Contribution à l'histoire du vocabulaire religieux contemporain 1935–1955* (Paris, 1964).

5 See J. Fuchs, 'Origine d'une trilogie', *RSPhTh* 53 (1969), pp. 185–211.

6 *Summa Theologiae* IIIa, q. 62, ad 5.

7 Cited in LPC, p. 201.

8 Pius XII, *Mediator Dei* (DS 3852)

9 Here Congar drew on J. Hashagen, *Staat und Kirche vor der Reformation: Eine Untersuchung der vorreformatorischen Bedeutung des Laieneinflüsses in der Kirche* (Essen, 1931).

10 Cf. V. Hove, 'Coutumes', *Dictionnaire de droit canonique* IV, cols 731–5.

11 For a less positive evaluation of Congar's theology of the laity see G. Angelini and G. Ambrosio, 'La *Summa* di Congar' in their *Laico e cristiano* (Turin, 1987), pp. 102–21.

6

Congar's ecclesiology: (c) The apostolic ministry

In *Lay People in the Church* Congar had offered a forthright account of Catholic teaching on the sacrament of Order, the continuing 'apostolic ministry' of the Church. He had distinguished between two modes of sharing in the priesthood, kingship and prophethood of Christ, the one by a 'title of dignity', a quality of existence, which would be common to all Christians; the other by a 'title of authority' and so of 'superiority', which is characteristic of the ordained ministry.

APOSTLESHIP AND COMMUNITY

Writing some years after the Council, in *Ministères et communion ecclésiale* (1971), though unsure as to whether this represents a happy way of proceeding, he considered that a distinction made broadly in this manner is required by Church tradition, in both East and West alike (MCE, p. 14). The Council had used the idea, found already in Pius XII, that the ministerial priesthood represents Christ as the Church's Head. This gives us a vital clue to construing the significance of the ordained ministry, which is to be, with respect to the community of the Church, the representative of Christ as the *vis-à-vis* or *gegenüber* of that community. The ordained ministry, in other words, represents the Head to the Head's own Body. Christ's relation with the Church is not only one of life and immanence, it is also a relation of superiority.[1] If the reflection of recent years on the ministerial priesthood is agreed on anything, it is on the notion of that priesthood as presidential within the Christian assembly.

However, looking back, Congar felt that he had been too influenced in his picture of the apostolic ministry by the account thereof given in such Neo-Thomist authors as Cardinal Charles Journet (1891–1975) of Fribourg and his own French Dominican predecessor Gardeil, for these men, in their analyses of the 'causes' of the Church in Aristotelean terms, had considered the only 'efficient causality' at work in the Church to be that of Christ forming the community of the faithful through the apostolic hierarchy. Unfortunately, this scheme leaves out the Holy Spirit, as well as the charisms, gifts bestowed in uncovenanted fashion for the upbuilding of the Church, and, with the latter, the variety of non-ordained 'services' through which God is also 'constructing' his people. The laity, after all, are not simply sharers in the apostolate of the hierarchy, or mere collaborators with the hierarchical priesthood. Though these two concepts, associated with the last Popes Pius, are far from passive, they carry with them the *risk* of passivity, for they imply a laity that is not creative, except in relation to assisting the ordained ministry. At the same time, Congar wishes to avoid what he terms a 'democratic' concept of the latter, where it would be seen, as in certain Protestant systems, as delegated by the congregation.

What, then, is his solution?

> We maintain that Christ willed a structured community. But it is *within* the community of his disciples that he chose the Twelve. Both at the outset of his ministry and during its course, as at the foot of the Cross and in the upper room of Pentecost, there were disciples together with the Twelve. (MCE, p. 18)

True, there were none such at the Lord's Supper. But Congar comforts himself with what the Decree of the Second Vatican Council has to say on the Church's mission: although a particular, explicit mandate for mission was given to the Twelve, yet the whole Church is missionary. As *Ad Gentes* puts it, 'The apostles were the germ of the new Israel; at the same time they were the origin of the sacred hierarchy'.[2] Congar comments on this, for him, crucial text:

> With the exception of special cases where a situation of authority is formally envisaged, what is founded on the Twelve is not only the hierarchy, but the entire Church. Let us say in brief that Jesus instituted a structured community, a community which is, in its entirety, holy, priestly, prophetic, missionary, apostolic, with ministries within it—some of them

freely raised up by the Spirit, others bound by the imposition of hands to the institution and mission of the Twelve. (MCE, p. 19)

FURTHER IMPLICATIONS

In this connexion Congar touches on two implications. First, community and ordained ministry are mutually conditioning. In the ancient Church, the election of candidates for the apostolic ministry was an organic part of the process which led to their ordination, and was regulated in a 'koinonial' or 'communionist' and collegial manner. However, Congar warns against the simple replacement of the present discipline, which has the merit of respecting more profoundly the personal liberty of a vocation, by some other in a wooden or mechanical fashion. Secondly, the theology of how the Church is apostolic concerns more than simply the apostolic succession of ordained ministers, vital though that is. As in his contribution to *Mysterium Salutis*, he insists that apostolicity of faith or doctrine is prior to apostolicity of order.[3]

Each of these two implications, Congar considered, would repay further thought. If the good health of a theology of the ministry depends on its conditioning by a preliminary perception of the Christian ontology of the *faithful community*, in relation to the action of God, through Christ, by the Holy Spirit (something indicated by the ancient practice of sending letters *either* to a Church community *or* to its head, and that indifferently), we must not be misled by this scheme into regarding only ministry *in general* as of divine institution, the community remaining unconditionally free to determine its concrete forms. On the contrary: Congar maintains stoutly that, in the case of the three offices of diaconate, presbyterate and episcopate, a new element intervenes, above the gifts of nature and grace active in other forms of serving in the Church. This new element is the *sacramental*. By a sacrament, a divine act relating to the messianic work of Christ, the ordained ministry, even if its work consists in 'functions', possesses a 'stability which is founded on an ontology of grace' (MCE, p. 46). Congar distinguishes this 'historic' ministry from two other generic types of service in the Church: those where gifts are placed at the service of others in an occasional, spontaneous and transient way, and those where analogous 'services'—perhaps in catechizing, or organizing Scripture study, directing a choir, or an evangelistic outreach, working for Catholic charities or Catholic Action—are offered in a more stable fashion, not least because they relate to permanent, or at any rate habitual, needs and activities of the Church.

Again, with respect to the primacy of apostolic doctrine over apostolic succession in the narrower sense, Congar is similarly careful to avoid *either* the defining of a Catholic position *over against* the Reformers in these matters, *or* the simple collapsing of the former into the perspective of the latter. In the Lutheran tradition, the succession of ordained ministers can be, and even must be, interrupted if this is necessary to safeguard the purity of the apostolic Word. The Church, in this view, is preserved not by the succession of episcopal consecration, but by succession in the preaching of the Gospel. Indeed, this view is typical of all the churches derived from the sixteenth-century Reformation, including the Anglican divines of the sixteenth and seventeenth centuries. Apostolicity consists for them in faithfulness to the fundamental teachings of the Gospel, of which the ministerial succession is at best a sign, rather than a guarantor. This tendency has been sharpened in much contemporary Protestantism, so Congar believes, by a certain 'actualism'. Christ is not seen as the historical foundation of a continuous chain of ministers, but as the 'actual', present, foundation. In Barth's ecclesiology, indeed, Christ's sovereignty is affirmed in such a way that the being of the Church is subsumed under that of Christ, as an 'event-like', *événementiel*, relation to him.[4] Can the notion of a conditioning of apostolic ministry by apostolic doctrine be presented in a fashion which avoids such excesses, taking on a genuinely Catholic sense that could, in addition, open the way to greater consensus among divided Christians?

For enlightenment, Congar turns to the history of doctrine, and, in the first place, to the Fathers of the Church. Drawing on the first letter of Clement of Rome, Congar suggests that the apostolic succession is inseparable from the apostolicity of the whole Church, and finds this conclusion confirmed in the practice of episcopal consecration, where, notably, one pastor does not consecrate his successor on the same *cathedra*. Such consecration is preceded by a scrutiny and a profession of faith: it is not separable from the confession of the catholic and apostolic belief. And here Congar cites Letter 6 of Pope Sixtus III (432–440) to the effect that no one is a successor of the apostles if he does not remain in the faith of the apostles.[5] Again, in Irenaeus, whom Congar describes as the 'doctor of the apostolic succession', we have a vision of the Church in which the legitimacy of the episcopal succession cannot be severed from continuity in the true faith. Not only Irenaeus but Augustine, Anselm of Canterbury (*c.* 1033–1109) and Thomas can be cited as holding that not even legitimate Catholic bishops can be followed where they teach what is contrary to the canonical Scriptures. Columbanus the Younger (543–615) will write to Pope Boniface IV (d. 615) that 'authority rests in your hands so long as you conserve the true rule [of faith]'.[6] Congar points out that these notions were assisted by the tendency to see the succession as the permanent presence of the founder in the line of those who succeeded him—a point of view which separated the person and his behaviour less from the function than is the case today. The mediaevals also discussed to what extent ordinations could be valid if carried out in opposition to the doctrinal, moral or canonical discipline of the Church, for example, by simoniacs selling entry to the apostolic ministry for hard cash. Although opinion was divided on issues of this kind, one school of thought allowing the sacramental order its own partial autonomy, the other regarding the existence, let alone the efficacy, of Order as doubtful outside the Church's communion, it was universally agreed, Congar reports, that there could be no valid transmission of that ministry without faith in at least the essential truths of the apostolic preaching (themselves never, apparently, listed). Moreover, mediaeval exegesis of the great Matthaean 'primacy text' (Mt 16:18) led to the conclusion that Peter (and the other apostles through him) were the Church's foundation inasmuch as they confessed and spread the true faith. For Thomas, erring prelates are normally to be fraternally corrected by their fellow Christians in a discreet fashion, but, in matters of faith, publicly.[7] Cardinal Humbert of Silva Candida (d. 1061), a pillar of the Gregorian reform and the fateful opponent of the Byzantine patriarch Michael Kerullarios, created the formula which would become classical in Western Canon Law: the Pope 'is to be judged by no one, *save in a case where he deviates in a question of faith*'.[8] As Congar sums up:

> The loss of the apostolic faith meant the loss of apostolic authority. (MCE, p. 80)

Congar's conclusions from his survey of the tradition on this point are threefold. First, the apostolic succession must not be sundered from everything else that makes the Church apostolic. As he writes:

> The apostolic succession is not isolatable from that reality which is the transmission of all that the Church is and that can

> be called, in its various aspects, its apostolicity or tradition (taking that word in its integral and true sense). (MCE, p. 87)

In particular, apostolicity cannot be severed from the other properties of the Church, notably her catholicity (of mission) and her sanctity. The apostolic ministry, Congar explains, is not a purely formal structure: it is essentially referred for its content as well as for its end to that which constitutes the Church, namely, faith and the sacraments of faith whereby the incarnate and risen Lord and his Spirit are given to all epochs and peoples.

Secondly, apostolicity must not be separated from the community of the Church. The Reformers appealed simply to apostolicity of doctrine: above all, conformity to the apostolic writings. But this hardly corresponds to the way in which the ancient Church saw its own continuity with the Church of the apostles. The 'place' of apostolicity is the ecclesial point of coincidence of succession and doctrine—the communion of the Church where a certain régime of 'reception' reigns.[9]

Thirdly and lastly, Congar asks that the full implications of the sacramental nature of the Church be inwardly digested: the bond whereby God has freely bound himself to the Church's sacramental structures derives from a covenant of grace, and this implies a relation of fidelity, not just from God to man (God is always faithful), but from man to God as well. As the lengthy preparation for ordination in modern Catholicism shows, entry into the apostolic succession presupposes grace and the charisms. As Newman put it, so Congar recalls, 'Apostolic Order is an ethical principle, or it is not worth much'.[10] Naturally, the *essence* of the apostolic succession is found in the self-identical office which perdures through the succession of bearers of that office—the self-identity of apostolic witness and doctrine being presumed. What Congar is stressing here is, rather, that it belongs to the nature of the apostolic office that it be exercised in a definite *spirit*. Congar is calling for the reintegration of spirituality into an ontology of ministry, something to which his Swiss contemporary Hans Urs von Balthasar (1904–88) has made a major contribution,[11] and which Congar himself has described under one important aspect, namely, *diakonia* or service.

COLLEGIALITY AND PRIMACY

Having thus outlined the general contours of the apostolic ministry, Congar turns to the principal internal differentiation of its plenary form, that which distinguishes the episcopate in its collegiality from the episcopal ministry of the bishop of Rome in its unique primatial character. As usual, Congar approaches the matter in an historical frame of mind. By his consecration a bishop of the pre-Nicene age was conscious of becoming at once head of a local church and a member of the episcopal order. At the time, the church and bishop of Rome was deemed 'an exemplary model' for other churches to follow, above all in matters of faith. Reference to that church and bishop constituted a kind of moral norm for the communion of local churches at large. Rome herself was aware of this—and so her bishop was asked to intervene, or did intervene, or at any rate made a claim to intervene, in the affairs of other churches.[12] Though an authoritative and even judicial aspect had already emerged, it would be anachronistic, Congar believes, to call the Pope as yet the 'head' of the episcopal college. For the first three centuries after Nicaea, that college was frequently referred to as the very structure of the Church's communion. But, within this concept, the idea emerges in the West that the Roman church is *caput*, 'head', in the ecclesial body; that her 'Church-quality' is different from that of any other church; that she is (theologically) the 'beginning' or 'source' of the rest, just as Peter was held to be the *initium episcopatus*, the 'start of the episcopate'.[13] For its part the East was perfectly familiar with the primatial principle, for in its early canons (approximately the time of Nicaea) the bishops of each region are to 'know which among them is their first and consider him as their head'. But this implied plural and somewhat localized 'heads', a notion finally focused in that of the patriarchal bishops. Congar stresses that, in the Eastern context, the primatial and synodal principles were seen as mutually complementing each other: the 'first' could make no decision without the rest, nor the rest without the first. In the West, prior to the Conciliarist crisis, something of the same attitude prevailed, in that a Council was seen not in opposition to papal authority, but as its 'helpmate and confirmation'. But with certain honourable exceptions, the idea of episcopal collegiality drained away from the consciousness of Western theology in the Middle Ages.[14] The notion of collegiality became the monopoly of the 'college' of cardinals. Although the cardinals were the *cardines*, 'hinges' of the Roman church, the ambiguity in the use of the term *ecclesia romana* in mediaeval ecclesiology, for which it could mean *either* the local church of Rome *comme tel, or* that church as 'containing' all the others as their 'mother' or synthesis, allowed the college of cardinals to appropriate part of the rightful heritage of the episcopal college.

As forming one body with the Pope they were held by such late mediaeval theologians as Pierre d'Ailly (1350–1420) to share in the government of the universal Church not as assistants to the papal primacy but as successors of the apostles, forming their college around Christ. The bishops, by contrast, were recorded as succeeding to the post-Pentecost condition of the apostles—dispersed through various parts of the world as founders of particular churches. Congar expects the attentive reader to gather one important, and alarming, point from this: if the proper typological relationship between the Pope and the bishops is that of *Christ* and his apostles (and not *Peter* with his fellow-apostles), then the bond linking Pope and bishops is no longer a matter of differentiation within the single apostolic ministry at all. This development was assisted, Congar believes, by the lamentable theology of Order passed on by Jerome of Bethlehem (*c*. 342–430), for whom presbyterate and episcopate were essentially one single order, though with two 'dignities'. Increasingly, the Pope is pushed beyond the episcopal order (which alone renders his authority sacramental) into the lonely pre-eminence of a 'pontifical monarchy', signalized in the title, at once juridical and mystical, of 'Vicar of Christ'.[15] Such claims raised up numerous enemies: Ockhamists, Conciliarists, Gallicans, but Congar stresses that the moderate figures in the Conciliar and Gallican movements provided precious nuggets of insight into the Pope's continued inhabitation of the episcopal order, as well as into the way that the 'supreme power' in the Church belongs not only to the Pope personally in his representing the whole Body but also to the episcopate with the Pope as its head.[16] These notions were vital at the *First* Vatican Council: indeed, Congar goes so far as to say that

> the First Vatican Council constitutes one of the *loci theologici* of collegiality. (MCE. p. 120)

And this not only for its decision to convoke residential bishops, or for the declarations of the *deputatio fidei* in these matters, but, above all, for the thesis of the dogmatic decree *De Ecclesia* which the Council, at the time of its enforced dissolution through the Savoyard seizure of Rome, was about to enact. There the bishops were said to hold the supreme power 'conjoined with their head' not only in Council but also as dispersed throughout the Church: the very doctrine that the Second Vatican Council would canonize almost a century later.

As one would naturally expect, however, Congar records the

achieved integration of primacy and collegiality in the documents of the Second Vatican Council as a major further step. But even those documents present, with the benefit of theological hindsight, certain *lacunae*, to whose existence post-conciliar tensions between the Papacy and segments of the episcopate testify. What is the nature of the reciprocity which should hold good between Pope and bishops? For Congar, the universal primate is required not by law but by the demands of communion to seek the help, support and co-operation of the episcopate *in the very exercise of his primacy*. Though the final decisions made by virtue of that primacy are his alone, the *conditions* of those decisions call for a certain freely-bestowed dependence of the Pope on the worldwide episcopate—since this is what communion, with its connotations of mutuality and exchange, necessarily implies. This is how Congar understands the theological significance of the Roman Synods which now meet at regular intervals, with a representative selection of the worldwide episcopate in attendance.

Congar wishes to marry a high doctrine and practice of the papal office, with a vigorous revindication of the synodal element in the Church's life. Though synods (and in that word Congar includes the meetings of bishops' conferences, but not of course their bureaucratic extensions) are creations of ecclesiastical law, they derive from a divinely-given quality of the Church, her 'conciliarity', which follows from her very existence as a brotherly communion. At the same time, and in connexion with that most flamboyant modern form of the Petrine ministry, the papal visit, he calls the desire to see the Pope the desire to see one who is the icon of unity, the icon of communion (FYCT, p. 55).

And yet, as Pope Paul VI remarked with characteristic candour during his visit to the World Council of Churches in Geneva, for many non-Catholic Christians, the bearer of the Petrine ministry of unity is, paradoxically, the greatest obstacle to unity, the unity of a remade Christendom. It is to Congar's lifelong interest in ecumenism that we should thus appropriately turn.

Notes

1 Cf. Acts 9:4; 1 Cor 11:3, 7; 12:12.

2 *Ad Gentes divinitus*, 5.

3 *L'Eglise une, sainte, catholique et apostolique* (Paris, 1970), pp. 208–11.

4 K. Barth, 'Das Sein der Kirche, das heisst aber Jesus Christus': *Kirchliche Dogmatik* I/1 (Zurich, 1932), p. 2.

5 Schwarz, *Acta Conciliorum oecumenicorum* I, 2, p. 109; cited in MCE, p. 67.

6 *Epistolae* 55 (PL 80, 280B).

7 *Summa Theologiae* IIa IIae, q. 33, a. 4 ad ii.

8 See A. Michel, 'Humbert von Silva Candida bei Gratian. Eine Zusammenfassung', *Studia Gratiana* I (Bologna, 1953), pp. 83–117.

9 For Congar's doctrine of réception, see his 'La réception comme réalité ecclésiologique', *RSPhTh* 56 (1972), pp. 369–484.

10 J. H. Newman, *Essays Critical and Historical* I (London, 1871), p. 370.

11 H. U. von Balthasar, 'Nachfolge und Amt' in *Sponsa Verbi* (Einsiedeln, 1961), pp. 80–147.

12 L. Hertling, 'Communio und Primat' in *Xenia Piana. Miscellanea Historiae pontificiae* VII (Rome, 1943), pp. 1–48.

13 P. Batiffol, *Cathedra Petri* (Paris, 1938), pp. 95–103.

14 See Congar's own 'Notes sur le destin de l'idée de collégialité épiscopale en Occident au Moyen Age: VII–XVI siècles' in *La Collégialité épiscopale* (Paris, 1965), pp. 90–129. Also J. Saraiva Martini, 'De collegialitate episcopali inde a saec. IV usque ad Concilium Tridentinum', *Claretianum* VI (1966), pp. 27–61, for further documentation.

15 See M. Maccarrone, *Vicarius Christi. Storia del Titolo papale* (Rome, 1952).

16 Cf. *L'Eglise. De saint Augustin à l'époque moderne* (Paris, 1970), pp. 305–42; see also G. Alberigo, *Lo sviluppo della dottrina sui poteri nella Chiesa universale. Momenti essenziali tra il XVI e il XIX secolo* (Rome, 1964).

7

Congar and ecumenism: (a) General principles

It is obvious from what we have seen so far of Congar's life and thought that ecumenism has played a major part in both. As early as *Divided Christendom* he laid down the basic principles that would guide him throughout his writing life. Firstly: in the light of the role of the theme of unity in the High Priestly Discourse of John 17, itself a solemn will and testament of the Incarnate Lord on the final night of his earthly existence, we must *do* something for unity—'if only to prepare ourselves to be God's instruments on the day when He is pleased to have mercy on us' (DC, p. 2).[1]

BEFORE THE COUNCIL: ECUMENICAL ANALYSIS AND PRESCRIPTION

In *Divided Christendom*, after accounts of both the Eastern Orthodox schism and that of the sixteenth-century Protestant West, Congar undertakes an initial analysis of the causes of continuing disunity. Fundamentally, he identifies three. In the first place, the mere fact that these schisms have endured for so long has its own momentum in prolonging their existence. One learns to live apart. Secondly, since the schisms, the Catholic Church has itself developed in ways that make it more, not less estranged from its detached children: it has developed as a society (in its institutional life), as a praying body (in its devotion) and as a thinking body (in its theological culture). Thirdly, this development has itself been one-sided, hardening tradition or concentrating it in a particular way which Congar sums up in the phrase 'Tridentinism'. This is, he stresses, not a fault of Catholicism alone: all the separated churches have known a similar sclerosis and partialness.

What does Congar regard as the solution to the problem of disunity thus analysed? He finds the key to a solution at both the theoretical and the practical levels in the distinction between faith—the faith as a totality of believing—and a faith-*value*, a notion which he drew from the Anglican A. Gabriel Hebert SSM. As Congar writes, in language which will persist in his work until the 1980s:

> Each of the great schisms which have become great Christian communities represents, in its positive aspect, certain genuine values, even if it is tragically astray in those aspects in which it is negative, exclusive and peculiar to itself. (DC, p. 40)

Or, varying the crucial terms somewhat, he speaks of a 'genuine spiritual impulse' which (as a rule) lay at the origin of the great secessions—an impetus which 'in so far as it was positive and disinterested, was truly Catholic' (DC, p. 41). Thus for instance, Congar takes such impulses or values to be instanced in Luther's *sola gratia*; in Calvin's *soli Deo gloria*. What then would Catholic ecumenism consist in? It would consist in co-learning with one's separated brethren how to subordinate particular values (as thus defined) to the divinely-given transcendent faith which 'should unite us all in God' (DC, p. 47).

Congar makes it crystal clear, however, that by 'faith' here he does not mean a vaguely-described spiritual relationship with the divine, shorn of all confessing, credal content—what the mediaevals might have described as the *fides qua*, sundered from the *fides quae*, with competing doctrinal claims rendered anodyne through their massive relativization as so many symbolisms or sensibilities expressing in diverse ways relationship with the single Christian God. His analysis of the 'liberal' theory of ecumenism (as he terms it), a theory he sees worked out above all in the 'Life and Work' Congress in Stockholm in 1925, is sharp and unremitting. He points out that the Life and Work movement married Anglo-Saxon origins redolent of a 'pragmatic outlook', and indeed an (ethical) 'idealism of the Woodrow Wilson type', to the personal inspiration of the charismatic Lutheran archbishop of Uppsala, Nathan Söderblom (1866–1931), himself, however, under the strong intellectual influence of the Protestant liberalism which followed in the wake of F.D.E. Schleiermacher (1768–1834).[2] Congar describes this liberal ecumenism in these terms:

> It is assumed that there is in Christianity an essential reality in which we are already united, and which only needs to be discovered, whilst there is also a whole order of non-essentials in and through which we are divided. The essential reality is a life of personal devotion to our Lord and service to our neighbour which results from it: the non-essentials are diverse and conflicting dogmas, forms of worship and ecclesiastical organization. In such things it is futile to seek a basis for Christian unity. (DC, p. 119)

And continuing to expound this 'liberal' notion of ecumenism, Congar goes on:

> Unity must be reached not on the basis of dogma and ecclesiastical order but '*in spite of* all our differing theological and ecclesiastical conceptions'. For these are only a body in which each one clothes the spiritual experience of grace according to his own categories; forms of human origin, necessary and useful ways of expressing the gift of God once it has been received. But the gift of God, in which every sincere soul is united to every other, and apart from which we can never hope to find unity, is the inward experience of grace and brotherly love inspired by Christ. The unity we must look for is unity in spirit with any form of ecclesiastical or dogmatic expression which will show itself tolerant of other equally legitimate expressions. One alone of these expressions is excluded, that one which excluded itself, refusing to meet in fraternal fellowship and putting itself, by its pretensions to the whole truth, into a state of universal schism. (DC, pp. 119–20)

Congar comments that it would hardly be possible to find a more radical opposition to the teaching of the Catholic Church; it is, moreover, a topsy-turvy use of words, which makes them mean what we want them to mean. How has such a picture of Christianity, and its unity, come to be painted?

Congar identifies three sources feeding liberal ecumenism, and thus rendering *Catholic* ecumenism more difficult to grasp and practise. First, there was a dualism of language and reality, visible and invisible, embodiment and meaning, which Congar ascribed to the influence of late mediaeval Nominalism, continued in Luther's view of faith. The Lutheran identification of the 'inward man' with 'faith', 'piety', 'freedom', 'the spiritual' and thus 'the Christian' *tout court*, most clearly evidenced in the 1520 *Liberty of a Christian Man*, had both consolidated and extended the split found in Nominalism, where, on the philosophical level, one symbolic manner of speaking might be held not really to conflict with another, since neither has any claim to be a statement of reality. In other words, various rational formulations, though incompatible with each other at their own level, may compatibly mediate the same 'communion in reality'. It was, Congar believed, virtually impossible for Lutheranism to hold together the 'organic union' between visible and invisible, human and spiritual.

A second factor underlying the liberal theory of ecumenism was identified by Congar as philosophical rationalism. Congar found in the 'anthropological turn' stemming from the Italian Renaissance and precipitating what the historian of ideas Paul Hazard had termed '*la crise de la conscience européenne*', a mentality centred on

> the study of man in himself, a contemplation and summing up of his innate possibilities from a reflexive and critical point of view, which in effect tends to invalidate all certitude imposed from without and results in the acceptance only of what is experienced as a spontaneous demand of consciousness or as a law of thought. (DC, p. 123)

And Congar suggested that because of certain formal correspondences between the idea of a religion without dogmas in such early modern rationalists as Spinoza (1632–77), and the theological notions of worship in spirit and truth in Lutheranism or the Calvinist (inner) *testimonium Spiritus Sancti*, such rationalism had been able to make deep inroads into the substance of the Protestant confession of faith.

Finally, there was the pragmatist positivism which Congar associated with the English-speaking world: this had much the same effect as the two already mentioned, namely, the disassociation of the order of understanding and reason, *intellectus* and *ratio*, from that of experience.

The upshot of the influence of these factors is wellnigh to reduce Christianity to the status of a philosophy of religion; it fails to grasp the nature of faith—which is not simply a relationship but a content—and the fact that faith is the very substance of the Church and its unity. (We recall that for Thomas the Church is defined by its sacraments, and those sacraments are precisely sacraments *of faith*.) It was an agreeable contrast to pass from the world of Life and Work (the earliest organized ecumenical movement in the modern period) to the somewhat later Faith and Order movement, whose Lausanne conference of 1927 had indicated a very different concept of what ecumenism might mean.[3]

The Faith and Order movement held, in sharp contrast to Life and Work, that the unity of Christians must be looked for in a creed and an ecclesial constitution: in effect, it was a movement Anglican in inspiration rather than merely Protestant—in the sense Congar has been exploring as regards the Stockholm event. Yet Catholics were forbidden to attend the Lausanne congress, and Pope Pius XI had devoted an encylical, *Mortalium Animos*, to an explanation of why. The chief reason was that the Conference based itself on the assumption that the Church of Christ is not an already existing reality. Congar notes that the representatives of Orthodoxy felt themselves compelled to make a declaration to the effect that the basis assumed for the foundation of the Reports to be submitted to the Conference's votes was incompatible with the principles of the Orthodox Church (DC, p. 133).

Congar argues—and takes encouragement here from some words of Barth in *The Church and the Churches*—that Catholicism's

> own way of helping the cause of oecumenism is simply to be herself. In refusing to enter the movement she has done more for its best interests than have the partial groups which compose it, and the more recent developments of the movement [he is thinking of the shift from Life and Work to Faith and Order] owe much to the uncompromising attitude taken by the Catholic Church.[4]

Moving on to consider the successors of these Congresses, the Oxford Life and Work Conference and the Edinburgh Faith and Order Conference, both of 1937, Congar considered that Life and Work itself had been transformed—something he ascribed to the effect of the 'confessional revival' within Protestantism, namely, the work of Barth. One of the consequences of this was the more lively realization that unity must be the work of God himself. Faith and Order, by comparison, had developed much less, being still inspired chiefly by Anglican theories of ecclesiology.

Did these developments open the way for Roman Catholic participation? Congar thought that motives of prudence, rather than strictly doctrinal reasons, were predominant in determining Rome's continuing opposition to such participation. He did not rule out, however, the movement's becoming more fully acceptable as it itself developed.

It was this inner evolution of non-Catholic ecumenism, as much as shifting attitudes within the Catholic Church itself, that made possible the new opening to other churches which was so marked a feature of the brief yet epoch-making pontificate of Pope John XXIII, and of the general Council which he convoked, which Congar attended and on whose texts he set his mark.

THE COUNCIL AND AFTERWARDS: EVALUATING OTHER CHURCHES

Not surprisingly, Congar's evaluation of non-Catholic churches and communities has been modified since the Second Vatican Council, whose own documents constituted a notable advance in this regard. Latin Catholicism's traditional view of schismatic Christian bodies was that worked out by Augustine, and notably in his *De Baptismo contra Donatistas*.[5] For Augustine, the sacraments are only genuinely salvific in the *unitas* of Christ's single Catholic Church, yet there are nevertheless 'traces' of that Church, *vestigia Ecclesiae*, in schismatic bodies which have taken into schism some or all of the sacraments and some or many points of the true faith. Moreover, prolonging Pope Stephen's (d. 257) theology as shown in the controversy over schismatical baptism with Cyprian a generation before, Augustine ascribes all sacramental acts (including, then, schismatical ones) to Christ himself. What is *ecclesial* in such sacramental operation is, however, according to Augustine, charity: that is, in his technical ecclesiological use of the word, *insertion into unity*. And this—which, by definition, is found only in the single Catholic Church—makes the sacraments actions of the Church too, actions vivified by the Holy Spirit, the 'soul' of Christ's Church-body. When we come to the mediaevals, we find that, for example in Thomas, heretics who administer the sacraments according to the 'form of the Church' are said to be in the Church *quantum ad formam Ecclesiae quam servant*, 'with regard to the form of the Church which they serve'.[6] In post-mediaeval Latin Catholicism, theology recognized a 'Church-value' in non-Catholic groupings in the context of apologetics. In discussing the 'notes of the Church'—one, holy, catholic, apostolic—such writers had to admit that certain other Christian communions shared these notes or marks to some degree.

Congar considers that his own *Divided Christendom* was the first work to consider in any systematic way how dissident churches and communities should be appreciated ecclesiologically. True, the matter had been touched on in an important address by the Polish Jesuit Urban to a Church congress in Bohemia before the Great War, mindful of the Russian Orthodox who shared with Catholic Slavs a debt to the mission of Cyril (826–869) and Methodius (*c*. 815–885).[7] Yet Congar felt that he himself had really blazed the trail. For in his book he had affirmed that ecumenism begins when we start to consider the Christianity not just of schismatic Christian individuals, but of schismatic ecclesiastical bodies as such. Reflection on such groups urged one to the conclusion, or so he argued, that the idea of schismatic persons being united to the single, visible Catholic Church through a *votum*, an 'implicit desire', was inadequate. For how could such a 'dissident Christianity'—that is, a group—have such a desire *as group*? Thus he was led to put forward his own concept that the schismatic communities retained *elements* of the *Una Sancta* in their schismatic situation.

Congar explains that his work was not slow to encourage a response in others. Following in his footsteps, Dom Jean Gribomont spoke of 'imperfect realizations' of the single sacrament of the Church in non-Catholic bodies.[8] Rather than speaking of a plurality of 'Church-elements' conserved by the dissident communions (as Congar himself had done), he insisted that the Church is so ordered that each element in her reality implies, objectively, all the rest: one cannot have one part without having, in some degree and in some manner, all the rest. In a different conceptuality again, but still one stimulated by Congar's efforts, his fellow Dominican Christophe Dumont saw in the separated Christian confessions 'potential parts' of the single Church. Such parts, Dumont explained, were not integral parts like the districts of a town, but rather the essential whole expressing itself partially, and thus deficiently, in its powers and activities.[9] Here the fundamental analogy was that of the soul with its faculties. As for a third writer whose interest Congar had awakened, Maritain, he preferred to speak of a 'supernatural created personality of the Church', present in a virtual and invisible way in the non-Catholic communities.[10] Congar had the satisfaction of finding his notion of the *vestigia Ecclesiae* adopted by the 1950 'Toronto Declaration' of the World Council of Churches. Though its phrasing was not, perhaps, especially gracious, its acceptance there was smoothed by its occurrence in the texts of Luther and Calvin.

Congar was also careful to chronicle references to major contributions made independently at a rather later date, in fact on the eve of the Second Vatican Council where a higher appreciation of the status of separated Christian bodies would be written into a conciliar document of the episcopate in assembly. These are, first, that of the German Jesuit Heinrich Fries who suggested the notion of participation, *Teilhabe*, as a key idea in this context.[11] Granted that the new members of dissident bodies were, at their baptism, members of the single Catholic Church, only becoming 'excommunicate' in later life as they consciously adopted non-Catholic teaching, and shared in non-Catholic worship, we are dealing with a situation where there is at once *Gemeinsamkeit* and *Verschiedenheit*, 'something in common' and 'something that differentiates'. The schismatic communities, in virtue of what is common, 'participate' in the single *Catholica*, and this notion of an already-existing participation rules out the idea that they will be reintegrated in the whole by a simple 'return'. Indeed, if it were Fries who put this viewpoint most clearly, he was only articulating, remarks Congar, a wider consensus by the opening year of the Council:

> On the eve of the decree on ecumenism, a certain consensus existed among Catholic theologians, in favour of a theology of the differentiated participation of the non-Roman communions in the treasure of the single Church, and in favour, too, of an ecumenism of integration which would be something other than 'return', pure and simple. (EOe, pp. 212–13)

The other source Congar cites is the august one of Pope Paul VI's first encyclical, *Ecclesiam suam*, of 1964. Paul VI unwittingly exemplified what the critics of Congar's *vestigia Ecclesiae* idea considered to be its excessive ecclesiocentricity, and tendency to make the concrete Roman Catholic Church the exclusive criterion of ecclesiality. For the encyclical is patterned in terms of four concentric cycles: world, non-Christian religions, non-Catholic churches and finally the Catholic family with the local church of Rome as *mater et caput*. However, as we shall see in a moment, Congar rejected these criticisms, regarding them as originating in a weakened sense of the Church in our present cultural ambience.

So far as the Council is concerned, Congar explains from the vantage point of his own intimate acquaintance with its workings that a number of the bishops sought a statement on the ecclesiality of non-Catholic confessions, along the lines of a theology of the *vestigia Ecclesiae*. Behind the scenes paperwork from the making of the Dogmatic Constitution *Lumen Gentium* shows that in the background of the text there was indeed *vestigia Ecclesiae* thinking, even though all that appears on the surface is the idea of a *conjunctio*, 'joining', between the Catholic Church and the faithful of other Christian communities.[12] Yet, as if to redeem this failure, *Lumen Gentium* enumerates in generous terms the realities which such 'conjunction' involves: Scripture; religious zeal; faith in the all-powerful God and in Christ his Son, the Saviour; baptism, and other sacraments. For some communions there could be added, the text explains, the historic episcopate, the Eucharist and devotion to the Mother of God. In every case there was communion in spiritual goods and in prayer. Another relevant feature of *Lumen Gentium* was its famous clause asserting that the Church of Jesus Christ *subsists in* the Catholic Roman Church, but is not exhaustively identical with that Church.[13]

The importance of this latter statement was that it rendered logically possible the companion affirmation of *Unitatis Redintegratio*, the Decree on Ecumenism, that the 'conjunction' asserted in *Lumen Gentium* derives from the existence of 'numerous elements' of the reality of Christ's Church outside the Catholic Church's visible boundaries.[14] These 'elements of sanctification and truth', being themselves proper elements of the Church of Christ, tend naturally, of themselves, towards Catholic unity. And *Unitatis Redintegratio* went on to express this more positive appreciation of the non-Catholic churches and communities in terms of the categories of 'perfect' and 'imperfect' communion. 'Imperfect' communion is a reality created by shared faith in Christ and by our common baptism. The value of this category consists for Congar above all in its power to synthesize the other key notions suggested in regard to this vital subject matter: namely, the implicit desire for, or tendency towards, unity, the 'traces of the Church', and the notion of participation, closely linked as this is to that of communion, *koinōnia*.

However, Congar points out that the Council nowhere specifies *which* elements, in their sum, truly constitute 'Church-ness', and so it fails to explain how a genuine ecclesiality can attach to a given separated communion. It is irrelevant that the Council speaks of individual baptized non-Catholics as *Ecclesiae appositi*, 'joined with the Church'. One can only note that, in fact, the Council calls the Orthodox churches *churches*, and the communions born of the Reformation 'churches or ecclesial communities'. The difference between these terms is clearly explained by *Unitatis Redintegratio*, 2: those communions which lack the sacrament of Order (in virtue of being outwith the apostolic succession) have 'not conserved the proper and integral substance of the eucharistic mystery'.

Since the Council, Congar reports, the language of *elementa Ecclesiae* (or *vestigia Ecclesiae*) has met with certain criticisms. It is said to be 'substantialist', forgetting that the Church proceeds only from the redemptive act of God, and moreover, both 'static' and 'juridicist'. But Congar defends the chosen language of the conciliar assembly, pointing out that the Council includes among the elements it specifies 'spiritual gifts' which involve an 'actualism of the Spirit', as well as institutions. Moreover, he reminds us that the gifts of God to the Church 'are not only those of an actual and vertical action, but also those which Christ and his apostles posed at the origin' (EOe, p. 226). And, moreover, the former depend on the latter. 'There is no valid pneumatology without a Christological reference' (EOe, p. 226). Congar shows himself firmly opposed to any attempt to bypass the sacramental, institutional questions by simply redefining 'church' in term of the living of the Gospel in view of the coming Kingdom, as desiderated by, for example, the Paderborn dogmatician Heribert Mühlen.[15] Congar does not think it appropriate indeed, that the term 'church' itself should be used of any and every Christian communion, since there is a danger that we will

> transfer or indiscriminately attribute to all other churches or ecclesial communities those qualities or qualifications which have their truth only in the Catholic Church. (EOe, p. 230)

And whilst admitting that the contemporary climate of Christian opinion, with its social-philanthropic mind-set, is not well placed for appreciating the concerns of traditional ecclesiology, he nevertheless insists firmly on the need to maintain those concerns:

> One cannot speak of *Church* in the full sense of the word except where the Christian spiritual *realities* are procured in their plenitude and authenticity by what is essential in the Christian *sacramentum*. That comprises the sacramental structure of the Church and ministry issued from the apostles, historically bound to the episcopate, and thus the 'apostolic succession' which includes apostolicity of doctrine and of ministry. The churches which verify this structure are classically counted as 'churches'. The Roman Pope has spoken

> in their regard of sister-churches. That implies the idea that, in the re-established communion with the Catholic Roman Church, they would keep their personality, and also that, from henceforth, they are of the same stock and blood, closely linked, alike, destined to live together. (EOe, p. 241)

DIVERSITY IN COMMUNION

How, then, does Congar see the ecumenical agenda in the post-conciliar epoch? With a remarkable continuity of thinking, he takes the ecumenical aim to be, fundamentally, that which he had already set out in *Divided Christendom*: the integrating of diversity into the unity of a single communion. He points out that all ecumenists now hold to the twin desiderata of diversity and unity *in some fashion*. This is so whether it be the notion of 'conciliar community' put forward by the Faith and Order Commission of the World Council of Churches in Nairobi in 1975, or the notion of 'types of Church' proposed by Cardinal Jan Willebrands, the president of the Roman Secretariat for Christian Unity, at Lambeth and Cambridge in 1972, or the concept of 'reconciled diversity' suggested by the sixth plenary assembly of the World Lutheran Federation in Dar-es-Salaam in 1977, itself a term coined by the Conference of Secretaries of World Confessional Alliances in 1974 (DivComm, pp. 3–5). Naturally, how one understands such reconciled diversity may vary a great deal in the concrete. For his part, Congar hopes for an ecumenical future in which the Catholic tradition, developed to the full and integrated with the resources of Eastern Orthodoxy, will be found to provide a sufficiently spacious home to house all the rest (DivComm, p. 5).

Congar considers the concept of diversity in the unity of a single communion well-founded, whether one looks at the New Testament, at the Fathers, or at the post-patristic Church of the early Middle Ages. While such writers as J. D. G. Dunn and Ernst Käsemann have stressed the diversity of the New Testament community, and Congar accepts the existence of variety and even of tensions in the primitive Church, he feels that justice has not always been done to the equally vital factor of *unity* in that Church.[16] After all, Paul excludes from the Church whatever would be incompatible with the truth of Christ, such as the denial of the resurrection, a Gnosticism allowing for a metaphysical dualism and quasi-divine intermediaries, justification by works, and Christological 'Docetism', the notion that Christ's coming in the flesh was only in seeming. *Pace* Käsemann, it is illegitimate to translate New Testament diversity into a plurality of separate and opposed Churches. Congar prefers the approach of the French exegete Jean Colson, for whom a 'Pauline' and 'Johannine' pattern in ecclesiology—the one with what would become a typically Western sense of universal mission and expansion, the other an analogously Eastern feeling for the significance of local episcopal churches—coexist, but are always capable of fusing as in, for example, the work of Irenaeus.[17] That the Church lives under a régime of grace means, among other things, that whatever is felt to be contrary to its life can be rejected as heresy, as invalid and ruinous diversity, without emasculating variety, valid and fruitful diversity as such.

> It is in the 'tradition' of the church, in the transmission of this life with all its diverse expressions, that diversities which might have proved discordant were harmonized. (DivComm, p. 14)

So far as the Church of the Fathers is concerned, Congar makes much of the controversy over the dating of Easter, the feast of feasts, which surfaced at various times from the Asia Minor of the mid-second century to the First Council of Nicaea, from the Anglo-Celtic church in the seventh century to the disagreement of St Boniface with Irish monks in Bavaria a century later. It was a test case for the principle of differences held in unity. Despite the desirability of sharing a common celebration of Easter, Congar insists that we must respect the appeal made by such men as Polycarp of Smyrna (*c.* 69–*c.* 155) and Irenaeus to the Popes of their day in terms of the legitimacy of two equally apostolic traditions. After all, as the decree of the Second Vatican Council on ecumenism itself has to say with regard to the separated Eastern churches:

> the heritage handed down by the apostles was received differently and in different forms, so that from the very beginnings of the Church its development varied from region to region and also because of differing mentalities and ways of life.[18]

But can the patristic student accept that there ever was an 'undivided Church'? Some Protestant writers have denounced this claim as a romantic fiction, and Congar agrees that the apostolic succession alone was never an adequate criterion. For Ignatius of Antioch (*c.* 35–*c.* 107), unity comes through union with the bishop, but some hundred and fifty years after Ignatius's day his own see,

Antioch, was occupied by the arch-heretic Paul of Samosata, while in the fourth century a notorious internal Antiochene schism lasted for several decades and produced three or, at one point, four bishops struggling for a place on the same *cathedra*! Nevertheless, Congar holds that there *was* a real unity, consisting not only in adherence to the fundamental dogmas of the *regula fidei*, the baptismal confession, but also, and even more profoundly, in the shared acceptance of the sacramental nature of the Church, its Godmanhood or theandrism. With Thomist caution on the point, Congar writes:

> I understand this to be essentially a union of supernatural and eschatological reality, with the tangible forms of the specific church that we know. When we speak of the undivided church, we are well aware that it had its diversities and tensions, not to mention differences, but we recognize this organic, sacramental or mystical unity of the body of Christ. (DivComm, p. 21)

And Congar appeals for a return not only to the witness of Scripture but to that of the Fathers and their age—something somewhat marginalized in the consciousness of post-conciliar Catholicism despite its great importance for the Council itself. We must return, he says, to the principles which inspired the Church's life during the epoch of the Fathers, when the liturgy, monasticism and the septet of the ecumenical Councils, from First Nicaea to Second Nicaea, had their moment.

Congar adds that expressions of the idea of diversity and unity, in matters not affecting the faith of the Church itself, can be found throughout the subsequent tradition up to modern times. The Eastern Church historians Socrates (*c.* 380–450) and Sozomen (early fifth century), as Jerome in the West, shared Augustine's conviction, expressed in a series of letters to Januarius, that

> anything that is neither against the faith nor against good morals must be a matter of indifference and observed with due regard for those in whose society one lives.[19]

This discussion of how far diversity in practice was legitimate and how far the local churches were free in this respect became classical for the Middle Ages and right down to the Council of Trent. As Pope Gregory I (590–604) told Leander of Seville (*c.* 550–601) in 591, 'If there is unity of faith, a difference of custom does no damage to

Holy Church'.[20] In the next millennium Fulbert of Chartres (*c.* 960–1028), writing in 1006, could say the same thing in almost the same words.[21] Even at the height of the controversy with the Byzantines over the kind of bread to be used for the Eucharist, Pope Leo IX (1049–54) could write to the patriarch Michael Kerullarios that 'customs differing according to times and places are not injurious to the salvation of believers when the same faith, active in love, commends them all to the one God'.[22] In the crisis of Conciliarism, which was also a moment of new opportunities for ending the Greek schism, Jean Gerson (1363–1429) and, above all, Nicholas of Cusa (1401–64) stress the same idea. However, Congar notes that a Roman sub-tradition, beginning with the later fourth- and early fifth-century Popes Damasus (366–384), Siricius (384–399) and Innocent I (401–417) tends to identify unity of faith with unity of discipline, and so to interpret unity as uniformity. But beginning with Pius IX (1846–78) and continuing in unbroken succession to John Paul II, the Popes' successors in the modern epoch have repudiated this sub-tradition as an abuse of the mission of unity of the Roman See. Whereas the pre-conciliar modern Popes had in mind chiefly the Eastern liturgies, John Paul II, in a 1979 address to a Coptic delegation from the patriarchate of Alexandria, has universalized the principle involved, holding that the richness of the unity of faith and spiritual life must be expressed in diversity of forms.

Congar grounds this papally approved pluralism on two considerations. First, the saving reality must be translated into history, whether we think of it at its Source, the Alpha, as it proceeds from God, or at its goal, the Omega, as it returns to him. And as no human expression will ever be fully adequate to either source or final outcome, 'a number of expressions are possible and even desirable'. Secondly, the saving reality is received by 'living subjects', with their own implicit philosophy, their culture and their characteristic problematic. Inevitably, then, they express it in different ways. This carries with it certain consequences, notably that tensions are inevitable, even when the unity of faith is safeguarded. Moreover, it tells us something about the nature of the mind of man, *l'esprit*, which is of enormous ecumenical importance:

> The spirit is ordered and open to the totality of truth, but it is limited in each person and even in each group of people. Each spirit, each group has only a certain number of experiences and realizes only a part or certain aspects of the truth. That is why

> the spirit is structurally in need of giving and taking. It is structurally directed towards dialogue, towards welcoming the other, towards what is *different*. If ecumenism is a quest for the purity and the fullness of the truth about God and the mysteries of salvation, it must be specifically and supremely a welcoming of differences on the basis of a common point of reference and a common destiny. (DivComm, p. 41)

In this respect, Congar feels, the present-day ecumenical movement has had the same effect on the Catholic Church as, in the fifteenth century, the internal strains of the Great Schism and Conciliarism had on the Latin Church of that day, rendering her more benevolently inclined to her Greek sister in Constantinople. The experience of Christian difference makes the Church more open to the legitimacy of pluralism in unity.

But does all of this mean that Congar looks with confidence to the immediate or to any currently foreseeable future, where the achievement of organic unity is concerned? As a preamble to answering this question, we must take note of his nuanced conception of the essentially *eschatological* nature of the ecumenical task. While recognizing that to say it is only at the Eschaton that our ecumenical concerns will finally be resolved may be to relieve our perplexities at no cost to ourselves, he considers that such a statement carries, nonetheless, a considerable degree of truth. Without giving way to defeatism about our present task, it is true that 'perfect unity will be *given*, eschatologically in the cosmic Easter when God destroys all temples "made with hands" ' (DivComm, p. 163). Moreover, the powers of the world to come are at work in earthly history for the sake of the *unitatis redintegratio*. The eschatological Gift, the Holy Spirit, has been at work since Pentecost, when the Last Days were ushered in. We are looking, then, not for a 'new Pentecost' but for further 'missions' of the Pentecostal Spirit. Finally, though work for unity draws on realities which derive from the historic incarnation and its consequences, namely Tradition, it 'envisages a consummation and can only be understood as a tension towards eschatological plenitude' (DivComm, p. 163). Here Congar cites the Orthodox lay theologian Paul Evdokimov, to the effect that the ecumenical imperative brings us into union with the Christ of Glory, He who is Coming. It is a question of the formation of the total, universal, eschatological body of Christ.[23]

WAYS TOWARDS UNITY: 'RE-RECEPTION' AND THE 'HIERARCHY OF TRUTHS'

Having done justice, then, to the eschatological dimension of ecumenism: short of the actual End, does Congar believe that body can be formed on earth? The awakening of a more eschatologically coloured sensibility within Catholicism gives grounds for hope. It is, Congar believes, the absence of an eschatological perspective in pre-conciliar Catholic ecclesiology which hindered ecumenical openness, imposing on it the theme of 'return', however nuanced by humility and the desire for friendship. Looking towards the End, by contrast, the Church is able and even obliged to recognize the relativity of her own concrete expressions of the Origin, the original, unique *Traditum* of the Gospel. By virtue of this principle, she could recognize the legitimacy of other expressions in other circumstances—*salvo iure communionis*, 'the requirements of communion being saved' (DivComm, p. 166). To Congar's eyes, that recognition may come about by an invocation of two principles: the idea of 're-reception', and the notion of a 'hierarchy of truths'.

What is re-reception? As already noted, reception is that process whereby, in the case of the dogmatic teaching of Pope and bishops, the faithful come to find such teaching beneficial and to live by it fruitfully. Re-reception means giving defined doctrine a new context, and a better equilibrium, through situating it more squarely within the overall witness of revelation—in the hope that even greater benefits and fruitfulness may come, not least for those who have had difficulty with an earlier formulation. Such re-reception will

> [take] account of the knowledge we have acquired of the historical, cultural and sociological conditioning of the [conciliar or papal] decision in question, of the current needs of the cause of the gospel which we seek to serve, of the connotations which have accrued since the first reception of the decision or doctrine, and finally of the criticisms and valuable contributions received from others. (DivComm, p. 171)

Naturally, this is not simply a matter of the re-reception of Catholic doctrines, rendering their fundamental dogmatic intention more intelligible to others; it concerns the doctrine of other churches too. Two doctrinal formulations ripe for re-reception, in Congar's view, are the Lutheran Augsburg Confession of 1530 and the Orthodox statements on the Uncreated Energies of God, 'Palamism', as laid out by Constantinopolitan synods of the fourteenth century. Recontextualized, modified, amplified, Congar is hopeful that these monuments to the history of other people's Christian teaching might one day be made acceptable to the Catholic Church.

The concept of a 'hierarchy of truths' also enters in here. In Congar's version of that concept, which has coloured the Decree on Ecumenism of the Second Vatican Council, it is conceded that there cannot be *degrees* of truth. Logically, any true statement is equivalent in truth-value to any other. Yet, as Congar writes:

> truth is truth *about something*, and is recognized and professed *by someone*. (DivComm, p. 129)

These apparently platitudinous statements yield two significant thoughts. That truth is always professed by a distinct *someone*, located in history, reminds us of the historicity of the human, and so Christian, grasp of truth. Here below, the same Church, at different points on her historical pilgrimage, may entertain, and embody, a perception of what is true in qualitatively variable ways. That truth is always truth about a definite *something*, one face of a constellation of aspects, may suggest how the corpus of doctrinal truths reflects the contours of a reality in which not everything is equally central.

In characteristic fashion, Congar has recourse to historical examples. The ancient Church recognized a hierarchy of errors, deeming, for instance, that the Novatians—dissidents over penitential discipline—were in a less unhappy position than the disciples of Paul of Samosata whose teaching undermined Trinitarian belief. In the mediaeval period Thomas distinguished between truths of faith which are such in a direct and intrinsic fashion by reason of their content, and those that are such only indirectly by reason of the relation they have with the former, *in ordine ad alia*. For his own part, Congar presents the notion of a hierarchy of truths under the image of a tree, where the smallest twigs are connected to the trunk, but via branches, and whose roots are Christ himself, 'the sacrament of our union with God' (DivComm, p. 130). However, Congar feels obliged to note the unhappiness of the Orthodox with the idea of a hierarchy of doctrines, above all in its most radical form, that of a distinction between fundamental and non-fundamental articles. Thus, in a theological encounter with Anglicans in Moscow in 1976, the Orthodox representatives found the concept to be in conflict with the unity of faith as a whole, although they recognized degrees of importance in matters of practices.[24] The vigour of this Orthodox rejection of the *hierarchia veritatum* concept should, Congar writes, give the Catholic ecumenist pause for thought.

The manner in which some future reunion Council might submit re-received doctrine for the assent of schismatic churches is controverted by Catholic ecumenists. While accepting that the French Jesuit Père Bertrand de Margerie has shown how historically ill-founded is the suggestion of some of their number that dogmas defined without the participation of others cannot be imposed as a *sine qua non* of communion,[25] Congar considers that

> what is at issue is not the precise conditions on which individuals may belong to the Catholic church *as it is*, but differences which may or may not stand in the way of restoring communion between Christian churches inspired by the new movement of reunion, raised up by the Holy Spirit in circumstances which the past could not know. (DivComm, p. 175)

He inclines to Karl Rahner's view that our attention must be focused on what is 'essential' and 'fundamental', which for Rahner was the doctrines explicitly formulated in the Creed of Nicaea–Constantinople of 381.[26] It may be that Congar has not appreciated the alarmingly radical force of Rahner's own proposals for a strategy of reunion. When published, with the co-operation of his confrère Fries, in book form, their intellectual despair of further doctrinal convergence called into question the value of continuing ecumenical negotiations, raised doubts in the minds of Rahner's erstwhile Catholic admirers as to his theological responsibleness, and went far beyond the modest notion of a hierarchy of truths whose negative effect on the orthodox had so impressed Congar.[27] The exact bearing of Congar's latest statement of ecumenical principles is, therefore, difficult to gauge. As a Dominican critic, Padre Daniel Ols, has pointed out, the proposals of *Diversity and Communion* are not notably coherent, even allowing for Congar's tendency to theologize through the making of *dossiers*.[28] Its author admitted, indeed, in his 'conversations' with M. Bernard Lauret on the fiftieth anniversary of the appearance of *Divided Christendom*, that the new book has 'more questions than solutions' (FYCT, p. 81). However, the following statement from Congar's 'middle period' sums up, I believe, his enduring fundamental conviction:

> We can freely admit . . . that if reunion does take place one day it will be *with a Church which differs in some ways* from the

present condition of the Catholic Church, different because it will have developed and been purified and reformed in more than one respect through living contact with its deepest sources, particularly with holy Scripture. It is not, and cannot be, a question of any substantial change in the Church, but of her attaining a stage in the concrete manifestation of her vitality at which the principles of her basic tradition shine out more clearly and in a more Catholic manner, irradiating culture and mentalities of more diverse kinds. (DBC, pp. 95–6)

Notes

1 For the context of Congar's ecumenical work, see E. Fouilloux, *Les Catholiques et l'unité chrétienne du XIXe au XXe siècle. Itinéraires européens d'expression française* (Paris, 1982).

2 An account largely borne out in N. Karlström, 'Movements for International Friendship and Life and Work, 1910–1925', and N. Ehrenström, 'Movements for International Friendship and Life and Work, 1925–1948' in R. Rouse and S. C. Neill (eds), *A History of the Ecumenical Movement 1517–1948* (London, 1954; 3rd ed. Geneva, 1986) I, pp. 509–44; 545–98.

3 T. Tatlow, 'The World Conference on Faith and Order' in R. Rouse and S. C. Neill (eds), *op. cit.*, I, pp. 405–44.

4 K. Barth, *Die Kirche und die Kirchen* (Munich, 1935); cited in DC, p. 133.

5 Augustine, *De Baptismo contra Donatistas*, I, 10, 4.

6 Thomas Aquinas, *In IV Sent.*, d. 25, q. 1, a. 2 ad i.

7 J. Urban, 'De iis quae theologi catholici praestare possint ac debeant erga Ecclesiam Russicam' in *Acta I. Conv. Velehrad* (Prague, 1908), pp. 13–35.

8 J. Gribomont, 'Du sacrement de l'Eglise et de ses réalisations imparfaits', *Irénikon* 22 (1949), pp. 345–67.

9 C. Dumont, 'Unité de l'Eglise et unité chrétienne' in *Les Voies de l'unité chrétienne. Doctrine et spiritualité* (Paris, 1954), pp. 123–8.

10 J. Maritain, *De l'Eglise du Christ. Sa personne et ses personnages* (Paris, 1970), pp. 47 and 188ff.

11 H. Fries, 'Der ekklesiologische Status der evangelischen Kirche in katholischer Sicht' in *Aspekte der Kirche* (Stuttgart, 1963), pp. 123–52.

12 *Lumen Gentium*, 15.

13 Ibid., 8.

14 *Unitatis Redintegratio* 4:3.

15 H. Mühlen, *Una mystica persona. Die Kirche als das Mysterium der Identität des Heiligen Geistes in Christus und den Christen: eine Person in vielen Personen* (Paderborn, 1964; 2nd ed., Munich, 1967).

16 E. Käsemann, 'Unity and multiplicity in the New Testament doctrine of the Church' in *idem, New Testament Questions of Today* (London, 1969), pp. 252–9; J. G. Dunn, *Unity and Diversity in the New Testament* (London, 1977); cf. DivComm, pp. 11–12.

17 J. Colson, *L'Evêque dans les communautés primitives. Tradition paulinienne et tradition johannique de l'épiscopat. Des origines à S. Irénée* (Paris, 1951).

18 *Unitatis Redintegratio*, 14, 3; cited in DivComm, p. 19.

19 *Epistolae* 54, 2, 2–3 (PL 33, 200–1)

20 Gregory the Great, *Epistolae* I, 43 (PL 77, 497).

21 Fulbert of Chartres, *Epistolae* 3 (PL 141, 192).

22 Pope Leo IX, *Epistolae et Decreta pontificia* XXIX (PL 143, 764B).

23 See Y. Congar, 'Notes préliminaires pour une théologie oecuménique', *Foi et Vie* 541.70 (September–October 1947), p. 562.

24 'La Conférence de Moscou (26 juillet–2 août 1976). I. L'Accord de Moscou conclu par la Commission doctrinale mixte anglicane-orthodoxe', *Istina* 24 (1979), p. 70.

25 B. de Margerie, *Vers la plénitude de la communion* (Paris, 1969), pp. 173–8.

26 K. Rahner SJ, 'Is Church union dogmatically possible?', *Theological Investigations* 17 (London/Baltimore, 1981), pp. 197–214.

27 A. Nichols OP, '*Einigung der Kirchen*: an ecumenical controversy', *One in Christ* XXI.2 (1985), pp. 139–66.

28 D. Ols OP, 'Diversité et communion. Réflexions à propos d'un ouvrage récent', *Angelicum* 60 (1983), pp. 122–50.

8

Congar and ecumenism: (b) Anglicans, Lutherans, Orthodox

Congar's discussion of the general principles of Catholic ecumenism raises the question of priorities in bilateral dialogue. Will the Catholic Church move in the direction of the separated Western churches, the shards of the splintered patriarchate of the West, re-receiving her own teaching in a manner more intelligible to them and invoking, if not a distinction between fundamental and non-fundamental articles such as Protestant confessional history has created, then at any rate an appeal to the hierarchy of truths? Or will she move rather in the direction of reunion with the East, where, again, a degree of re-reception will be required but with far less disruption of the continuity and coherence of her own faith, both as lived and as defined? How, in fact, did Congar view the principal historic Christian bodies with which, in the wake of the Second Vatican Council, the Catholic Church would initiate negotiations aimed at overcoming the differences which impede organic reunion?

A. ANGLICANISM

At the time of writing *Divided Christendom* Congar's principal interests were in Anglicanism and Orthodoxy. His later absorption in the figure of Luther, though originating in his youthful sentimental journey through Saxony, was barely hinted at. Later on, it would be Lutherans and the Orthodox who most concerned him. Orthodoxy was the fixed star in his firmament of interests. Indeed, he came to regard it as in some sense a model for the renewal of Catholicism through its own fidelity to the apostolic tradition, as expressed in a rich totality of doctrine, liturgy and spirituality all inseparably united.

Congar was, nevertheless, concerned to keep up his study of the history of Anglican theology, of which he attained a remarkable grasp. He opens his chief account by saying:

> There is no other Christian communion which is so difficult to understand apart from its history as Anglicanism; the prime characteristic of its theology is to share in this relatively unique inseparability from the march of national history and of the general movement of ideas within the nation. (DBC, p. 249)

And Congar connects this tendency of Anglicanism to act as the 'spiritual mouthpiece' of the life of the English nation with its other main distinguishing quality: namely, its comprehensiveness, falling as it does into three main parties representing three trends:

> a traditional and Catholic trend, a Protestant and Puritan trend, a critical and rational trend. (DBC, p. 250)

For, like English social and institutional life at large, at least in Congar's generous perception, Anglicanism tries to be simultaneously 'traditionalist, reformed, critical and humanist' (DBC, p. 250).

Congar regards the Elizabethan period as the true origin of the Anglican Church: up to the Queen's accession, the very existence of the Reform, never mind its concrete form, was in question. He sees the reigns of Elizabeth (1558–1603) and James I (1603–25) as a time for working out a *via media*, whereby Anglicans would tread a delicate dance between, on the one hand, Puritanism and Presbyterianism, and on the other, the Church of Rome. Congar cites approvingly F. J. Shirley's comment that Richard Hooker (*c*. 1554–1600), writing exclusively in Elizabeth's reign, is the real 'father of the Church of England'.[1] He stresses the Catholic and Thomist qualities of Hooker's *The Laws of Ecclesiastical Polity*, but is also conscious of their peculiar view of the relation between Church and State. In regard to the former aspect, he goes so far as to say that

> England has remained to a certain extent both Catholic and medieval because she has kept the idea of natural law. This she owes in large part to Hooker. (DBC, pp. 252–3)

(Had Congar known of Hooker's possible relation to the plays of Shakespeare, this point could have been more fully made.) As Congar presents him, Hooker did not ascribe a divine right to the episcopate, though he denied that the Presbyterian polity is required by the New Testament texts. He connects the institution and sacraments of the Church with the Incarnation in a way 'more Catholic than Protestant'. By contrast, Congar cannot underwrite Hooker's view that the Church is one aspect of a *respublica christiana* of which the queen (or king) is the head. Hooker erected into a theory the state of affairs existing in his own country—a procedure which, Congar ruefully remarks, has not been unknown either before or since. Though Congar does not mention in this context that great student of Hooker, Samuel Taylor Coleridge (1772–1834), his analysis of Hooker's view of society and the Church is remarkably Coleridgian in tenor. For Hooker, he explains,

> Society as a whole . . . consists, in its political aspects, of the state, which is the affair of the laity and, in its cultural aspects, of the Church, which is the business of clerics. (DBC, p. 253)

Congar concludes his account of Hooker by noting that many Elizabethan Anglicans tended to a much lower doctrine of the Church, seeing it as fundamentally invisible, known to God alone, though this point of view made no appreciable impact on Anglican formularies or the wider Anglican tradition at large.

From these thoughts, Congar passes to the more congenial topic of the Caroline divines, approached by way of Lancelot Andrewes (1555–1626) whose life forms a living link between Hooker and those masters of the reign of Charles I. Congar notes Andrewes's work as pastor, spiritual writer, preacher and controversialist (much of his polemics was conducted with Frenchmen, whether Catholics such as Jacques Davy du Perron [1556–1618] or Protestants like Pierre du Moulin [1568–1658]). He describes his theological method as a matter of appealing not only to Scripture but also to the Fathers and to the early history of Christianity:

> all references compatible with a Church which is traditional but bereft of any hierarchical magisterium. (DBC, p. 254)

From his reading, Congar considers the Caroline divines themselves to be remarkably unequal as theologians. William Laud (1573–1645) can barely be classed as a dogmatician at all, being rather the 'English Cyprian', patron and martyr of Church government by the 'priesthood', that is, as the original Cyprian would have understood, the *episcopate*. Congar points out that while some of the Laudian school regarded the episcopal office as of the *esse* (being) of the Church, others deemed it to be necessary only for her *bene esse* (well-being), a providential fact rather than a divine institution. Laud's death at the hands of Parliament and Presbyterianism was followed not only by Commonwealth and Protectorate but by an increasing determination of the survivors of the Caroline school to secure, with the return of the Stuart house, a new settlement that would 'resume Laud's line but without any compromise with Presbyterianism'. Nevertheless, the 1662 Prayer Book revision was so modest that in Congar's opinion it could have permitted Puritans to remain more or less at their ease within the Church of England. He characterizes the new settlement as a fresh *via media*, 'found even in the middle of a restoration which was resolutely episcopal and monarchical' (DBC, p. 257). Not until the 'Glorious Revolution', so-called, of 1688 would a clear 'High Church party' emerge—a reference to the study of that name by George Every, now of Oscott College, Birmingham.[2]

These later Stuart High Churchmen cannot be understood, however, without some awareness of the increasingly rational and liberalizing trend which other Anglican milieux were evincing. Between the 'Laudians' and the Puritans of the 1630s and 1640s there had been placed, if rarely emphasized, a moderate faction led by Lucius Cary, Viscount Falkland (*c.* 1610–43) and his Great Tew circle. As the Calvinist soteriology which marked the dominant force within the Jacobean church declined in attractiveness, this moderate party began to take on that liberal tinge which would later earn for it the name of 'Latitudinarians'. The experience of the Civil War had shown that

> the uncompromising attempt to impose one's ideology on others led to nothing but catastrophic deadlock. (DBC, p. 258)

Accordingly, the Cambridge Platonists and their Latitudinarian successors translated Christianity into terms of values which rationalists and humanists might share, thus paving the way for the widespread theistic trend of the eighteenth century. Congar regards the precursor of such a non-dogmatic theism as Edward Herbert of Cherbury (1583–1648), but its chief proponent he identifies as the author of the significantly named *Christianity not Mysterious*, John Toland (1670–1722). The High Churchmen, marginalized by the new ideology which grew powerful as it found with the Revolution of 1688 those social and political conditions that favoured its triumph, defined themselves over against 'Low Churchmen', those who showed no interest in the Church as such, or care for her authority. Excluded from the episcopal sees, they became internal emigrés, most often Jacobites, holding that non-resistance to the prince was part and parcel of the doctrine of the Church of England.

Like most historians of Anglicanism, Congar regards the age of the Georges as a period of apathy. Although some notable figures defended Church principles, not least Samuel Johnson (1709–84) whose convictions Congar finds 'on the whole, Catholic', the scene was dominated by the liberal-minded ecclesiastics anxious to bridge the gap between the Church and the rationalist tendencies of the times. Such Churchmen sought a revision of the Prayer Book radical enough to keep the Nonconformists within the Anglican fold, the removal (under Arianizing influence) from the Book of the (pseudo-)Athanasian Creed and the dropping or mitigation of the obligation, incumbent on all clerics, to subscribe to the Thirty-Nine Articles.

It is against this background that the rise of the Methodist movement must be seen. While mentioning the influence on the first Methodists of the spiritual writings of the Non-Juror William Law (1686–1761), Congar does not really bring John Wesley's High Church background into clear focus. However, he describes Wesley's debt to Lutheran pietism as

> modified . . . by an almost Catholic sense of the reality of spiritual effort (works) and of the Christian life. (DBC, p. 264)

After the year 1747 it became customary to dub Methodists 'evangelicals', a term earlier used for Continental Lutherans, though Congar finds some reason to think it may also have denoted Anglicans who stressed personal conversion and the doctrine of vicarious redemption. Methodists were also described as 'enthusiasts', a term carrying some of the same derogatory overtones occasionally attached to the word 'mystics' in Catholic contexts: and here Congar notes J. Orcibal's description of the influence on the Wesleys of the French and Spanish mystics of the Counter-Reformation.[3]

The departure of the Methodists from the Church of England left, as Congar explains, an Anglican residue—the Evangelicals. While admiring the zeal of these Evangelical parish clergy who followed in Wesley's wake, Congar does not look to them for any great theological Enlightenment.

> Most of them simply sought, by means of a sort of revivalist preaching similar to that practised nowadays by Billy Graham, to bring the largest possible number of their congregations to the point of following the way of personal conversion: a sense of sin, in a somewhat sentimental atmosphere; abandonment of oneself to Christ through faith; conversion to Christ and a decision to follow him; to give such an example as would contribute to the conversion of others. (DBC, pp. 265–6)

Their chosen instrument the pulpit, such Evangelical parsons and their lay sympathizers did not establish theological colleges until the second half of the nineteenth century. Earlier they had preferred to found missionary and biblical societies, and as Congar notes, this was the time of the first great expansion of Anglicanism outside England to the wider world, the first painful steps towards the creation of a worldwide 'Anglican Communion'.

In dealing with such subsequent Anglican figures as Coleridge and F. D. Maurice (1805–72), Congar shows, perhaps, a less sure touch. Coleridge is yoked somewhat unceremoniously with Thomas Arnold (1795–1842) and Charles Kingsley (1819–75) as a liberal who tried to harmonize the biblical revelation with that disclosure of truth connatural to the human mind by

> minimizing the positive and dogmatic affirmations of Revelation while preserving its value as an inspiration and an ideal. (DBC, p. 269)

If Coleridge is too complex and subtle a thinker to be thus easily classified—one thinks of his 'struggle back towards a Trinitarian theology'[4]—Maurice's ambivalences are, by contrast, duly registered by Congar. Maurice's attempts to explore the divine immanence in Bible and Incarnation, but also in history and nature at large, as in the human conscience, leave Congar somewhat baffled. Maurice's 'system-phobia',[5] as his son and earliest biographer termed it, has defeated more than one enquirer. What Coleridge and Maurice have in common is reverence for Plato, and a high doctrine of the Word of God rather than theological liberalism, though Congar rightly draws attention to Maurice's place at the fountainhead of Anglican socialism.

From these unclassifiable figures Congar moves with an almost audible sigh of relief into the more familiar world of the Oxford Movement. Stressing the intense personal spirituality of its leaders, from John Keble (1792–1866) to R. W. Church (1815–90), and the indirect debt they owed to the renewed interest in Christian history which Romanticism had fostered, Congar describes Tractarianism as the effort to realize

> a theological restoration and religious reform on the basis of a sound knowledge of the Christian past, the Fathers, the liturgy, medieval theology and the great Anglican classics of the sixteenth and seventeenth centuries. (DBC, p. 271)

Surpassing the Caroline divines in their willingness to draw on Catholic tradition, the Tractarians managed to disengage the High Church party from the political entanglements by which, since its fateful alliance with the house of Stuart, it had been encumbered. Rightly, Congar finds the heart of the Oxford Movement to lie in its affirmation of the Church as a divine institution, whose ministry enjoyed apostolic authority to teach, to celebrate the sacraments and to administer the Church's discipline. A sign of good taste is the praise he heaps on the comparatively little-known dogmatic works of R. I. Wilberforce (1802–57), whose conversion to Catholicism he does not mention. Congar regards the Anglo-Catholic movement, with its ritualistic preoccupations, as a genuine product of Tractarianism, since the high doctrine of the sacraments propounded by the Tractarians could not but produce 'certain practical reforms and restorations'.

So far as the later nineteenth century is concerned, Congar singles out for scholarly commendation the 'Cambridge triumvirate' of J. B. Lightfoot (1828–89), B. F. Westcott (1825–1901) and H. B. Swete (1835–1917) (they succeeded one another, in that order, as Regius Professor of Divinity). In this connexion he draws attention to the fact that, from at least 1889—the year of the controversial *Lux Mundi* onwards—Anglican theology has been preoccupied with Christological problems. Congar does not accept the view of the last Tractarian, H. P. Liddon (1829–90) that *Lux Mundi* was a capitulation to rationalism—though a trend in that direction was already manifest in an earlier collective volume, the 1860 *Essays and Reviews*. However, the old Latitudinarianism reappeared in full dress in the Churchman's Union for the Advancement of Liberal Religious Thought, founded in 1898, and its journal *The Modern Churchman*, which began publication in 1911. Congar finds the qualities of the 'modern churchmen' much the same as those of Catholic Modernism:

> immanence, evolution, appeal to experience, the moral and spiritual interpretation of traditional formulas, the letter of which is thus preserved but not really the sense. (DBC, pp. 280–1)

Given the multiplicity of Anglican viewpoints, and the lack of a concept of 'hierarchic magisterium', it is difficult, in Congar's view, for the Church of England to have a doctrine. Highly significant to his mind was the title given to the Report of the Commission appointed in 1922 by the archbishops of York and Canterbury to consider Anglican doctrine—a Report not in fact published till 1938 during William Temple's (1881–1944) tenure of the latter see. That title was *Doctrine in the Church of England*, meaning, or so Congar interpreted it, a study of the doctrine to be found *de facto* within Anglicanism, rather than of the doctrine of the Anglican Church as such. Dr Temple's biographer, indeed, commented unfavourably on the superabundance in its pages of such locutions as 'It is felt by many that . . .', 'on the other hand . . . many feel', or while 'Many of us hold . . .', on the other hand 'there are some among us who hold . . .'. The same author concluded without mercy, and in some unwitting sympathy with Congar's reaction:

> The general opinion of readers was on the same lines: while it was 'felt by many' that the Report displayed the irritating inconclusiveness of Anglican compromise, 'on the other hand many felt' that it was a triumph for toleration and for the comprehensiveness of the National Church.[6]

The subsequent publications of the same commission do not wholly dispel the sense that classical Christian doctrine is somewhat insecurely housed in the modern Anglican establishment.

Looking at Catholic–Anglican relations from the standpoint of the 1970s, Congar naturally cannot fail to draw attention to Paul VI's remark about the 'sister church', at the canonization of the Forty Martyrs of England and Wales on 25 October 1970. But he also points out what is sometimes overlooked: that, in contrast with the case of the Orthodox churches, the Pope spoke of sisterhood status as a future, rather than a present reality. As Congar puts it:

> The two churches are not 'sisters' now; in their reunion, which of course presupposes unanimity in faith, they will recognize each other, embrace each other and behave as sisters. (EOe, p. 240)

And Congar goes on, striking a more positive note, in his spelling out of the implications of this future (hypothetical) happening:

> That means that they will have their own personality; that the one, the younger, will not be absorbed by the other so as to be, on the level of customs and spiritual patrimony, no more than the other's quantitative extension. (EOe, p. 240)

This is, of course, the concept of an Anglican Uniate church spelt out most clearly, on the Catholic side, by the Benedictine ecumenist Bishop B. C. Butler.

The internal divisions in Anglicanism which Congar so learnedly charted have not become markedly less acute since the writing of his chronicle in the 1950s. Thus one must presume that he has preserved the same critical stance towards the prospect of Anglican–Catholic reunion. As he puts it, whilst the English temperament may be tolerant of intellectual inconsistency, and such tolerance doubtless makes a positive contribution of its own to the stability of British institutional life, nevertheless:

> the absence of any real magisterial authority permits the coexistence of extreme and even logically contradictory views within the national organization constituted by the old Church of England. (DBC, pp. 250–1)

The pursuit of a *via media* by Anglicans may not, then, be altogether desirable:

> To us they often appear to be precariously balanced between authentic Catholic principles which are not pursued to their logical conclusions and Protestant and humanist points of view which they are reluctant to renounce. (DBC, p. 284)

Increasingly, it would seem, Congar has tended to the view of the Orthodox theologian and ecumenist Alexander Schmemann (1921–83), that a 'new ecumenical triangle' is emerging, consisting of Rome, the Orthodox and Lutherans.[7] Doctrinal disorder, even on matters once held in common by the three historic parties or trends, is presumably responsible for this shift of attention from Canterbury to Wittenberg. In Congar's judgement, as we have already seen, succession in the apostolic faith (something which, to a remarkable degree, many Lutherans manifest) is more important than a putative succession in apostolic order. Indeed, the latter is deprived of meaning in the absence of the former. It is to Congar's view of Luther and Lutheranism that we must now turn.

B. LUTHERANISM

There can be little doubt that Lutheranism has displaced Anglicanism as Congar's chief centre of interest among the churches which stem from the sixteenth-century Reform. As he wrote in 1983:

> The Reformation is first and foremost Luther. It was through Luther that the first crater was hollowed out in the solid crust of the Western Christian world. The molten lava which flowed out has not yet been exhausted. (ML, p. 7)

Not that this imagery is meant to be as infernal as it may sound: Congar considers that Luther, though containing in himself, as an earlier generation of Catholic scholars had perceived, substantial ingredients of moral mediocrity (Heinrich Seuse Denifle [1844–1905]), philosophical subjectivism (Maritain), and even psychological pathology (Hartmann Grisar [1845–1932]), was more—much more—than the sum of these defective component parts. Congar esteems Luther highly for the quality of much of his Christian understanding, while stolidly maintaining that Luther at the same time did indeed deny major articles of the Catholic faith. Some of the latter are, fortunately, being rediscovered by his contemporary disciples. Even for Lutherans themselves, Luther cannot be the touchstone of Christianity or of what it is to belong to the Church.[8]

What, then, are Congar's conclusions about Luther and his Reform? Congar's position is subtle. First, there had to be a reform, as so many *gravamina* of critics in the late mediaeval Church bear witness. Yet Luther was not merely the sounding-box of such complaints; he was, rather, the organ of a liberating discovery. In the *Dictata super Psalterium* of 1513–15 and the commentary on the letter to the Romans of 1515–16, Luther echoed, indeed, such criticisms of abuses. But:

> the monk Martin Luther lived quite otherwise than in ideas, or in theses, the drama of the salvation of sinful man. (ML, p. 71)

His question was, How might I have a favourable God? and, in answering it, he found himself helped by the work of those he termed the *lebemester*, the 'masters of life and awareness' in the mediaeval Church, over against its *leremester*, the 'masters of doctrine', whom he repudiated. In Bernard of Clairvaux (1090–1135), Bonaventure, John Tauler (*c.* 1300–61), the author of the *Theologia Germanica* (late fourteenth century), and in the spiritual consolation these writers brought him, he found assistance.

But he needed to experience personally that which—or so he intuited, with the aid of these figures—alone could satisfy him. Either suddenly or, as some have argued, through a progressive illumination, he came to the discovery of what he would call *fides specialis*: faith that is 'special', that is, individual, to me. God is Saviour *for me*; Christ is my justice before God, simply through faith. He reread Romans 1:17 and found in that verse about the mercy of God who gives sinful man both pardon and righteousness in Christ the heart of the Gospel. He would devote the rest of his life to communicating this discovery.[9] The crazily distorted preaching of indulgences which came to his attention some little while after gave him the opportunity to publicize his discovery, but was not its cause. The *Disputation against Scholastic Theology* belongs to early September 1517; the 95 theses '*pro declaratione virtutis indulgentiarum*' belong to the last day of October of that year (ML, p. 18). Luther's attack on indulgences was a symptom of something wider, a message that was 'new', in both a positive and a negative sense.

Luther, whilst holding firmly to the traditional authority of Scripture and the Fathers, deliberately sought a new language, a new *modus loquendi*, which would replace that of Scholastic theology, and, unlike the latter, would scorn to be trammelled by the constraints of philosophy. *Spiritus sanctus habet suam grammaticam*: 'The Holy Spirit has his own grammar'. But philosophy was not his only target. As Congar writes:

> Luther had two enemies to fight: Scholastic theology, with Aristotle, Porphyry and the Thomists; and the papal power which required adhesion to its decretals and canons. (ML, p. 48)

Roman criticism, and antagonism to his message radicalized Luther's attitude to the Papacy, which he now suspected of being the anti-Christ. In 1520, at Elster, he burned the papal bull issued against his teaching, and with it the books of canon law; this in his double capacity as a Christian and as a sworn doctor of Holy Scripture.

Congar has been much exercised by the sense in which Luther, on the basis of this theology, wished to reform the Church in a strong sense, that is, to refound it. Luther did not give up hope for some years that the universal Catholic Church might accept his doctrine. His 95 theses were not affixed to the door of the Wittenberg church but, as E. Iserloh has established, sent to the bishops and universities in conformity with correct ecclesiastical procedure.[10] Up to the end of 1520 he multiplied his protestations of obedience. As late as 1522 he addressed the Catholic bishops in a Catholic way. But as Congar points out, given the nature of Luther's positions at this time, it is difficult to make much sense of these statements. In the event, Luther, was obliged to set up new churches on the threefold basis, as he argued, of the Gospel preached, baptism and 'the sacrament' (of the Eucharist). For these churches, Congar comments:

> Luther took Scripture as his normative reference. He admits the Fathers and the ancient Councils inasmuch as they conform to Scripture. That is not equivalent to what the Orthodox and ourselves call Tradition: that presupposes an awareness of the Church as mystery, as a union of the visible and the invisible; of the earthly and the heavenly—which seems to us insufficient in Luther's case. (ML, p. 67)

With his violent, extremist temperament, and his conviction that his cause was that of Christ himself, Luther saw everything in black and white. His hatred of the Pope was an 'outlet for his neuroticism' of such a kind that it could not but distort his evaluation of the 'old' Church. In such conditions, Congar goes on:

> Luther gravely shook the equilibrium of important realities held in organic synthesis by the undivided Church: the equilibrium, that is, the mutual relationship of such realities as Scripture–Tradition–Church, the *ecclesia* and the authority of ordained pastors; community and its ministers; faith and sacrament; diverse components of the sacraments (for example, of Penance), law and the exercise of authority, Pope and Council. (ML, p. 68)

And Congar feels that Luther's Dominican contemporary Thomas de Vio, Cardinal Cajetan (*c*. 1480–1547), was perhaps speaking in prophetic guise when he said of the German Reformer's 'special faith' and his view that Penance must entail believing the promise of God in Christ to be 'for me', 'This would be to make another Church'.[11]

How, then, does Congar see the Reform of Luther? As already mentioned, he stresses that *a* reform was necessary. Luther was right to make the norm of such a reform the grace and mercy of God incarnated in Jesus Christ, the Gospel to which Scripture witnesses. But the manner in which he saw that norm was defective.

> It is here that, while recognizing the greatness of Luther and the soundness of his intention, we cannot follow him in the way in which he exercised it. The intention was to establish as the principle of reform the sovereignty of the Word of God. The application was made in the sense of a *Scriptura sola* which we believe we must reject. We cannot accept the break which an extremist pessimism made between nature (creation) and grace (redemption). And Scripture—we may even say here the *Word*—is it the only gift which God has given us that there might be a Church-body of Christ? The Church as a sacrament of Christ, a sacrament of salvation, is made up of gifts, instituted means of grace, which have been placed in position as such without their institution being necessarily attested in Scripture. (ML, p. 75)

In criticizing, sometimes with justice, the faith and life of the mediaeval Church, Luther wounded much that was pre-mediaeval and non-Western; Congar regards the Orthodox critique of Luther as especially valuable in this connexion.

Though not wishing to found a new Church, rather to purify the old, Luther nevertheless regarded the 'papal' Church, i.e. those who remained in communion with Rome, as lacking in conformity or continuity, despite appearances, with the 'true, the ancient Church'. The Pope's Church belongs to the anti-Christ, though it retains elements of the Gospel. However, Congar notes that a number of Lutherans have held a very different position from this, holding that the Lutheran Church is itself an 'interim Church', provisionally necessary since the Catholic Church was unreformed, a country occupied by a foreign power, like the France of 1940 by the Nazis, to use a striking if uncomplimentary comparison proposed by the American Lutheran dogmatician George Lindbeck (ML, p. 78). The fact that the Lutheran churches have preserved so much, so jealously, of the faith of the patristic Church in their own preaching and theology encouraged Congar to seek a way of somehow integrating the flawed figure of Luther into the Catholic inheritance. How could such a repatriation of Luther be achieved? For Congar, Luther must be reinterpreted as a spiritual teacher, rather than as a source of doctrine, in which he is an unreliable guide: using a distinction that Luther would have understood, Congar proposes to accept him as a *lebemester*, while rejecting him as a *leremester*.

> The idea has become increasingly common among informed Catholic historians and theologians, that Luther's starting

> point was a profound and authentic intention, itself inspired by a correct and, fundamentally, fully Catholic spiritual perception.[12]

What became debatable or false in its subsequent general theological formulation earlier existed in the shape of a spiritual language where like statements may be found in the Fathers, the Doctors of the Church and the saints: in Augustine, in Bernard and, above, all, in Thérèse of Lisieux (1873–97) with her cry, 'I have no works . . . he must render to me according to his own'.[13] The 'spirituals' have a language of their own, which is not that of theological doctrine. They have recourse to hyperbole and contrast in order to evoke the experience of a reality beyond the humanly imaginable and conceptually expressible. They succeed in articulating something that is true on the level of spiritual attitude: proceeding directly from attachment to the unique Absolute, it neither goes into detail nor offers distinctions. Whereas in the Gospels Jesus tells his disciples that 'Whoever loves his life shall lose it', a Scholastic divine is obliged to point out that

> he who loves his life with a love *contrary* to charity will lose it. He will not, however, lose it from the fact that he loves his life with a natural love which is *distinct* from charity without being contrary to it.[14]

Is it possible that, by a similar contrast, Luther's passionate commending of the Gospel of grace may be allowed to stand, without calling into question the doctrinal truth that justification demands commitment to subsequent sanctification? Posing a question, rather than commending a solution, Congar's ecumenical energies were, in any case, directed more wholeheartedly to the situation of the Orthodox, in which we must now follow him.

C. THE ORTHODOX

From *Divided Christendom* to *Diversity and Communion*, it has become ever more clear that, for Congar, the principal ecumenical partner to which the Catholic Church must look is Eastern Orthodoxy. While not oblivious of, nor ungrateful for, the witness of the Oriental Catholic churches, only by reunion of Catholic and Orthodox will the one Church be able to breathe with her two 'lungs' (ECFM, p. 9).

Congar sets great importance on the 'dialogue of charity' between Rome and Constantinople whose most significant monument so far has been the mutual raising of the excommunications of 1054, at Rome and at Istanbul, something described by Congar as 'a liberation, a clearing of conscience'. His own work on the origins and development of the schism has shown how vital such a charitable catharsis must be.

In *After Nine Hundred Years* Congar considered four contributing causes of the rupture between the Chalcedonian East and the Western Church. The relevant factors were, he believes, political, (religio-)cultural, and, finally, ecclesiological. In the first place Congar draws attention to what may be called the 'Constantinian' concept of the Church: a Church within the Empire, and, more than this, an imperial Church. Whilst not doubting Constantine's religious sincerity, Congar believes that, nonetheless:

> it still is the old pagan system which became Christian only in the person of the Emperor, and which was transferred in large part to the shores of the Bosphorus. (ANHY, p. 8)

The imperial power, operating within the domain of the Church, not only designated the patriarchs, changed diocesan boundaries and the location of sees, convoked councils and presided over their sessions, but, and this for Congar is the essential point, gave to their decisions the force of imperial law. The significance of this, in Congar's eyes, is that the juridical attributes of the Church, necessary to her as a society with its own organs of authority, were in practice understood not as apostolic but as imperial. Congar also lends his support to the view of the Anglican church historian T. G. Jalland who considered that in the period following the Edict of Milan, Emperor and Papacy constituted two alternative ways of uniting the Church of the *oikoumenē*.[15] Jalland believed that in the period opened by Diocletian's (284–313) reforms an ever more insistent attempt was made to unify an empire which, hitherto, had consisted rather in a federation of provinces and cities. The Church, which had herself existed in the ante-Nicene age as a brotherhood or communion of local churches, was obliged by this development, notably when she achieved *Christian* form in Constantine, to think out her own ecumenical organization and to elaborate a theory of ecumenical authority.

> The persistent theme of the Popes' opposition to the *Basileus* and the Patriarch of Constantinople was their refusal to accept

> the idea that any exercise of juridical power on the part of the Church in the Empire derived from some political or imperial statute. They insisted, in these cases, that it flowed from an Apostolic law, one properly ecclesiastical, particularly in the case of supreme authority in the Universal Church, which it is the divine prerogative of Rome to exercise. (ANHY, p. 11)

The crisis, already endemic in the age after Nicaea, became acute as soon as the Roman see had emancipated itself from imperial control and was thus able to seek with greater independence of action the right to determine the whole canonical life of the Church of the *oikoumenē*. Every event in the political history of the West which rendered the Roman Church more autonomous *vis-à-vis* the empire had, therefore, repercussions of an ecclesiological and canonical kind.

As Congar presents the matter, Rome followed the logic of a universal Church centred on her own primacy; in this she was obedient at once to her 'profound vocation', founded on the Lord's own institution and the 'apostolic presence' of Peter and Paul, and to the impulses of the political genius of the Roman élite, heirs to the ideological and sentimental inheritance of imperial Rome, and in a Western Europe increasingly occupied by barbarian tribes the sole apparent source of civilizing influence. Thus conditions were ripe for the emergence of a 'universalist' ecclesiology as well as, alas, for the *abuses* of that ecclesiology which overemphasis on the role of Latin Christian culture and the need for apostolic authority in governance might bring in their train.

In the East, by contrast, Christianity developed from the outset in very ancient, and diverse, regional cultural settings. Even the Byzantine church, with its pretensions to imperial coverage, ended up as, in effect, a national church of the Greeks. Congar borrowed from the German liturgical historian Anton Baumstark (1872–1948) the contrast between a Western 'universalist' picture of the Church, a picture for which the Church is basically one, with an appropriate hierarchical organ of this unity in the Pope, and the local churches its parts, and an Eastern 'particularist' alternative, where one starts out from the local church, construing the whole Church as a communion or brotherhood of such bodies.[16] In the West one prays, as in the Roman Canon, 'for your holy catholic Church, watch over it, Lord, and guide it; grant it peace and unity throughout the world. . . . for N. our Pope . . .'. In the East one prays, as in the Liturgy of St John Chrysostom, for the 'prosperity of the holy churches of God'. While in the West a separation of Christians is seen, accordingly, as a scandal, the amputation of a limb, in the East unity is regarded more as an ideal, a family gathering in which all may not, for one reason or another, be able to share at some given time. Ruptures of communion, east of Ravenna, were more easily tolerated.

Cutting across these considerations is, however, to Congar's mind, the peculiar claims of the church of Constantinople, which are to be seen against the backcloth not of this widespread, if often implicit, Oriental ecclesiology, but of the transfer to the 'New Rome' of the potent imperial ideology of the city on the Tiber. Expanding what he has already said on the role of the Emperor, Congar explains:

> Christian society [for the East Romans] is in the image of the Heavenly Kingdom, and of the *politeia* of Heaven. It embraces in a unique order, under the authority of the Emperor, all the aspects of life. By right, it covers the whole world. (ANHY, p. 16)

Following the fate of this idea from the Aristotelean *de mundo*, through the writings of Philo Judaeus (*c.* 20 BC–AD 50) to Eusebius of Caesarea (*c.* 260–340), Congar notes that the unitary order sought by Byzantine people under its ideological sway was essentially political, not ecclesial. The notion that the unity of the Kingdom should be reflected in the visible pattern of the Church was elided; such a reflection remained 'altogether mystical', in the order of prayer and of the sacraments.

The ensuing estrangement of two politico-cultural 'worlds' is chronicled by Congar in its main phases. With some reservations Congar accepts the celebrated thesis of Henri Pirenne in *Mahomet et Charlemagne*[17] to the effect that, with the Muslim expansion of the seventh century, the Mediterranean ceased to be a 'Roman–Byzantine sea', the means of unity between the two halves of Christendom. Economic and social life underwent a certain displacement from south to north, Mohammed thereby anticipating Charlemagne. The coronation of the latter on Christmas Day 800 marks the end of the concept of a single *Romania*, a break with the Eastern Empire and, in Byzantine eyes, the passage of Rome to the barbarians. The occasional alliances of the Popes with the declared enemies of the Byzantine state, notably the Normans, in the early mediaeval period confirmed this surmise. Congar records the judgement of the ecclesiastical historian Claude Fleury (1640–1723) that it was, however, the Crusades which fundamentally created the schism.[18] The role of the Fourth Crusade, and the capture and sack of Constantinople in 1204 which it entailed, as a poisoner of minds is undeniable. Congar stresses in particular the effort at Latinization made wherever Westerners held power in the East.

> It is clear that at this period, which saw the development of ecclesiastical power, of canon law, and of Scholastic philosophy, the lack of an historical sense and of curiosity towards other men and other worlds gave Western Christianity that self-confidence which comprised its strength. On the other hand, it deprived the Latins of the feeling of legitimate diversity in the matter of rite, of ecclesiastical organization, of canonical tradition, and even of doctrine. (ANHY, p. 25)

If previously the East had failed the West in matters of 'an attitude of communion in the respect for differences', something most clearly signalled in the patriarch Michael Kerullarios's attack on Latin Eucharistic practice in the early 1050s, now it was the turn of the Latins to 'show proof of a spirit of univocity'. The inevitable outcome was the cry, 'Rather the turban than the tiara!'.

Moving to 'facts of the religio-cultural order', Congar singles out four which played a part in the estrangement. These were: language; the greater traditionalism of the Byzantine East; the factor of liturgical difference; and lastly, divergence in theological method. The loss of Greek in the West and of Latin in the East was not merely a matter of a tedious need for interpreters: *language* is, Congar points out, a fashioner of ideas. That Greek has no obvious equivalent of *infallibilis* or *vicarius* had momentous consequences for ecclesiology; that its word for 'cause', *aitia*, signified a first principle has bedevilled the controversy over the *Filioque*, the Spirit's procession 'from the Son'. As to '*traditionalism*', Congar maintains that the Byzantine state, held in check as it was by Islam, naturally presided over a culture that looked to the past as its golden age, whereas in the West, the advent of the Germanic peoples rejuvenated Latin Christianity, whose Scholastic movement was 'a fruit of youth'. Thirdly, there is the problem of *rite*, which Congar understands as more than rubrics, for it is the concrete style of Christian worship and life. Because the Christian East saw the 'ritual symbol' as nothing other than 'enacted faith', while many Latin Christians (not excluding Popes) were Latin*izers*, it was wellnigh inevitable that lists of liturgical *gravamina* should be drawn up on either side. Finally, in matters of *theological method*, the West underwent a revolution at the turn of the eleventh and twelfth centuries. It passed, in the words of de Lubac, from symbol to dialectic; from a world where exemplary causality manifested the archetypes of the transcendent realm to a universe where efficient causality made the world go round—or, if not go round, then at any rate pass incessantly from potency into act.[19] Intellectually, Westerners were ceasing to live under a régime of tradition, where perception was synthetic, and moving towards a régime of scholarly research, where perception was, by contrast, analytic. Although Congar's brush-strokes are swift and broad, the picture he paints has considerable historical verisimilitude. However, it may be that, under the influence of Sergei Bulgakov's (1871–1944) 'Neo-Orthodox' concept of Eastern 'sapiential knowledge', he has exaggerated the degree to which philosophy, theology and mysticism were a unity in Byzantium.[20] His interpretation of the development (or non-development) of East Roman religious culture encourages him to hope that Orthodoxy has maintained, by its 'relative indetermination', a degree of plasticity which one day might be solidifed in a sense favourable to reunion. However, Congar's acquaintance with the more recent history and present-day attitudes of the various 'autocephalous' (self-governing) Orthodox churches also suggests to him a countervailing thought: the 'absolutization' of (national) culture in later Orthodoxy has erected new obstacles of a psychological kind to the work of unity.

Moving on to the strictly ecclesiological causes of the progressive estrangement between Latin West and Byzantine East, Congar's discussion turns on differing attitudes to the Roman primacy, and to the synodal element in the Church's life. Although the East, in its Councils and Fathers, recognized the primacy of Peter, and of Rome as the first See, to a far greater extent than some modern Orthodox are prepared to allow, Congar agrees with the Church historian Pierre Batiffol (1861–1929) that it lacked the concept of a universal primacy *by divine right*.[21] West and East did not give to the Roman primacy, in other words, the same concrete content—something exemplified in the Oriental tendency to accept papal interventions in matters of doctrine, but not in those of ecclesiastical life or discipline. The Eastern canonical tradition opted fundamentally for the administrative autonomy of local churches (guided by the fifth canon of Nicaea I and the eighth canon of Ephesus), with matters of grave moment taken for judgement to councils. In a manner heavy with implication for the future, the Roman see, conscious of its responsibility for the solidary good of the whole Church, tended increasingly to elide the distinctions which had formally governed its relations with the churches of its metropolitanate ('suburbicarian' Italy), the churches of its patriarchate (the West) and the churches beyond (the East). The schism of 1054 cannot be adduced simply to the personal ambition of the Constantinopolitan patriarch, though that factor was certainly present. More deeply, in that moment when Patriarch and Papal Legate confronted each other in the city on the Bosporus, 'two ecclesiological régimes' brusquely collided.

How may the 'progressive estrangement' be halted and put into reverse? Congar insists on the necessity of *Wiederbegegnung*, 're-meeting', before there can be *Wiedervereiningung*, 're-union'.

> If the historical process of the schism was a gradual and general estrangement, and if in substance it consists in the acceptance of a situation of non-rapport, then the reunion, which should be the cure of the schism, can only be the result of a resumption of contacts full of esteem and sympathy—two words that really stand for charity. (ANHY, p. 88)

What will its modalities be? 'What the heart desires', Congar answers, 'the mind will invent.' Before theological discussion, before canonical or diplomatic parleying, there must be a psychological and spiritual *rapprochement* aimed at creating sentiments of confidence, of genuine sympathy: in a phrase, at remaking the 'mutual affinity' of the two Churches. Prophetic words: this was exactly the means of approach taken by Pope and Ecumenical Patriarch in the wake of the Second Vatican Council: a 'dialogue of charity', recorded in a *Tomos Agapis*, or 'Book of Charity', a record of respectful, indeed affectionate greeting and encounter, regarded as the necessary preliminary to a dialogue of doctrine.[22]

But in and of itself the dialogue of charity will not suffice: there must be genuine theological underpinning for its progress, and a serious theological attempt to confront the limited, yet real, doctrinal obstacles to its perfecting. Congar finds the theological underpinning of the dialogue in the concept of 'sister Churches'. On the whole, the patristic occasions when the Roman bishops called their Eastern Churches 'sisters' turn out to be invocations of their common filiation from Peter: in other words, they are restricted to the relations between Rome and Antioch, the two Petrine sees. A wider use of the phrase seems to have originated, so Congar's researches indicate, among Byzantine spokesmen, who, in the wake of the Gregorian reform, with its tendency to see the universal Church as an extension of the Roman patriarchate, protested that

Rome was not so much mother as elder sister. As Nicetas of Nicomedia told his Western interlocutor, Anselm of Havelberg, in 1136: 'We do not refuse the Roman Church the primacy among its sisters'.[23] Congar relates how, in the providentially concurrent reigns of the two great hierarchs, Paul VI of Rome and Athenagoras I (1886–1972) of Constantinople, this language was revived on both sides of the Catholic–Orthodox divide, most notably of all in the bull *Anno ineunte* sent personally by Paul to Athenagoras on 25 July 1967.

From his own perspective Congar sees this latter as affirming that, first of all, the Catholic and Orthodox Churches are the same Church—on the level of the ancient conception of the Church as 'a unity of faith, a sacramental reality and spiritual organism' (DivComm, p. 89). At Florence, he points out, it was a question of restoring *unio* or *unitas* between two Churches where a schismatical situation had not affected a profound substantial community. This unity, which is, therefore, in great part still present (though not all Orthodox commentators would agree with Congar here), persists as two different traditions.

> Between East and Catholic West, everything is similar and yet it is all different, even what is essentially the same thing! (DivComm, p. 90)

The reason why the Orthodox Churches, with their distinctive tradition, are sisters, and not daughters, is that the substance of faith and sacramental reality common to the Orthodox and Catholic Churches 'does not come from the Roman Church, as is the case with the Protestant communions of the Reformation'. For, following the Decree on Ecumenism, that ecclesial substance must be linked with apostolicity, and the West has none save via Rome.

Given Congar's understanding of Florence, where both sides recognized that a Council could only be fully ecumenical if both East and West were represented, it will not be surprising to report that he proposes both a revision of the list (Robert Bellarmine's, 1542–1621) of ecumenical Councils currently used by the Catholic Church, and the introduction—in harmony with the views of a number of Catholic writers—of a two-tier concept of the ecumenicity of Councils. Echoing Père Louis Bouyer, Congar reassures his readers that from this it does not follow that the dogmatic decisions of the general Councils held subsequently to the separation should not be allowed a very high authority.[24] 'Partial

Councils' may in fact express the *mens ecclesiae* in a definitive way; this will be the case, at least to a marked degree, in all general Councils of the West summoned by the Pope and confirmed by him, provided that there was substantial episcopal representation. And Congar believes that this approach was sanctioned by the letter of 5 October 1974 from Paul VI to Cardinal Jan Willebrands for the celebration of the Second Council of Lyons.[25]

Whittling down the ecumenicity of Councils hitherto regarded as ecumenical is, however, a perilous affair—not least because, if followed through consistently, it would undermine the authority of that very Council, the Second Vatican, whose call for a more generous appraisal of the separated Eastern Churches was the starting-point of this whole process! More satisfactory is de Margerie's notion of 'analogical ecumenicity' whereby the general Councils of the West are, through the role of the Pope as head of the universal college of bishops, genuinely, but not maximally, ecumenical.[26]

From Congar's view it would seem to follow that what the West should, at this stage, ask of the East is a provisional acceptance of these general Councils of the West as providing positive elements needful for an adequate consideration of the issues involved. The West should also, he proposes, offer the East the same considerate benevolence towards those Councils the East judges to be equally important. Congar could hardly make this proposal with any show of plausibility unless he were already convinced that the apparent doctrinal divergences of East and West do not amount to irremediable contradiction. In this connexion he invokes the idea of complementarity introduced into the study of theoretical physics by the Danish natural scientist Niels Bohr (1885–1962) in 1927.[27] While recognizing that this idea could be employed too easily, too uncritically, to resolve problems only in seeming, Congar was brought by, in particular, his study of the procession of the Holy Spirit in Greek East and Latin West to believe that

> there are two constructions of the mystery, each of which is coherent and complete—although each is unsatisfactory on some point—and which cannot be superimposed. (DivComm, p. 76)

We should not leave Congar's remarks on Orthodoxy without noting his palpable love of the Orthodox Church, as well as his sharp criticisms of its anti-Latinism. He speaks of a quasi-equivalence of

Church, tradition and liturgy in the East. A world transfigured in anticipation by Uncreated Grace is experienced for what it is in the holy liturgy, which is

> penetrated throughout by the mystery of the Trinity, by Easter, by the presence of the Mother of God and the saints. (DivComm, p. 72)

At the same time, he finds that the Orthodox are all too ready to label everything Western 'legalistic' and 'external'. In 'spitting in that direction as against the Devil', the Orthodox manifest a culpable uninterest in whatever does not originate amongst themselves. However, it would betray the tenor of Congar's writing on the separated Churches of the East to end an account of that writing on this note. Better to imitate the close of the preface to his own attempt to resolve the disputed question of the *Filioque*, where he makes his own some words of Pope Paul VI:

> The East provides us with an example of faithfulness to our doctrinal inheritance and reminds us of a rule which is also our own and which we have often reaffirmed recently, at a time when so many attempts are being made—many of them full of good intentions, but not always with happy results—to express a new theology that is in accordance with present-day attitudes.[28]

Returning from the pilgrimage to Constantinople (Istanbul) and Ephesus which prompted these remarks, the Pope declared:

> The East is a master, teaching us that we, as believers, are not only called to reflect about the revealed truth, that is, to formulate a theology which may rightly be described as scientific, but also obliged to recognize the supernatural character of that revealed truth. That character does not entitle us to interpret that truth in terms of pure natural rationality and it requires us to respect, in the texts, the very terminology in which that truth was stated with authority.[29]

Giving his support to these statements, Congar added that 'I should like to place myself in a tradition common to both East and West'. This is the deepest sense in which Congar is an ecumenical theologian: he has sought with all his powers to recreate the theological unity of the *oikoumenē* which preceded the drifting apart of East and West. How that is so is best seen in his theology of the Holy Spirit, the subject of the next chapter.

Notes

1 F. J. Shirley, *Richard Hooker and Contemporary Political Ideas* (London, 1949), p. 256.

2 G. Every, *The High Church Party 1688–1718* (London, 1956).

3 J. Orcibal, 'Les spirituels français et espagnols chez John Wesley et ses compagnons', *Revue de l'histoire des religions* 139 (1951), pp. 50–109.

4 B. Willey, *Samuel Taylor Coleridge* (London, 1972), p. 26.

5 F. Maurice (ed.), *The Life of Frederick Denison Maurice, Chiefly Told in his Letters* (New York, 1884; 3rd ed. London, 1884) I, p. 308.

6 F. A. Iremonger, *William Temple, Archbishop of Canterbury. His Life and Letters* (London, 1948), pp. 465–6.

7 See his 'Bulletin d'ecclésiologie oecuménique. I. Approches théologiques luthéro-catholiques. II. Le troisième partenaire: L'Orthodoxie', *RSPhTh* 71.1 (1987), pp. 123–31. Cf. R. J. Neuhaus, 'Lutheran connection', *30 Giorni* III.3 (March 1985), pp. 66–9.

8 J. S. Preuss, 'La discussion luthérienne sur Luther', *Concilium* 118 (1976), pp. 91–8.

9 P. Hacker, *Das Ich im Glauben bei Martin Luther* (Graz, 1966).

10 E. Iserloh, *Luther zwischen Reform und Reformation* (3rd ed., Münster, 1966).

11 Cited in ML, p. 68.

12 'Langage des spirituels et langage des théologians' in STPT, p. 154.

13 Cited ibid., p. 154 from the texts collected in A. Combes, *Introduction à la spiritualité de sainte Thérèse de l'Enfant Jésus* (Paris, 1946).

14 Words of Congar's old mentor R. Garrigou-Lagrange OP in his 'Le langage des spirituels comparé à celui des théologians', *La Vie spirituelle* 49 (December 1936), p. 272. Cited in STPT, p. 148.

15 T. G. Jalland, *The Church and the Papacy* (London, 1944).

16 A. Baumstark, *Grundgegensätze morgenländischen und abendländischen Christentums* (Rheine, 1932), p. 18. Cf. 'De la communion des églises à une ecclésiologie de l'Eglise universelle' in Y. Congar and B. D. Dupuy (eds), *L'Episcopat et l'Eglise universelle* (Paris, 1964), pp. 227–60; *L'Ecclésiologie du haut Moyen Age* (Paris, 1968), pp. 324–93.

17 H. Pirenne, *Mahomet et Charlemagne* (Paris/Brussels, 1937).

18 C. Fleury, *Histoire ecclésiastique* XVI, p. 10.

19 H. de Lubac SJ, *Corpus Mysticum. L'eucharistie et l'Eglise au Moyen Age* (Paris, 1944).

20 Cf. K. Pfleger, 'Sinn und Sendung des neuorthodoxen Denkens' in J. Tyciak *et al.* (eds), *Der christliche Osten* (Regensburg, 1939), pp. 259–74.

21 P. Batiffol, *Cathedra Petri* (Paris, 1938), pp. 75–6.

22 *Tomos Agapis: Vatican–Fanar 1958–1970* (Rome/Istanbul, 1971).

23 Anselm of Havelberg, *Dialogi* III. 8 (PL 188, 1219 A–B), cited in DivComm, p. 87.

24 L. Bouyer, *L'Eglise de Dieu, corps du Christ et temple de l'Esprit* (Paris, 1970), pp. 678ff.

25 'Lugduni, in urbe Galliae nobilissima', *Acta Apostolicae Sedis* 66 (1974), p. 624.

26 B. de la Margerie, 'L'analogie dans l'oecumenicité des Conciles, notion clef pour l'avenir de l'oecuménisme', *Revue thomiste* LXXXIV, 3 (1984), pp. 425–45.

27 See N. Bohr, *Essays. On Atomic Physics and Human Knowledge 1958–1962* (London, 1963).

28 Paul VI, audience of 2 August 1967; cited in IBHS III, p. xix.

29 Ibid. Cf. 'J'aime l'orthodoxie', EE, pp. 71–5.

9

Congar's pneumatology

From what we have seen of Congar's fundamental theology and ecclesiology, it is not surprising to find that he opens his pneumatological trilogy *I Believe in the Holy Spirit* by promising to follow 'the classical rules of faith seeking understanding'. Congar takes the content of Anselm's definition of the theological imperative to be an interrogation of Scripture and Tradition, but, with a characteristic humane *pietas*, he presents this as a conversation with the 'generations of believers [who] have reflected about faith before us and . . . have also experienced the Spirit' (IBHS I, p. vii). Yet he sees the pneumatologist's resources as extending to contemporary experience too, since the Spirit blows today as yesterday. Such calling on the Christian experience of one's fellows is especially necessary in this area since the revelation of the person of the Spirit is marked by a 'certain lack of conceptual mediation'. The Holy Spirit is known to us, and here Congar echoes Bernard of Clairvaux, not in himself but in his effects, in the Christian life as lived. In this connexion, Congar shows himself sympathetic towards Mühlen's suggestion that the Spirit, by a *kenōsis* parallel to that of the Son in Incarnation and Atonement, empties himself of his own personality in order to become the personal bond linking human beings and the Father in Christ.

THE SPIRIT IN SCRIPTURE AND TRADITION

The first volume of Congar's pneumatological trilogy presents the doctrine of the Spirit in terms of a dialectic of revelation and experience, first and foremost in the Scriptures but also, in dependence on the canonical writings, in the later Church. Although the Scriptures are normative for later faith, nevertheless God has continued to act in history and in human life after the era in which divine revelation was constituted, and to do so, more precisely, through his Spirit. Because of this, our sources of understanding comprise not only revelation itself but also, though always in relation to the norms we receive from that constitutive epoch, Christian experience in the post-apostolic Church. By 'experience' Congar means, as he explains:

> our perception of the reality of God as he comes to us, is active in us and operates through us, drawing us to him in communion and friendship, as one being exists for the other. This experience falls short of vision and does not do away with the distance that we are aware of in our knowledge of God himself, but overcomes it at the level of a presence of God in us as the beloved end of our life, a presence that makes itself felt in signs and in the effects of peace, joy, certainty, consolation, enlightenment and all that goes with love. (IBHS I, p. xvii)

As this list perhaps indicates, Congar has in mind here both the high points of strictly mystical experience, and the lower plateaux of the signs of God's presence in ordinary living in the Church, where we pray, share in the sacraments and try to love God and our neighbour.

In the *Old Testament*, Congar stresses that the Spirit (or 'Breath') is primarily what causes people to act so that God's plan in history may be fulfilled. In this way, the Spirit which is of God differentiates itself from any other spirit, that is, any other principle of action. It should be noted that here there is no particular relation to personal sanctification, associated more in the Hebrew Bible with the observance of the Torah. To speak of the Spirit as the principle which enables God's plan for history to be carried forward enables Congar to unify what the Old Testament has to say about heroes ('judges'), prophets and the messianic line which stretches from David to his coming 'son', the Christ. And if, in the Isaianic corpus, the work of the Spirit is extended to the place of all the nations in the divine plan, in an 'election' which is universal in extent though Israel remains its centre (Isaiah 60 – 61), in the sapiential literature the Spirit is virtually identified with the divine Wisdom itself. To the Hellenistic sensibilities of the sapiential authors, Wisdom appears as a kind of sublimation of the part played in the Old Testament by the Spirit. This explains why some of the Church Fathers regarded

Wisdom as prefiguring not the Word, the Son, but the Holy Spirit. In concluding his section on the pneumatology of the Old Testament, Congar stresses the fact that Wisdom (and so the Spirit) expresses the *intimate* action of God: in the New Testament, the Spirit will be regarded, as above all, responsible for sanctification, divine indwelling, the inhabitation of the heart.

However, Congar begins his account of the *New Testament* witness to the Spirit, and very properly, with an investigation of the role of the Spirit in the *public* ministry of Jesus. As he writes:

> At his baptism by John the Baptist, Jesus is marked out and dedicated as the one by whose words, sacrifice and activity the Spirit enters the history of mankind as a messianic gift and, at least as *arrha* or earnest-money, as an eschatological gift. (IBHS I, pp. 15–16)

While a first sending of the Spirit made the little Jesus, brought to life in Mary's womb, 'holy' and the 'Son of God', a new communication or mission was initiated in the event of his baptism, where he was declared the Messiah—the one on whom the Spirit rests, who will act through the Spirit, and who, once he has become the glorified Lord, will give the Spirit. It was as one led by the Spirit come upon him at his baptism that Jesus undertook his evangelical ministry. It is a royal and prophetic anointing for a messianic ministry. For Congar, although these vital New Testament givens about the crucial role of the Spirit in activating and animating the work of Jesus were not forgotten in the post-apostolic Church, the Arian crisis encouraged the orthodox to trace the saving and sanctifying activity of Jesus Christ to the personal union of the Word with Jesus' humanity rather than to the Spirit's descent on Jesus at his baptism. What led Athanasius (*c.* 296–373) and the Cappadocian Fathers to take up this stance was echoed in the very different context of the twelfth-century West, with its theology of Christ the Head and his 'capital' grace. Thus in Thomas, the coming of the Spirit in the form of a dove is simply a 'visible mission': that is, a sign given for the sake of others of an *invisible* mission which has already been fully realized. Congar cites as a corrective the contemporary theology of Mühlen for whom Jesus' humanity receives a twofold 'anointing'. In the hypostatic union there is a pneumatic anointing which concerns Jesus only; in the baptism a prophetic anointing which is bestowed on him for others. The unity of the two lies in their being from the Spirit in each case; but Congar protests that this is too much of a distinction, verging on a separation: in Christ personal grace and 'capital' grace, what he is *in se* and what is he for us, are identical.

What, then, does Congar have to report about the testimony to the Spirit of the various New Testament theologians? In his discussion of the Pauline texts he comes to the conclusion that the ultimate content of the promise and of the Spirit, and the real fruit of his coming, is that

> we are and will be the subjects of a quality of existence and activities which go back to God's sphere of existence and activity. (IBHS I, p. 32)

The Spirit's sphere of action is ecclesial: he plays a decisive part in building up the Church. The Spirit can be the principle of communion, not only between God and ourselves but between us and our fellow human beings, because of what he is as Spirit:

> sovereign and subtle, unique in all men and uniting persons without encroaching on their freedom or their inner lives. (IBHS I, p. 33)

Though Paul made no attempt to restrain the Corinthians' 'exuberant manifestations of the Spirit', he provided them with a fuller context for their appreciation. This meant, in Congar's eyes, three things. First, he traces everything back to Christ, who is *le Tout du christianisme*, 'the Christian whole'. Secondly, in dependence on this, Paul draws the Corinthians' attention to the personal subject which is the Spirit, a subject who is transcendent *vis-à-vis* his own gifts. Thirdly, he teaches that the gifts of the Spirit and their use are for the common good. In all these ways, Paul insists that there can be no Church of the Spirit based on individual inspiration or on a 'greedy personal enjoyment' of the Spirit's gifts. Congar sets his face resolutely against any contrasting, in this connexion, of charisms and office in the Pauline, or more widely, New Testament churches. The charisms are gifts or talents placed by the Spirit at the service of the building-up of Christ's body. While a place must be allowed in any ecclesiology for a degree of tension between free inspiration and the institution, it is vital not to let this consideration so influence our reading of Paul's teaching about the charisms that it changes its whole meaning. On another controverted point: whereas some exegetes have considered that Paul hardly distinguished between the Spirit and the (exalted) Lord (Jesus), Congar begs to differ. In speaking of the 'Spirit of the Lord' as he does in 2 Corinthians 3: 16–17, Paul has in mind Christ's present

> mode of existence and . . . the power in which he is coming forward to meet his community. The apostle, then, is pointing to the sphere of existence and activity of the glorified Lord. That sphere is the eschatological and divine sphere of the Spirit. This means that, from the functional point of view, the Lord and his Spirit perform the same work, but in the duality of their roles. (IBHS I, p. 39)

So far from being a mere impersonal divine force, Paul's 'Spirit' is 'God himself, insofar as he is communicated, present and active in others'. God is present in the Pneuma as he is present in the Son.

The other New Testament writers Congar considers are the author of Luke-Acts, and the Johannine circle. For Luke, the Spirit is the means of assuring the continuity of Christ and the Church: the Spirit who brought Jesus to iife in Mary's womb also brings the Church into the world. Thinking back, no doubt to his own *The Mystery of the Temple*, Congar observes that just as the new sanctuary is the Jesus Christ who is open to all the nations (in his passion and resurrection, the new Passover), so the new Law is the Spirit bearing witness to Jesus for and in all peoples—in the new Pentecost, itself in Jewish tradition a celebration of the gift of the Mosaic Law on Sinai. Congar accepts the patristic exegesis which regards the miracle of Pentecost as, above all, the reversal of Babel. Consonant with his own preoccupation with the dialectic of the One and the Many in the Church, he stresses that

> The distinctive aspect of the Spirit is that, while remaining unique and preserving his identity, he is in everyone without causing anyone to lose his originality. This applies to persons, peoples, their culture and their talents. The Spirit also makes everyone speak of the marvels of God in his own language. (IBHS I, p. 44)

For the second part of the Lucan corpus, the book of Acts, the contribution of the Spirit is described by Congar as one of making present and spreading the salvation gained in and through Christ, and—more especially—of doing this by the bearing of witness. Congar is heavily dependent on the Anglican Swete in his account of the pneumatology of Acts.[1] He insists, citing that late Victorian scholar, that an understanding of the universal call of faith was only achieved by the apostles after 'several fresh interventions' of the Spirit, beyond the first Pentecost. There is a *history* of the coming of the Spirit, which involves a series of various kinds of Pentecost: in

Jerusalem (Acts 2; 4:25–31); Samaria (Acts 8:14–17); at Caesarea (Acts 10:44–48; 11:15–17) and Ephesus (Acts 19:6). At each of these moments, the Spirit's intervention is indicated by the sign of giving praise to God in the gift of tongues and 'prophesying'.

The Twelve themselves, Congar thinks, were never baptized (except, perhaps, with the baptism of John). Instead they were, so to speak, 'plunged into the Spirit, who came upon them' (IBHS I, p. 45). However, they themselves, from that time onward, practised a baptism of water in the name of Jesus—that is, in reference, through faith, to his saving Passover and his power as Lord. This baptism was accompanied by the gift of the Spirit. With the exception of the case of Cornelius, where the Spirit has an absolute initiative, his coming follows the baptism of water, though on occasion by means of a second rite, namely, that of the apostolic laying-on of hands (Acts 8:16; 19:17).

In an interesting discussion, Congar considers whether Luke really considers the Spirit to be the principle of interior personal sanctification or merely, as the exegete G. Haya-Prats has suggested, simply the principle of a 'dynamic testimony accompanied by a confidence, *parrhēsia*, that is borne out by the experience of speaking in tongues'.[2] Congar concedes that Luke does not provide a theology of the fruits of the Spirit, that is, of the Spirit's effects in the Christian life. Nevertheless, he holds, Luke shows in his pages the 'dynamism of faith and the growth of the Church', in which it would be artificial—indeed, impossible—to separate out the 'disciples' impulses for mission' from their 'spiritual life'. Luke's understanding of the Spirit cannot be reduced, in other words, to Old Testament proportions. In fact, Congar argues, the Book of Acts shows a remarkable development in the direction of a personalization of the Spirit. Though the distinction between the Spirit and the Father (= YHWH) is not explicitly posed by Luke, his repeated attribution of definite and important interventions in the history of salvation to the Spirit strongly suggests that he saw the Spirit as a distinct subject of attribution, in some way different, therefore, from the God of Israel *tout court*.

Turning to the Johannine corpus, Congar reports that, for the Gospel of John, Jesus is, first, the one who gives the Spirit and secondly, in the Last Supper discourses of that Gospel, the one who proclaims the sending of the Paraclete. The Spirit given by Jesus is, more exactly, the Spirit as relating to the messianic period. When John says that in the time of Jesus' discourse on the Spirit at the feast of Tabernacles, 'the Spirit was not yet given', this must naturally be interpreted in a way conformable to John's belief that Jesus himself, and his apostles, had already, in some sense, received the Spirit. Congar sees the giving of the messianic Spirit as expressed in John in four ways. First, that giving is expressed by the *double entendre* of John's phrase for the death of Jesus as the 'handing over of his spirit'. The dying Lord breathes out over Mary and John who are, as the Church, at the foot of his cross, and thus hands over his 'spirit'. So intimate is the connexion between Jesus' sacrifice and the gift of the Spirit that there is, Congar believes, at the symbolic level, a relation between this 'spirit' and the Holy Spirit himself. Secondly, Congar gives tentative support to F. M. Braun's contention that the water which flowed from the riven side of the Crucified stands for the Spirit—by analogy with the Tabernacles discourse of John 7.[3] Thirdly, there is the promise of the Paraclete, so important that Congar devotes to it a whole new section of his first volume. Fourthly and finally, there is the scene (to which we shall return in a moment) in John 20 where the risen Christ makes a paschal gift of the Spirit to the apostles. Congar sees this as the 'beginning' (only) of the promised gift of another Paraclete. It is not a gift of the *person* of the Spirit (there is no article preceding the words 'holy spirit') but of the *power* of the Spirit for the apostolic mission, itself a continuation of that of Christ.

Returning, then, to the topic of the Paraclete, Congar sums up the relevant material from five Johannine passages in the course of the Last Supper Discourse as follows:

> The revelation of the Father, as the source of faith and love, must be experienced by the disciples in a hostile world and in faithfulness to that revelation. This is the function of the Spirit-Paraclete, the Spirit of truth. He continues, after Jesus' departure, to do Jesus' work, that is, to welcome by faith the one who is sent by the Father to reveal the Father and to keep his words and his commandments. He enables us to bring about the new relationship between Jesus and his own after Jesus has withdrawn his tangible presence from us. (IBHS I, p. 56)

Congar stresses the intimate connexion between Jesus and this 'other' Paraclete: the latter does not introduce a new and different economy from that of the Son, perhaps an excessive statement on Congar's part. Following Swete once again, for John, Jesus is the way, *hē hodos*, and the Spirit the guide, *ho hodēgos*, who enables us to go forward on that way.[4]

It is eminently understandable, then, that for the Johannine letters, the Spirit acts first and foremost to make disciples believe that the Son was sent in human flesh, and to make them know and confess him. The Spirit adds his testimony to that of Jesus, making it present in the Church by baptism and the Eucharist—the 'three concordant witnesses of 1 John 5:6–8, the Spirit, the water and the blood. This same Spirit, moreover, arouses in the Johannine disciples a feeling of communion. By reason of this communion, they were, through faith and love, in God, as he in them.

From Scripture Congar moves on to *Tradition*, to offer a series of soundings—hardly more—in the development of the doctrine of the Spirit in the patristic Church and at a variety of other select points since. And first, he treats of the early Church which, as Congar describes it, saw itself as subject to the activity of the Spirit and filled with his gifts. This was, indeed, how that Church saw the glorified Lord exercising his authority over her. In the beautiful text which he cites from the (Syrian) *Odes of Solomon*, the early believer could say:

> As the hand moves over the zither and the strings speak, so does the Spirit of the Lord speak in my limbs and I speak through his love.[5]

Congar's account of the workings of the Spirit in the sub-apostolic community is dominated by the need to take issue with a problematic of charism versus institution which in the modern period can be associated with the Lutheran Rudolf Sohm (1841–1917), though it existed also in the ancient Church, above all in the later work of Tertullian (*c*. 160–*c*. 225). Congar describes both the 'spontaneous' and the 'official' patterns of the Church's life as *equally* the work of the Spirit, active in the one community. The increasing affirmation of the part played by the bishops did not in any way minimize the charismatic life of the Church, since so many of the bishops were spiritual men in the sense understood by Paul in 1 Corinthians (2:10–15). Though the life of the early Church is studded with visions, warnings and suggestions attributed to the Spirit, for many of which terms like *inspiratio* and *revelatio* could be used by contemporary authors, this did not in any way stand over against the apostolic succession of bishops and presbyters. For they too were deemed to have charisms, notably knowledge and teaching. Thus, Ignatius of Antioch claimed that he enunciated his essential message under the action of the Spirit, Polycarp was called by the anonymous author of his *Martyrdom* a 'teacher who was both an apostle and a prophet', and Melito of Sardis (d. *c.* 190) was said to 'live entirely in the Spirit' by one of Eusebius's sources.

Nor does Congar believe that this position changed fundamentally in the post-Constantinian period. Though it has become a convention to regard the monastic movement as a covert form of protest against the relaxation of the Church's 'eschatological tension', the fact is that many bishops were themselves monks, or at any rate men who had been educated within the framework of the religious life and had retained many of its attitudes. Both the later patristic bishop and the monastic founder are described in Latin Christian literature as *viri Dei*, men of God, in whom the active presence of the Spirit is manifest.

It was on such continuing experience of the Spirit, as well as with reference to the canonical Scriptures, that the Fathers drew for their construction of a *doctrine* of the Spirit, to which Congar now turns. Naturally enough, Congar's account centres on the achievement of the Cappadocian Fathers, who are crucial in the emergence of orthodox pneumatology. Whereas certain post-apostolic writers have difficulty in distinguishing the Spirit from the Son, the Pneuma from the Logos (notably Hermas [second century], and Justin Martyr [*c.* 100–*c.* 165]), the crisis generated by the insistence of Macedonius of Constantinople (d. *c.* 362) and his followers that the Spirit was simply a power or instrument of God, created so as to act in us and in the world, obliged the Church to clarify its doctrinal mind. Stimulated by Athanasius, who had already, in his *Letter to Serapion*, concluded from the baptismal formula that the Spirit shared the same divinity as Father and Son in the unity of the same substance, Basil the Great (*c.* 330–379) produced the doxological formula 'Glory to the Father, with the Son, with the Holy Spirit', and defended it as well-founded in Scripture and Tradition in his treatise *De Spiritu Sancto* of 374–375. His argument recapitulates what he has to say in various of his letters of the period: it is necessary to be baptized according to the received form—but one must believe as one has been baptized, and to praise God as one believes. In other words, the baptismal initiation founds doctrine and doctrine founds worship, and these three converge on the notion that the Spirit is worthy of the same honour and adoration as are the Father and the Son. At the Council convoked at Constantinople by the Emperors Gratian and Theodosius I (d. 395) in 381, the Spirit is described as

Lord and Life-giver, proceeding from the Father, object of the same worship and the same glory with the Father and the Son. (DS 150)

Congar notes that, whilst this statement does not describe the Spirit in so many words as consubstantial God, the following year the bishops sent to Pope Damasus and certain of his Western colleagues a letter which described the work of the Council as the setting out of our faith in 'one substance, the uncreated Trinity, consubstantial and eternal'. Congar regards it as faithful *both* to the motivation of this teaching in the minds of the Eastern Fathers *and* to the contemporary mind-set, to regard it as a truth not only about God but also about man and man's destiny.

If the Spirit is not God in substance, then we cannot be truly deified. (IBHS I, p. 75)

And, the better to show how far all of this is from mere cerebration, Congar describes its consequences in Christian worship: the development of the 'epiclesis' or invocation of the Spirit over the Eucharistic bread and wine, and the celebration of the feast of Pentecost as a distinct moment within the totality of the Easter festival.

Congar passes briefly over the other patristic witnesses subsequent to the Council of Constantinople, who would need to be assessed in any complete history of pneumatology, so as to concentrate on Augustine. He considers that Augustine's mature doctrine of the Holy Spirit, as laid out in the *De Trinitate* (399–419), was dependent for its inspiration on the Neo-Plotinian Milanese Catholicism of Marius Victorinus whose conversion had so impressed him thirty years before. In his *Hymns* the latter had written:

Help us, Holy Spirit, you who connect the Father and the Son!
When you are resting, you are the Father; when you proceed, the Son;
in binding all in one, you are the Holy Spirit.[6]

Augustine, echoing not only this text but also his own earlier reflections in the *Tractates on John*, considers that the Spirit, whilst being a quite distinct person, is what is *common* to the Father and the Son, their shared holiness and love

They are therefore no more than three: the one loving him who has his being from him, the other loving him from whom he has

> his being, and that love itself. And if that love is nothing, how can God be Love?[7]

For Augustine, as Congar expounds him, there is both a general or essential, and a distinctive or personal meaning with which the terms 'Love' and 'Spirit' are used. Being common to both, the Spirit receives as his own the names that are common to Father and Son, that is, 'Spirit' and 'Holy'.[8] To Augustine's mind, the *Filioque* is an 'obvious necessity', as indeed it was for Ambrose who had affirmed it in no uncertain terms despite the fact that his own Trinitarian theology was inspired above all by the Greek Fathers. Because the Spirit is the Spirit and the Love of the first two Persons, he must be said to proceed from them. In the first place, however, he proceeds from the Father, since the Son derives his being from the Father, though he is also, with the Father, the origin of the Spirit. While in St John's gospel Jesus remarks that the Paraclete 'proceeds from the Father' (John 15:26), this is meant in the same sense, or so Augustine believed, as Jesus' earlier statement there that 'My teaching is not mine, but his who sent me' (John 7:16).

That is, the Spirit proceeds *principaliter*, 'in the first place', from the Father, since the Father gave the Son life in him and the power to communicate that life. Congar is careful not to overestimate the place Augustine gives in his pneumatology, as in his Trinitarian theology at large, to his celebrated psychological analogies and other extended images. They are simply useful theological tools, helpful in, for instance, pointing to the difference between the procession of the Word and that of the Spirit. For Congar, reading Augustine with the interests of one who is above all a theologian of *the Church*, it leaps to the eye that this pneumatology leads directly into ecclesiology. Commenting on Augustine's habit of calling the Spirit the 'Gift' of God, Congar writes:

> It is true that the Spirit is only 'given' when there are creatures who are capable of 'possessing' and enjoying him, but at the same time he also proceeds eternally as 'giveable' and, in this sense, as Gift, so that this can be regarded as one of his attributes and one of his proper names. When the Spirit is given to us, he unites us to God and each other by the same principle that seals the unity of Love and Peace in God himself. It is not enough to speak here of the created gift of grace, even though it is in effect through that gift that the Spirit is given to us. The Spirit, however, is given as the principle of the Church's unity. (IBHS I, pp. 79–80)

For Augustine, however, as *communio sacramentorum*, the 'communion formed by the sacraments', the Church is the work of Christ; as *societas sanctorum*, a society created by sanctifying holy *gifts*, fashioning holy *people*, it is the work of the Spirit.

Congar goes on to look at the theme of the Holy Spirit as the mutual love of Father and Son in a variety of Western mediaeval authors, from Anselm to Thomas Aquinas, all of whom were deeply influenced by Augustine. In fact, he suggests, Anselm is not particularly Augustinian here: for him the procession of the third Person is primarily the Love of the Supreme Spirit proceeding from his memory and his thought.[9]

Congar finds this too austerely rational an approach, too close to that of the deduction of faculties or properties from an essence, and chides Anselm for not expressing more clearly the 'demands made by the personalization of the three Persons' (IBHS I, p. 86). William of St Thierry (*c.* 1085–1148) and Richard of Saint-Victor (d. 1173) receive higher accolades from Congar for building up their theology of the third Person much more with reference to prayer and personal experience. In Richard, the Spirit is posited as the *condilectus* of the Father and the Son: a 'common friend' or 'a third equally loved', since, according to Richard, the perfect charity we must ascribe to God requires a *consortium amoris*, that is, a co-loving of a third and a common enabling of that third to share in the happiness of the first two. Bonaventure, too, Congar finds to be fully in sympathy with Richard's theology of 'unselfish and communicative love' (IBHS I, p. 87). As for Thomas, whilst for the Dominican master it is illuminating to present the Holy Spirit as the friendship of Father and Son or as their mutual love, such a view cannot be utilized metaphysically, since it does not provide a consistent analogy for our understanding of the third Person. For what two friends have in common to unite them is not the reality experienced in their act of love. Each experiences his own act: there are two loves, two acts of loving. Rather, what they have in common is an object in which they find their good. Thomas, therefore, preferred to present the Spirit in more Anselmian terms as the Love which God bears for his Goodness, or the Love that proceeds from the divine Knower and Lover, and from his Word. However, Thomas is clear that the Persons are not modes or faculties of the divine Essence. For him, everything active in God is done by the Persons: *actiones sunt suppositorum*. As Congar sums up Aquinas's teaching:

> The essential knowledge and love of self exist only as

> hypostasized in personal subjects, which can be distinguished only by the opposition in the relationships which constitute them. These relationships are established in the divine substance, which is absolute existence, and are therefore themselves subsisting, in other words, they make the Persons exist according to the divine substance. (IBHS I, p. 89)

But all of this austere speculative theology must be set within the wider context of life and worship in the Latin Church of the Middle Ages if justice is to be done to how contemporaries saw the Holy Spirit west of Ravenna. This takes Congar into consideration of the role ascribed to the Spirit in the liturgy of Baptism, above all in the solemn celebration provided by the Gelasian Sacramentary (*c*. 750) for the Easter Vigil, and in Confirmation. Congar compares the 'two-in-one' form of Baptism–Confirmation to the twofold anointing of Jesus by the Spirit: that which constituted his human and divine 'holy being', and that which made him, or at least declared him to be, Messiah, the minister of salvation. Again, the Spirit is not absent from the consecration of the elements in the Eucharist (something Congar postpones to Volume III of his work), while in Order, and notably the consecration of a bishop, all the bishops present 'were ministers of the Spirit within the epiclesis of the entire assembly' (IBHS I, p. 107). So as to restore a more explicit pneumatological dimension to sacramental theology, Congar has revived the idea of a sacrament in Isidore of Seville (*c*. 560–636). Isidore would have celebrated the Hispano-Visigothic liturgy, whose Eucharistic Prayer included a *post pridie* in which the Holy Spirit was invoked over the elements. Isidore believed that the consecration of those elements was effected by all the prayers between the *Sanctus* and the *Pater noster*, and he distinguished within those prayers between two aspects: the *sacrifice*, or consecration of the gifts by the 'mystical prayer' in memory of the Passion (a Christological aspect), and the sanctification, which makes the action into a *sacrament* by the invisible working of the Spirit (a complementary pneumatological dimension).

> There is, then, in the celebration of the Eucharist—and, with the necessary modifications, also in the other 'sacraments'—a commemorative aspect, recalling a Christological act, and a sanctifying aspect, in which the commemoration receives its fruit, this aspect being the work of the Holy Spirit. (IBHS I, p. 108)

Congar sees the twelfth and thirteenth centuries as something of a high point in Western devotion to the Spirit. Many hospitals, hospices and churches placed themselves under his protection; pilgrimages and the common life of the *vita apostolica* had strong pneumatological overtones; the great antiphon and sequence *Veni, Sancte Spiritus* were composed. Despite the lack of a real epiclesis directed to the Holy Spirit in the Roman Canon, Pope Innocent III required Waldensians re-joining the Church to affirm that in all the sacraments the Holy Spirit was operative, indeed, co-operative by his 'inestimable and invisible power' (DS 793). In such divines of the period as the Augustinian Hugh of Saint-Victor, the Church-body whose Head is Christ was seen as made by the Holy Spirit. Iconography shows Christ as giving the seven gifts of the Spirit, and in the black monk Rupert of Deutz's (*c.* 1075–1130) theology of history, the same sevenfold gift is linked with the seven days of creation and the seven ages of the world. Congar brings all this material to a climax by an account of the gifts in Thomas, for whom they are lasting realities, distinct from the virtues, which make the Christian 'ready to grasp and follow the inspirations of the Spirit'. They amount to a disposition which

> makes the disciple of Jesus permanently open to have his activity guided, beyond the power of the virtues, beyond his reason as animated by faith, beyond his supernatural prudence, by another who is infinitely superior and has sovereign freedom, in other words, the Holy Spirit. (IBHS I, pp. 119–20)

This work of the Spirit, most clearly seen in the saints and the prophetic men and women of the Middle Ages (the women being especially notable for the quality of their interventions in the life of the Church), is, Congar concludes, 'his secret, and it is as spacious as the love and mercy of the Father'.

Since the Counter-Reformation, Congar finds, the Holy Spirit has remained active in Catholicism, yet he has been insufficiently related by theologians to the life of the Church. For Henry Edward Manning (1808–92), for instance, the Spirit is the principle of holy living in individuals, and the guarantor of the acts of the institution, notably its infallible teaching—yet this hardly constitutes a sufficient pneumatological ecclesiology worthy of the name.[10] The texts of the Second Vatican Council, on the other hand, provide a fuller foundation for an account of how the Holy Spirit is co-

constitutive of the Church. It is to this subject, the relation of the Spirit to the Church, that Congar turns in his *second* volume.

THE SPIRIT IN THE CHURCH

Congar opens his second volume by pointing out how intimately the Creed of Nicaea–Constantinople relates the article of the Spirit to that on the Church. Indeed, the mediaeval Scholastics did not hesitate to paraphrase the latter by reference to the former as

> I believe in the Holy Spirit, not only in himself, but as the one who makes the Church one, holy, catholic and apostolic. (IBHS II, p. 5)

The tradition witnesses to the fact that the Church is born and lives by two missions: those of the Son and of the Spirit, whereby human creatures enter into a wholly new relation with the Father who is the Sender of Spirit and Son. The Spirit is, therefore, the 'co-institutor' of the Church. Congar illustrates the point by reference to the history of the sacraments and of the ministry. For the Catholic theologians who replied to Luther's denial of a Scriptural basis to the sacraments of Marriage, Order, Confirmation and the Anointing of the Sick, Christ determined the communication of their sacramental graces, but it was the Spirit, acting in the Church, who gave them precise form. Again, Jesus instituted the Twelve, but neither Trent nor the Second Vatican Council attributes the degrees of the apostolic ministry—bishop, presbyter, deacon—to Christ's intervention: this was the Spirit's work. Between the institution (the Son) and the charism (the Spirit) there is not opposition, but the complementary unfolding of two styles of divine acting, both ordered to the same goal, the completion of Christ's work. While not retracting wholly his distinction between 'structure' and 'life', Congar regrets that he did not, in his earlier writing, underscore the (functional) identity between the Holy Spirit and the glorified Christ.

In his account of the Spirit's relation to the Church, Congar describes him as the principle of the Church's unity, catholicity, apostolicity and holiness—in that order. First, then, he is the principle of unity, and so of communion. The Spirit is given to the community as such, but also to the persons within it. The Church is not, as Arthur Koestler said of Soviet Communism, a great system where the individual is the sum of a million divided by a million. Congar ascribes to the Spirit the harmonization of community with persons, each of whom is an original, autonomous source of sensibility, experience, relationship, initiative. Only at the cost of destroying such richness could the Spirit unify the Church through pressure or reduction to a uniform pattern: so he adopts the finer way of a communion. Interior to all believers, at once subtle and sovereign, the Spirit is both 'able to respect freedom and to inspire it' (IBHS II, p. 17). Heeding his promptings, we live and act as conscious members of an organic whole. Congar speaks in this connexion of a supernatural created personality of the Church, but that 'personality' is still in a state of becoming. It is the goal of the realization of God's mysterious plan, the fruit of the twofold mission of Son and Spirit. By 'appropriation', however, the Spirit is the Subject who effects everything that relates to grace, and so, in a phrase of Journet, the 'supreme and transcendent efficient personality of the Church'.[11] Descending from the sublime to the street, Congar insists that the mystical communion of which the Spirit is the principle must find translation into an effective human communion of welcome and support.

The Spirit, moreover, 'catholicizes' the Church in her outreach across both space and time. Congar finds the work of the Spirit in connexion with the Church's 'note' of catholicity signalled in Paul, who, for his vocation as apostle of the Gentiles, ushering the Church out of the Jewish domain, had not known Christ according to the flesh, but only the Lord 'who is the Spirit'. But above all his discussion takes the form of reflection on the mystery of Pentecost.

> The Church was established in the world by Pentecost, which gave it a vocation to universality, which was to be achieved not by means of a uniform extension, but by the fact that everyone understood and expressed the marvels of God in his own language (Acts 2:6–11). Through the mission and gift of the Holy Spirit, the Church was born universal by being born manifold and particular. The Church is catholic because it is particular, and it has the fullness of gifts because each has his own gifts. (IBHS II, pp. 25–6)

The Church reversed Babel not by a return to a pre-Babelic uniformity, but by rooting the same Gospel, and the same faith, in markedly different kinds of cultural soil. Hence the multiplicity of charisms, all given for the 'common use', despite their startling variety. Hence too the structure of the Church as a communion of particular churches.

On a rather different tack, Congar also speaks of the Spirit as catholicizing the Church 'in advance of time'. By this somewhat curious locution he means to say that the Spirit gives the Church the fullness of its own truth in the Word, and in dependence on that Word, in the Tradition which renders it actual in various ways. In another sense of the same expression, and taking his cue from von Balthasar's description of the Spirit as the 'Unknown One beyond the Word',[12] Congar sees the Spirit as, additionally, pushing forward the Gospel into the 'not yet happened' of future time. The 'once and for all' of Christ's work must be made fruitful in all subsequent history until the Eschaton.

Thirdly, the Spirit is he who maintains the Church in her apostolic quality. Apostolicity, for Congar, is at once conformity to the apostolic origins of the Church, and fidelity to the goal of her apostolic mission.

> Apostolicity is the mark that for the Church is both a gift of grace and a task. It makes the Church fill the space between the Alpha and the Omega by ensuring that there is a continuity between the two and a substantial identity between the end and the beginning. (IBHS II, p. 39)

In the messianic and eschatological era inaugurated by the mission of Christ and the gift of the Spirit, two 'values' must be united: on the one hand, memory and attestation of what has already happened for our salvation, and, on the other, the affirmation of the real efficacy of these events and their continuance through the apostolic mission sprung from them, even until the close of the Age. In all this, the Holy Spirit is the Church's 'transcendent principle of faithfulness'. The Spirit is given to the Church so that she may keep indefectibly the faith received from the apostles—as dozens of texts, beginning with Irenaeus, bear witness. This is true, first of all, for the 'total' Church; it is also true, more particularly, of ecumenical Councils, of the pastoral government of the bishops and, more specifically still, of the *magisterium* of the bishop of Rome. Congar stresses that it is only in the communion of the faithful people, themselves apostolic in serving, witnessing, suffering, struggling, as well as in transmitting the faith, that the 'apostolic succession' in the technical sense of that term has its reality: that is why a bishop is co-consecrated before the people, who are called on to testify that the candidate possesses the catholic and apostolic faith.

Finally, the Spirit is the principle of the Church's *holiness*. In writing which is at times almost ecstatic, Congar celebrates the Church's (corporate) holiness as the Spirit's temple, and Christ's Bride in the one Spirit. However, he is not so overcome as to forget the realism of *Vraie et fausse réforme*: the union of Bride and Lord is still imperfect; she possesses the Spirit only as 'first-fruits'; her marriage feast will be joy unalloyed only in the banquet of the Last Day. Yet the Spirit himself inspires reform, and initiatives of every evangelical description, thus rendering the Church a 'hagiophany', a sign of the real presence of another World, an anticipation of the Kingdom where God will be all in all. Congar stresses in particular the hagiophany of the Spirit in and through beauty, in iconography and in Church music at its finest, as also in the lives of the faithful, in souls wholly surrendered to God like the Russian hermit Seraphim of Sarov (1759–1833) or his Catholic counterpart the Frenchman Charles de Foucauld (1858–1916).

This brings Congar to the second main theme of his second volume: the Spirit's role in personal holiness, in which he devotes particular attention to the hopes and temptations of the 'Charismatic Renewal'. A pneumatic ecclesiology will be in part a theological anthropology, for man is restored to the divine image by an *askēsis*, or discipline of purification, achieved through the Spirit, as well as by the Church's sacraments, whose agent is the Spirit, the Sanctifier.

The Christian mystery is that the Son of God was born as man so that men might be born as sons of God. In Catholic theology this is called 'grace', but the word carries a danger that it may condemn what it denotes to 'reification'. For what is at stake here is the action of the Spirit, the 'Uncreated Grace' whereby God sanctifies us in his Son, by his Spirit. Unlike many writers in the Western tradition from Augustine onwards, Congar underlines the difference between the spiritual condition of the just of the Old Testament and the New Testament with its radically new gift of the Spirit. He allows the Old Testament fathers of Israel certain *effects* of grace, a supernatural righteousness which was the privilege of those who looked to the fulfilment of the promises of God in the far distant future. But in them, grace was not able to produce its proper fruits: the inhabitation of the divine Persons whereby we become sons, and share the life of God. The 'spirits in prison' needed contact with the living Christ on Holy Saturday before the potentialities of the grace they had received could be brought to their term. While recognizing the inconveniences of this scheme, which calls into question the substantial unity of grace, Congar insists that the internal rhythms of the sacred history must be respected: grace is actuated in different ways, according to the unfolding of God's design (IBHS II, pp. 73–7).

It is at any rate clear that in the New Testament dispensation the Holy Spirit is not merely present but present as one who inhabits the believer. Congar cites Eusebius's account of how Origen's father, on his way to martyrdom, uncovered his sleeping son's chest and planted a kiss there, for he was a temple where the Holy Spirit dwelt on earth.[13] And, faced with the embarrassment of riches of the Christian mystics on the same theme, Congar calls to the witness stand Teresa of Avila and Marie de l'Incarnation (1599–1672) in the West, and his favoured Symeon the New Theologian in the East. What these mystics speak of, the Spirit's coming to the soul to take sovereign possession of it, to be with it and in it, as it is with and in him, is described by Thomas as the Uncreated Gift of the Spirit—a self-giving of the divine Person which is logically and causally prior to that transformation of our being called created grace. Though, with the Trinitarian Persons there is always a 'communion of activity and a sort of concelebration on the part of the three Persons' (IBHS II, p. 86), they come to the soul according to their own inner-Trinitarian order and with the personalizing mark which is proper to each. Likewise, their action assimilates the soul they sanctify to the Godhead by bringing it to God via a distinctive relationship with each of the Persons.

In this distinctive relationship the Spirit makes the common 'life in Christ' real, personal and interior for each member of the Church, both now and in the final consummation of all things. In prayer, the soul cries out to the Spirit, as in the *Veni, Sancte Spiritus*, or the invocation St Symeon placed at the head of his hymns, appealing thereby for the sending of the Spirit by Father and Son.[14] The Spirit assists the Christian in all the modalities of his prayer, from the meditative study of Scripture to the prayer of petition, and from these to the prayer of simple regard which seeks God only for himself, for the savouring of his love, in attentive waiting on his will. The Spirit converts the sinner, making him free and strong in goodness, and, as Congar has already registered in his first volume, pours into his life the fruits that make faith, hope and charity perfect in their exercise.

Finally, Congar turns to that most spectacular movement of the present time which has claimed the Holy Spirit by name: the 'Pentecostal Movement' or 'Charismatic Renewal', within the mainstream historic Christian churches and notably in the Catholic Church. While recognizing that the sociological analysis of this phenomenon is in part accurate, for in a rationalized world from which the magic of existence is fled people will naturally seek warm, spontaneous, yet communitarian spirituality in small groups, Congar maintains that this is not the whole story.

> What is remarkable is that it has taken place directly within the Christian and even within the Catholic faith and, what is more, within the framework of a very categorical Trinitarian faith. If we recall that, according to the fourth gospel, Jesus' trial continues throughout history, the Holy Spirit, in the Renewal, greatly strengthens Jesus' disciples by convincing them that the world is wrong (Jn 16:8–11). They are disciples of Jesus *Christ*, of the Jesus *the Lord*, and not simply of the 'Jesus of Nazareth' called on by politically orientated and secularized Christians. In addition to this, physical miracles and divine interventions in human history were eliminated from Christianity by the thinkers of the Enlightenment and later by Bultmann and his followers in demythologization, yet the Renewal claims to have experienced the direct intervention of divine power in the lives of its members and insists that God is 'living'. (IBHS II, p. 150).

As Congar sees it, the Charismatic Renewal is excellently placed to reassure believers of the authentically supernatural quality of the Christian life; to give visibility, a 'face', to the gifts of the Spirit, and to introduce into the ordinary life of the Church such activities as 'prophecy', defined by him as an opening of the Church to 'new ways for and a new understanding of its future' (IBHS II, p. 177), and healing, not only spiritual but physical.

However, Congar is also concerned to issue *caveats*. The very name 'Charismatic Renewal' is ambivalent: for if a charism be the 'locus' of the felt action of the Holy Spirit, the monopoly of such experience which the title implies deprives the ordinary faithful of their rightful claim to know the Spirit, his gifts, his fruits. The restriction of the charisms to what Paul terms *pneumatika*, the pneumatic gifts of a spectacular kind such as speaking in tongues, prophecy, healing would be impossibly narrowing, and in any case fails to correspond to the New Testament itself. Congar takes with great seriousness the charges that the Renewal gives excessive weight to immediacy, involving a false childlikeness and anti-intellectualism; that it is greedy for experience of the Spirit, against the counsels of 'sobriety' and 'vigilance' given by the masters of East and West; and that it leads to a weakening of the impulse towards social service of the neighbour. But all things considered, he believes that these perils can be avoided, while their very existence is a salutary reminder that no one movement can be the Church, since 'the Church is fullness' (IBHS II, p. 169). The condition of their avoidance is that its supporters

> above all form part of the great Catholic community with its sacraments, its pastors, its activities, its mission and its service to the world. They should fully accept its history and its life, in solidarity with their brethren who do not belong to the Renewal, but who are also animated by the Spirit and in whom the Spirit also dwells. (IBHS II, p. 210)

In addition, they must remember that the Spirit does no other work than that of *Christ*. If only these conditions are satisfied, Congar looks with hope to the future irradiation of the Renewal, not least in the context of ecumenism, where ecclesiastical negotiations cannot be expected to bear fruit unless they are themselves immersed in the deep communion of prayer.

THE SPIRIT IN EAST AND WEST

The *third* volume of Congar's pneumatological trilogy is essentially concerned with the differences in this particular realm between East and West, between Orthodox and Catholics. It is, in effect, an extended historical and theological reflection on the *Filioque*. Reasonably enough, Congar opens by situating not simply that knotty problem of the manner of 'proceeding' of the Holy Spirit, but the doctrine of the Spirit at large within the diverse Greek and Latin approaches to Trinitarian theology as a whole. On the Orthodox side, the lay theologian Vladimir Lossky (1903–58), on the Catholic the Jesuit historian of doctrine Théodore de Régnon, have succeeded in exaggerating this diversity—or so Congar believes. The way in which such writers stated the (undoubtedly real) difference of approach has produced in their lesser disciples a caricature of the Catholic or Western position. On this account, with Augustine and for ever afterwards, the Catholic doctrine of the procession is described as

> an impersonal subordinationism, in which the *deitas* or deity is the primordial metaphysical basis and, in this sense, the sufficient foundation or the cause of the hypostases.[15]

In the hope of doing better than this, Congar invites us to consider the peculiar methodologies which, typically, have distinguished East and West in their approaches to the mystery.

Congar presents the Greek tradition as attempting to synthesize two rules for theological thought derived from the great Fathers. First, they drew on the resources of rational education in the Hellenistic world: the riches of Greek *paideia* of which Julian the Apostate (361–363) had tried to deprive them in closing the schools to Christians. Until the mid-Byzantine period, these resources were, however, primarily directed to the training of theologians, and to the refutation of heretical positions rather than to the explication of the revealed data themselves. In the positive treatment of the mystery, one 'simply had to follow Scripture, the Fathers and the Councils'. To some extent, this Greek-speaking consensus about theological method was disturbed, Congar believes, by the work of Photius, the controversial patriarch of Constantinople (858–867, 878–886) and especially his *Mystagogic Discourse on the Holy Spirit*.

> Photius did not confine himself to scriptural arguments and references to patristic or papal texts—he also made extensive use of his critical reason. Since his time, the debate between Orthodox and Catholic Christians over the dogmatic construction of the mystery has at least partly consisted of rational theological argument. (IBHS III, p. xviii)

Paradoxically, Congar is saying, the mid-Byzantine figure in whose person the future schism was most clearly anticipated had the most 'Western' theological method. For, in the case of that great fount of subsequent Latin theology, Augustine, we find doctrine being construed on the foundations of Scripture, yet with the added principle that an *intellectus fidei*, an 'understanding of faith', should be sought through reasoning and meditation and so, if need be, outside Scripture. Drawing on the work of the historian of Byzantine thought Georg Podskalsky,[16] Congar argues, however, that in the late Byzantine period, and under the influence of the monastic and mystical revival associated with the name of Gregory Palamas (*c*. 1296–1359) the new theological methods diverged once again. Thus in Nilus Cabasilas, Palamas's successor as archbishop of Thessalonica, we find Latin theology accused of a wholesale rationalizing of the mystery of God by the misplaced use of the syllogism: a point of view which dominated the anti-Unionist voices at the reunion Council of Florence a hundred years later.

Congar does not deny, indeed he affirms, that a different attitude of the spirit distinguishes Eastern and Western Christians. The first are

> more symbolic and the second more analytical in their thinking, and this different spirituality has manifested itself in the thought, liturgy and art of the East and the West and in the entire theological approach to the same Christian mysteries. (IBHS III, p. 8)

Nevertheless, common understanding is possible, and Congar's own theological method, as a Western Catholic, is so shaped as to be at once sympathetic to the Eastern Orthodox reader. For he affirms without equivocation that our first source of knowledge where the Spirit, and so his mode of procession, are concerned is revelation itself. The data must be, as already laid out in the first volume of the trilogy, those of the 'whole economy of grace', Old Testament and New Testament, extending their life as these do into the entire subsequent history of the Church. The texts in question, then, are preeminently those of Scripture, but secondarily, those of Tradition: Fathers, saints, theologians. *Within* Scripture we find both statements and images. What is necessary is to consider and weigh the meaning of the statements, and to discover the coherence which holds good among the images. Yet in this, as the introduction of the term *homoousios* into the creed of Nicaea indicates, it is impossible to confine oneself wholly exclusively to the Bible. In using the developed language of theology, Congar promises, however, that he will try to preserve the sense of 'the mystery that exists far beyond our hesitant efforts'. And, not for the first time, he reminds a possible Orthodox audience that the Catholic tradition too knows of the imperative of apophaticism, of affirming the unknowability of God.

However, at the same time, Congar cautions that we must, in this matter, take care just *how* we invoke the apophatic idea. He mentions how, for a Dutch theologian such as Piet Schoonenberg, the immanent Trinity—God in himself—is unknown and unknowable, God's tri-personality qualifying simply his 'economic' outreach to us in history.[17] Congar describes this in sharp terms as to place oneself 'outside the whole Christian tradition of reflection based on the inspired evidence of Revelation' (IBHS III, p. 14). On the other hand, Congar *does* recognize a distance between the economic and the immanent Trinity, for:

> this [divine] self-communication takes place in the economy in accordance with a rule of 'condescendence', humiliation, ministry and 'kenosis'. (IBHS III, p. 15)

Revelation is limited in that the Incarnation, as a created work, imposes its own conditions on the revelatory process. And taking over Luther's concept of the *opus proprium* of God found in an *opus alienum*, which Congar regards as also the understanding of the early Byzantine theologian Maximus the Confessor (*c.* 580 – 662), he writes:

> The Father is 'omnipotent', but what are we to think of him in a world filled with the scandal of evil? The Son, who is 'shining with his glory and the likeness of his substance', is the Wisdom of God, but he is above all the Wisdom of the Cross, and so difficult to recognize that blasphemy against him will be pardoned. Finally, the Spirit has no face, and has often been called the unknown one. (IBHS III, p. 15)[18]

The relevance of all this to the *Filioque* is sufficiently indicated when Congar remarks that were Trinitarian theology to be the straightforward retrojection of the data of the economy back into the eternity of God, then the Church should have to teach, rather, that the Son proceeds *a Patre Spirituque*: from the Father and the Spirit!

How does Congar understand the development of the divergent positions of Orthodox East and Catholic West in the matter of the Spirit's relation to Jesus Christ and his Father? He surveys in turn the Greek and Latin Fathers, scouring their pages for illumination. On the Greeks up to and including Athanasius, Congar believes that they did not deny to the Son or Word a part in the eternal coming-to-be of the Spirit. However, they did not apply to this possible role of the Son the verb *ekporeuomai* used in St John's gospel (John 15:26) to speak of the Spirit's procession from the Father. Naturally enough, they did not raise the question in the polemical form which it took from the time of Charlemagne (771–814), and especially from that of Photius, onwards. For such post-Athanasian fathers as Basil, the Spirit's relation with the Son can be compared to that of the Son with the Father—a relation of expression or manifestation.

This manifestation and assimilation clearly place us within the order of the economy and God's action in and for his creatures, but the word used—*proēlthen*—points to intra-divine relationships between the Persons. (IBHS III, p. 30)

Whether this was so in Basil's treatise *De Spiritu Sancto* would be a hotly debated point at the reunion Council of Florence more than a thousand years later. Basil's brother, Gregory of Nyssa (*c.* 330 – *c.* 395), despite his stress on the monarchy of the Father—the way that the Father is the single source of the whole Godhead—indicated an intermediary role for the Word in the procession of the Spirit. Using the image of a lamp giving its light to another lamp and, through that lamp, to a third: the Spirit 'shines' eternally through the Son. However, Gregory does not say that he is *ek tou Huiou* 'from the Son'. In manuscripts of his commentary on the Lord's Prayer where this seems to be so, we are dealing with an interpolation: a sign of the doctrinally troubled times to come. Congar goes to the heart of the matter when commenting on the tentative and imagistic character of the Greek description of the Son's role in the Spirit's process, where he has this to say:

> All the Greek Fathers . . . believed that this 'mode of coming to be' of the Word and the Spirit is inexpressible. All that man can do, they insisted, is recognize, respect and affirm it. The Son, the Father's Word, was begotten *huiokōs*, filially, and the Spirit was begotten *pneumatikōs*, as Spirit, according to Didymus of Alexandria. The analyses made by the Latin Fathers, which are fundamentally in agreement with the teaching of the Greeks, seemed to the latter to be a rational elaboration which lacked discretion and went beyond what could properly be said about the inexpressible mystery of the divine processions. (IBHS III, p. 34)

Congar's confidence that the Greek and Latin doctrine here is essentially the same is confirmed by his investigation of the work of Cyril of Alexandria. Over against Nestorius, Cyril was concerned to show that the Spirit was not unrelated to the incarnate Son at the level of being. Cyril describes the Spirit, indeed, as not only 'proper', *idion*, to the Son, but as 'from', *ek*, that Son, and as 'proceeding', *proienai* or *procheitai*, from him, or more precisely, 'from the Two', *ex amphoin*, that is, the Father and the Son (or, sometimes, the Father *through* the Son). Although Theodoret of Cyr, Nestorius's fellow Antiochene, at once pounced on such statements as a chink in Cyril's armour, the Alexandrian bishop stood by them. But as modern patrologists have pointed out, because Cyril's aim was the defence not of the *Filioque* but of the divinity of Christ (for the Son who distributes such a gift as the Spirit as his own cannot be a creature), these texts are not without a certain ambiguity which, in the middle and late Byzantine periods, Monopatrists and Filioquists, Photians and Latinophrones would wrestle over inconclusively.

A slightly later writer hiding under Cyril's mantle, the 'Pseudo-Cyril', introduced another concept of close relevance to the *Filioque*, that of the Trinitarian *perichōrēsis*. The Persons are *in* each other. Each is 'turned towards the other and is open and given to the other'. This concept will be drawn on by Congar in his own proposed solution to the *Filioque* dispute. A second notion taken from this pseudo-Cyrilline author by the extremely influential summarizer of the earlier Greek tradition, John Damascene, is that of a procession of the Spirit 'through', *dia*, the Son: a preposition already, found, as we have noted, in Cyril himself. Following the close analysis of John's texts by J. Grégoire,[19] Congar holds that, for Damascene, the Spirit's distinguishing quality, his 'hypostatic property', namely the mode of his coming-to-be, is only accessible and understandable by reference to the Son. The Spirit can disclose his own cause, the Father, by his procession—but only *via* the Son; our understanding cannot pass directly from Spirit to Father. Going beyond the patristic scholar whose work he is using here, Congar considers that the phrase 'through the Son' signifies the genetic expression of the Trinitarian *perichōrēsis*. The mutual indwelling of the Persons, in other words, is the eternal 'result' of the procession *dia Huiou*. Before leaving Damascene Congar notes, in conclusion, how many different Greek words for 'coming forth' have to be crammed into the single Latin term *procedere*.

Less than fifty years separates the death of John Damascene in 749 from the opening of the Filioquist controversy, which may be dated to 787. For in that year, as Congar explains in a sustained historical excursus, the letter of the Byzantine patriarch Tarasius (d. 806) to the Seventh Ecumenical Council, meeting to determine the Church's doctrine on the cult of images, arrived at the court of Charlemagne, along with the decrees of that Council, and caused grave offence by its reference to the procession of the Spirit 'from the Father *through* the Son'. Charlemagne, accordingly, assembled the Frankish bishops, who condemned the notion at the (local) Council of Frankfurt in 794. Some few years later, a Greek monk in the monastery of Mar Sabas, outside Jerusalem, noticing that the Frankish monks on the Mount of Olives had inserted the *Filioque* into the Creed, began a campaign against them in which they appealed for support to Pope Leo III (d. 816). The Pope, who was as adamant in his belief in the truth of the *Filioque* doctrine as he was hostile to its insertion into the ecumenical Creed, wrote unsympathetically to Charlemagne about the abuse. Charlemagne's synod of Aachen in 809, in ratifying nonetheless what was already the liturgical practice of the imperial chapel and the imperial episcopate, threw down the gauntlet to the Roman See. Leo III picked it up the following year by ordering that the text of the Creed, without the *Filioque*, should be engraved in Latin and in Greek on two silver shields and placed at the *confessio*, or entrance to the high altar, of St Peter's, *ad perpetuam rei memoriam*. Ten years later, Photius was born.

Congar's foray into early mediaeval Church history stops short at this point, and, abstracting from the complex political and religious situation which Photius inherited on becoming patriarch of Constantinople in 858, turns to consider his theology instead. According to Congar, Photius either passed over in silence or else suppressed those texts of the Greek Fathers which were 'open to the idea' that the Son plays a part in the eternal coming-to-be of the Spirit. In Photius's view,

> there were only two possibilities—an activity that is common to the three Persons and goes back to their nature, or one that is strictly personal. To admit, as the Latins did, that the procession of the Spirit came both from the Father and the Son, as from a single principle, was to withdraw that procession from the hypostases and to attribute it to their common nature. (IBHS III, p. 58)

In other words, the affirmation of the *Filioque* would be, in an important sense, the depersonalization of God. But, as Congar points out, in the Latin construction the divine nature only exists *in* the divine Persons, who are, as Aquinas would later remark, 'subsistent relationships': the Father *being* Fatherhood, the Son *being* Sonship and so forth. However, Congar does concede that the word 'procession', when applied by the Latins to the origin of the Spirit, does not in itself make clear how it is the Father who is the 'absolute and primordial origin' of the Spirit. Father and Son are not here on the same level. He holds it to be self-evident that Photius gave Eastern pneumatology a form that ruled out agreement with Western Christians, and even with those Latin Fathers (such as Ambrose) whom the East had taken to its heart. But all is not lost—the 'victory of confrontation has not been total, nor is it definitive' (IBHS III, p. 59). One *sign* of this for Congar is that the thirteenth-century successor of Photius, Gregory of Cyprus, and in his wake that crucial figure in the development of Eastern Christian doctrine, St Gregory Palamas, were willing to allow that the Holy Spirit, not precisely as hypostasis but as 'inhypostasizing' or personalizing the 'energies' of God—his glory, face or power: that is, his being as turned towards ourselves—is poured out from the Father through the Son (or even *from* the Son). Emboldened by this discovery, such twentieth-century Orthodox theologians as Lossky and Olivier Clément have suggested that, even if the 'monarchic' character of the Father as unique principle of Son and Spirit is an absolutely incommunicable hypostatic character (which cannot be shared with the Son), it may be that his 'fontal privilege' of being the source of the divine energies (and even essence) is communicated to the Son and then, from Father and Son (*Filioque*) to the Spirit, there to become our deification.[20] Unfortunately, despite its eirenic intention this suggestion runs up against an obstacle: for the dogmatic theology of the Latin tradition, the hypostases are themselves identical with the divine essence. For the Holy Spirit to be dependent on the Son as regards the divine essence is, therefore, for him to be dependent on the Son with regard to his hypostasis also.

It is time for Congar to turn to look at that alternative Latin tradition for itself, and this he proceeds to do. He has already had occasion to point out that the West professed the *Filioque*, through such Fathers as Hilary of Poitiers (*c.* 315–*c.* 367), Ambrose, Augustine and Leo the Great, and through its Councils, at a time when full communion reigned between West and East. Congar discusses the development of the Latin understanding of the *Filioque* in terms of the four figures who dominated his account of Western pneumatology in the first volume of his trilogy: namely, Augustine, Anselm, Richard of Saint-Victor and Thomas Aquinas. As early as his account of Augustine, he sketches out the contours of a possible solution to the *Filioque* issue. He points out that, over and above Augustine's desire to be faithful to the biblical evidence for *some* causal role for the Son in the Spirit's coming-to-be, his wider aim was to guarantee the 'perfect consubstantiality of the three Persons'.

> He made sure of this by making the distinction between them consist in a relationship which opposes them correlatively to each other and which is a relationship of procession. The relationship between the Father and the Son does not give rise

> to any questions—it is clear, and our own experience provides a striking analogy. The Spirit is distinguished relationally from the two in the unity of the divine essence only by proceeding from the two as their common Spirit. If he did not proceed from the Son, he would not be distinguished from him by that relationship which safeguards the divine equality and consubstantiality. (IBHS III, p. 87)

This is how Congar understands Swete's statement that the Western *Filioque*, in its Augustinian form, is virtually an inference from the *homoousion* of Father and Son as defined at Nicaea.[21] In the Greek tradition, by contrast, the divine consubstantiality was justified in terms of three factors: the monarchy of the Father, the *perichōrēsis*, and the triune character of all the relationships of Father, Son and Spirit. This being so, a part, at least, of the doctrinal intention of the *Filioque* in the West may be said to be secured in the East by other means. But more than this, Congar detects two points at which a new theological convergence of West and East might be feasible. The first has been noted before: it is the difference between the Latin *processio*, as a general word for 'coming from another', and the Greek *ekporeusis*, with its unmistakable connotation of an absolute, aboriginal source. May it not be said that the Spirit stands to the Son in a relation of *processio*, but not of *ekporeusis*? Secondly, although the idea of the Holy Spirit as the communion of Father and Son—at once a ground and a consequence of the *Filioque*—is rarely encountered in the East, it is not unknown, and the incidence of its use appears to be increasing. Such representatives of the Russian Orthodox diaspora as Bulgakov and Evdokimov do not hesitate to appeal to it, the latter in his interpretation of Andrei Rublev's marvellous icon of the Trinity.[22]

Congar argues that Thomas Aquinas sensed the complementarity of the Latin formula 'from the Son' and the Greek 'through him'. In this, he can be acclaimed as a forerunner of that luminary of the Council of Florence, Cardinal John Bessarion (1403–72), who observes that *ex Filio* means equality, whereas *per Filium* points to order, yet the divine life of Father, Son and Spirit is both equitable and orderly.[23] Congar insists that, contrary to Greek charges, Thomas, as the classical theologian of the Latin Church, was careful in his Trinitarian writing to preserve the full truth of the monarchy of the Father, even though that monarchy was not the 'axis' of his triadology, as it was for the Byzantines. Indeed, Congar provides an entire *catena* of citations, from Augustine to Cardinal Pierre Bérulle

(d. 1629), in testimony to the Western conviction that the Father is the absolute source, *fons et origo*, of the divinity.

In his attempted 'solution' of the issue, Congar maintains that the Latin and Greek traditions on this disputed question constitute two dogmatic expressions of the same mystery, and that the conversion of the one to the theology of the other is neither necessary nor, in the light of history, feasible. The formulae 'from the Father, as the absolute Source, and from the Son' and 'from the Father through the Son' must be recognized as equivalent and complementary. If this were done, and the non-heretical character of the *Filioque* fully accepted by the Orthodox, he personally would be willing that it should be excised from the Western Creed since

> the one-sided introduction of the *Filioque*, without consulting the Eastern Church, into a creed of ecumenical value was not only a way of behaving that was canonically illicit, but also an action which devalued the unity of the Christian family. (IBHS III, p. 205)

While recognizing the strength of this argument, and Congar's own sensitivity to the pastoral aspect of the issue—for one cannot tamper with an inherited creed without some shaking of the foundations—it may be suggested that his conclusion is unnecessarily drastic. The abandonment that must follow of the Latin Church's myriad musical settings of her Creed—some of them, from plainsong to Cherubini, of stunning spiritual beauty—should give one pause, especially if one is a lover of the liturgy such as Congar. Perhaps, as an alternative, a sufficient act of brotherly reparation would be to turn into a custom an initiative of Pope John Paul II, on the fifteen-hundredth anniversary of the First Council of Constantinople in 1981, and say that whenever Western Catholics and Orthodox come together in prayer, even in the great basilicas and cathedrals of Latin Christendom, the Creed will be recited in its original ecumenical form.

But an account of Congar's pneumatology should echo the pneumatological trilogy itself and close not on such a controverted point, but with a reference to the secure truth of the Spirit's life-giving presence in the Church. For, following on an investigation of the Spirit's role in Confirmation and the Eucharist and, more briefly, in the other sacraments, Congar concludes that the entire life of the Church may be thought of as 'one long epiclesis', or invocation of the Spirit.

> What we have here is an absolutely supernatural work that is both divine and deifying. The Church can be sure that God works in it, but, because it is God and not the Church that is the principle of this holy activity, the Church has to pray earnestly for his intervention as a grace . . . the Church does not in itself have any assurance that it is doing work that will 'well up to eternal life'; it has to pray for the grace of the one who is uncreated Grace, that is, the absolute Gift, the Breath of the Father and the Word. (IBHS III, p. 271)

This seems an appropriate point at which to turn to the last of Congar's particular themes to be considered in this book: how it can be that *Holy* Church is *semper reformanda*, always in need of reform.

Notes

1 H. B. Swete, *The Holy Spirit in the New Testament* (London, 1909), pp. 63–109.

2 G. Haya-Prats, *L'Esprit force de l'Eglise. Sa nature et son activité d'après les Actes des Apôtres* (Paris, 1975).

3 F. M. Braun, 'L'eau et l'Esprit', *Revue théologique* 49 (1949), pp. 5–30; *idem, Jean le Théologien* (Paris, 1972), III. *Sa théologie* 1, pp. 167ff.

4 H. B. Swete, *op. cit.*, p. 160.

5 *Odes of Solomon* VI; quoted in IBHS I, p. 65.

6 Marius Victorinus, *Hymns*, I, 3–5; in *Sources chrétiennes* 68 (Paris, 1960), pp. 620–1; quoted in IBHS I, p. 77.

7 Augustine, *De Trinitate* VI, 5, 7; quoted in IBHS I, p. 78.

8 Ibid., XV, 19, 37.

9 Anselm, *Monologion* 50.

10 H. E. Manning, *The Internal Mission of the Holy Ghost* (London, 1864); *idem, The Temporal Mission of the Holy Ghost* (London, 1866).

11 C. Journet, *L'Eglise de Verbe incarné* (Paris, 1943–69) II, pp. 96, 232–4, 490, 508.

12 H. U. von Balthasar, 'Der Unbekannte jenseits des Wortes' in *idem, Spiritus Creator* (Einsiedeln, 1967), pp. 97ff.

13 Eusebius, *Historia ecclesiastica* VI. 2, 11.

14 'De notre Père saint Syméon prière mystique: Invocation au Saint Esprit, par celui qui déjà le voit' in Symeon the New Theologian, *Hymnes* I: *Sources chrétiennes* 156 (1969), pp. 151–3.

15 IBHS III, p. xvii, citing S. B. Bulgakov, *Le Paraclet* (Paris, 1946), p. 68.

16 G. Podskalsky, *Theologie und Philosophie in Byzanz. Der Streit um die theologische Methodik in der spätbyzantinischen Geistesgeschichte 14–15 Jh. Seine systematischen Grundlagen und seine historische Entwicklung* (Munich, 1977), pp. 124ff.

17 P. Schoonenberg, 'Trinität—der vollendete Bund. These zur Lehre von dem dreipersönlichen Gott', *Orientierung* 37 (1973), pp. 115–17.

18 Cf. Martin Luther's commentary on Galatians in *Werke* 15 (Geneva, 1969), pp. 282–95; for Maximus's *Quaestiones et Dubia* 12 (PG 90, 793), see J.-M. Garrigues, *Maxime le Confesseur. La charité avenir divin de l'homme* (Paris, 1976), p. 160.

19 J. Grégoire, 'La relation éternelle de l'Esprit au Fils d'après les écrits de Jean de Damas', *Revue d'histoire ecclésiastique* 64 (1969), pp. 713–55.

20 O. Clément, 'Grégoire de Chypre, "De l'ekporèse du Saint Esprit" ', *Istina* 17 (1973), pp. 443–56.

21 H. B. Swete, *The Holy Spirit in the Ancient Church* (London, 1912), p. 353.

22 P. Evdokimov, 'L'Icône', *La Vie spirituelle* 82 (1956), pp. 24–7.

23 Ioannes Bessarion, *De processione Spiritus Sancti* (PG 161, 397C–400A).

10

Congar as Church reformer

Both before and after the Second Vatican Council, Congar devoted much energy to questions of Church reform. Such reform, in his eyes, concerned the entire manner in which the Christian faith is embodied in the Church community in the world of today: it is not an affair for bureaucrats, but for prophets. Granted that the internal difficulties facing the Catholic Church have changed so markedly across the watershed of the conciliar divide, Congar's desiderata for the life of the Church were, naturally enough, notably different before 1962 and after 1965.

A PRE-CONCILIAR CALL FOR REFORM

After the Second World War Congar was much concerned, not with the making or enactment of particular reforms within the Catholic Church, but with the formulation of principles whereby faithful or true reform could be distinguished from false. Or, as he put it himself in the preface to his *Vraie et fausse réforme dans l'Eglise*, we must discriminate between those reforms which are necessary in the Church's life and those which, by contrast, cannot be carried out at all without damage to her communion (VFRE, p. 8). It was not that he lacked conviction about particular reforms; indeed, almost the contrary was the case. In the light of the biblical and liturgical movements, and the revival of the lay apostolate, the kind of reforms needed was virtually self-evident to him. But somebody had to confront the underlying issues of principle involved. Accordingly, his book has two main sections, which correspond to his general concern. First, why does the Church never finish with reforming herself, and in what sense *can* she be properly said to reform herself in history? Secondly, on what conditions can reform be 'true' and take place without a rupture that would harm her life?

Congar opens by describing the Church's life in such a way that reform must be regarded as an essential aspect of that life. Every active movement, as he puts it, in the Church involves a transcending of what went before. It takes place thanks to a new curiosity about the permanent 'sources and animating principles' of ecclesial life. And so, all active movement implies, by that very fact, 'a certain reform-value' (VFRE, p. 21). Nor was this statement made in a void. The immediately post-war years had produced, as Congar points out, a ferment of 'reformist' agitation in France, Italy, Germany, which touched on many vital points: the liturgy, preaching and catechesis, forms of parochial organization.[1] The Church has frequently inhibited internal self-criticism—intelligibly enough, thought Congar, since it could so easily be turned against her, as when Luther obtained a copy of Cardinal Gasparo Contarini's (1483–1542) memoir on Curial reform. This is especially true in the modern world where no respect for office or spiritual function can be presupposed. Yet such self-criticism was a necessity: we can learn, if from no higher example, from that of the Nazis who were weakened by its impossibility within their system.

Congar gives four characteristics of the self-criticism which he observed around him in the Church of Western Europe. First, it was a 'loving and respectful self-criticism'. Second, it had pre-established solid foundations in the actions of the Church's supreme pastors: notably in the theological and liturgical renovation carried out by Leo XIII and Pius X. Thirdly, it activated the role of the laity who, especially in grave circumstances, are 'in a certain sense responsible for the whole body'. Fourthly, it was motivated by a profound desire to 'get back to the sources': especially the Bible and the Fathers. The first cause of this phenomenon that Congar mentions was a 'taste for sincerity', that is, personal authenticity. This, he felt, could also be superficial, a conformism of the *avant-garde* already noted as a danger by the social critic and personalist philosopher Emmanuel Mounier (1905–50). The second factor at work was a more realistic awareness of the true apostolic situation, namely the effectively unchurched condition of so much of the nominally Catholic population. Congar stressed that the post-war reformism of which he was speaking had nothing in common with that of Modernism at the turn of the century.

> It is not a matter of reforming abuses, for there virtually are none. It is a question of revising structures. That goes beyond a simple reminder of what the canons require. It demands a climbing higher up towards the sources (VFRE, p. 59).

It was not enough to restore a deviant form to its canonical pattern; what was needed was to invent new forms, always 'starting from the deep tradition of the ever living Church, under the superintendence of the *magisterium*'.

But some will say, Congar remarks, 'Reform yourself! Reform your own lives, and everything will go well. What we need is men of God.' That was good advice at the turn of the century, when civil society and culture were in a relatively, or apparently, settled state, but there was turmoil in the Church, about her own ultimate principles of thought and action. Today (that is, in 1950), the situation is quite different. The situation within the Church is untroubled; her essential structure is 'not in the slightest way put in question'. Current reformism has profited by numerous features of the antecedent situation, not the least of which is the 'strengthening of the Church's doctrinal tradition over against Modernism'. Whereas, on the other hand the state of culture, of civil society, and so of the conditions in which evangelization must operate in the modern world, is unstable. And Congar concluded his lengthy preamble on the aim of his book:

> It is not alongside, or against, the Church's tradition that we are seeking a solution, but in that tradition's very depths. (VFRE, p. 59)

So Congar turns to the first of his two great questions: how, and in what sense, does the Church reform herself? This is really the question of how the Church, composed as it is of sinners, can still be holy Church. The early Fathers were intuitively aware of the problem, which they referred to in such images for the Church as the moon—one light side, from Christ, the other side, from man, dark—or the *casta meretrix*, the 'chaste harlot', elected in her impurity. But not till the Donatist crisis, and its aftermath of emotion recollected in tranquillity, did the beginnings of a solution suggest themselves, in the idea of an objective holiness of the ecclesial institution itself—stemming from the holiness of the

Church's faith, of her sacraments, and of the apostolic authority of her priesthood, which no amount of sinfulness could destroy.

Congar's account builds on this notion, rendering it more supple and nuanced in the process. He points out that in one sense the Church is made by its members, but in another sense it makes them, and thus is (logically and ontologically) anterior to them. First, in the Incarnation itself the Church existed insofar as Christ was the predestined head of the Church, the One who assumed human nature as the Bridegroom of his future Bride. The reality of the Church's mystery exists before her reality as the congregation of the faithful. Secondly, as an institution the Church is, in a sense, prior (logically, ontologically and even chronologically) to her own members: that is, in virtue of 'the totality of means by which Jesus wished to form and unite faithful disciples to himself'. This involves the deposit of faith, and the sacraments of faith, instituted as these were by Christ so as to unite us to the mystery of his passover to the Father. It also includes the apostolic ministry, with its powers, or, as Congar prefers to say, 'energies'. All of this has its fruit in the community of the faithful (VFRE, pp. 95–9).

How, then, can the Church be termed necessarily holy, and how contingently sinful? With regard to the Church as institution, composed, as the mediaevals would say, of faith and the sacraments of faith, there can be no question of sin or fault. This is not triumphalism, for, as Congar reminds us from the texts of Thomas, '*hoc ad excellentiam Christi pertinet*'.[2] But with regard to the fruit of this perfect excellence among the faithful, those who regard the Church as consisting only of the just and the predestined fail to see one of her essential features. As Congar puts it:

> The belonging of sinners to the Church is not an accidental thing, a peripheral concession. It represents something structural. The whole idea of the Church is engaged here. If the Church is only a communion, wholly spiritual, with God, then one leaves her by sin, even interior sin, and in the measure that one commits sin. For sin destroys communion with God in Christ. But the Church is not only a communion in Christ; she is also, and at the same time, the means of this communion: the means to procure it through the proclamation of faith and baptism; the means to nourish it and bring it to its perfection by everything she ceaselessly develops in terms of illumination, assistance, grace; it is also a question of the means to repair it by the exercise of the power of the keys. (VFRE, pp. 110–11)

However, what troubles our contemporaries is not so much personal sins which are, as Congar's analysis has shown, 'the work of the Church's members, not of the Church herself', but rather what he terms the 'historico-cultural faults' of the Church. For the ministerial priesthood, even in its magisterial, teaching office but especially in its pastoral, governing office, is delivered over to the conditioning process of historical time. Through that conditioning—the state of ideas and of customs, of politics and even economics in a given period—the Church's leadership take on modalities which do not belong to them in any essential way yet, phenomenally, become one body with them in their concrete exercise. The priestly office of the apostolic ministry becomes bound to cultic and devotional forms characteristic of a given time; the *magisterium*, 'at least in its minor forms', is bound to a certain state of information and expression. As for the governing power, this is much more closely associated, historically speaking, with particular forms of authority. This helps to explain how, though the hierarchical functions of the apostolic ministry are themselves holy, the way they are exercised partakes in human limitation. Before considering more closely the basis on which the Church, *semper reformanda*, can undertake such reform, Congar concludes with the rueful reflection that such faults in the Church's members, and narrowing, distorting constraints in her ordained ministry, touch us all. In the organic solidarity by which each good deed profits the whole Church, so each sin and shortcoming diminishes it. No critic dare disregard his own deficiencies: everyone says at Mass, *Confiteor*: 'I confess'.

By what title, then, does the People of God need to reform itself? Under this heading, Congar draws his readers' attention to two great temptations of the Church: he called them, with reference to New Testament history, 'the temptation of the Pharisees' and 'the temptation of the Synagogue'. 'Pharisaism' here is taking means for ends; absolutizing religious observance rather than the spiritual good of persons which it is meant to serve. The 'temptation of the Synagogue' is the refusal to go beyond those forms in which the work of God has come down to us—even when this entails retarding the development and the fruitfulness of the Church in the world. By contrast with these temptations, a right will to reform will want to restore to the routine gestures of the life of faith their full spiritual truth, and to adapt various forms of the Church's life to the needs which new situations carry with them. Aware that all this *might* be construed as iconoclast *insouciance* towards the tradition, Congar immediately adds:

> It would be a grave mistake to interpret what has just been said as a call for change for change's sake, and a relativization of the Church's life as no more than a succession of wholly transitory historical forms. Development, which is the law of that life, involves respect for inherited forms and for the past; it comprises fidelity, rootedness, continuity. But it also means movement, growth, adaptation, and it is this latter aspect which our theme leads to underline in a special way. (VFRE, p. 177)

What Congar sought was a reform not of abuses (as we have seen, he denied that there were any worth speaking of), nor of doctrine (he insists that the 'self-criticism' he is calling for has nothing to do with early twentieth-century Modernism), but of patterns of life—above all, those relevant to the apostolic outreach of the Church community. He did not see how the Church could be effectively *evangelical* without a certain evangelicalism of lifestyle, even in matters 'external and economic'. The same '*élan de ressourcement évangélique*' would, he held, if effected, also bring the Church to harmonize herself more generously with the style of a new society—a society she was called to baptize, as she had others in the past. If in this last statement Congar shows himself much influenced by the search for imaginative pastoral strategies close to the heart of his old teacher, Chenu, those he regards as 'prophets' of such evangelical generosity are a larger band. Ozanam; Henri-Dominique Lacordaire (1802–61), the political Liberal and restorer of the Dominicans in France; the Comte Albert de Mun (1841–1914), pillar of French 'social Catholicism'; the fiery and uncomfortable novelist and pamphleteer Léon Bloy (1846–1917); Péguy: this is his roll call of his favoured 'ecclesial prophets' and, believing as he did that poetry was an especially apt vehicle for prophecy, it is not surprising that Péguy's name figures here. The controversial character of those personalities and their 'message' led him to reflect upon the ambivalence of the reformist impulse, and to work out the conditions on which reform could avoid the perils of potential schism. The negative object-lesson of the sixteenth-century Reformation was evidently at the back of his mind.

Congar specifies four such conditions. First, any would-be reformer must take seriously the primacy of charity, and hence of the pastoral.

> Successful reforms in the Church have been those made in view of the concrete needs of souls, in a pastoral perspective, by the way of charity. (VFRE, p. 252)

And citing the seventeenth-century spiritual writer and archbishop of Cambrai, Fénélon (1651–1715), Congar warned that no reform conceived in the spirit of a 'bitter and arrogant criticism' would have enduring results for the good. Secondly, a sound reform will be saturated from start to finish with the desire to 'remain in the communion of the Whole'. Drawing on his beloved Möhler, he insists that only by willingness to learn from the whole Body, whose communion is guarded by the *magisterium*, can a reformer enjoy the advantage of correction, complementation and, ultimately, fullness of truth. Thirdly, a reform requires patience: as the example of Luther shows, an impatient reformer tends to become a schismatic and heresiarch. The patience Congar speaks of is not simply tolerance of delay, but

> a certain docility of spirit, a diffidence about self, a distance *vis-à-vis* solutions that are rushed, extreme, 'all or nothing', and therefore *simpliste*. (VFRE, p. 311)

Fourthly and finally, true reform takes place 'by return to the principle of Tradition', something that Congar contrasts with 'innovation by mechanical adaptation'.

> The grand law of a Catholic reformism will be to begin by a return to the principles of Catholicism. First and foremost there will be a searching of the tradition, and an immersion of the self in that tradition—it being understood that 'tradition' does not mean what is 'routine' nor even, strictly speaking, 'that which is past'. (VFRE, pp. 335–6)

As Congar explains, while tradition includes a past aspect, in which it is the treasury of texts and realities handed down in Church history, tradition is also much more than that. It is the presence of the Beginning in all the stages of its development, from Scripture and Fathers, through the Liturgy and the explorations of the doctors and spirituals. It is the development of the piety and doctrine, the thought and life of the Church, up to the present day where still she labours perpetually in her work of faith and praise, contemplation and apostolate, under the guidance of her *magisterium*.

Congar closes his appeal for true reform with a series of human vignettes in which 'faithful' and 'revolutionary' reformers are compared and contrasted. In the great gallery of figures with which his reading of Christian history had acquainted him, one reformer stands out for his combination of the desirable qualities Congar had specified, the refounder of the Dominicans in France, and prophet of 'Christian Democracy', Henri-Dominique Lacordaire. Speaking of Lacordaire's withdrawal into silence after the first controversial conferences in Notre Dame de Paris, Congar writes, thinking perhaps of his own case also:

> The future is prepared in the waiting when the seed, once deposited, puts forth a shoot and grows. What is essential is to have sown the seed. . . . There is a plan of Providence, a general conduct of things, and in this plan, each is solidary with others, and must know how to await the hour that God has fixed. (VFRE, pp. 567–8)

POST-CONCILIAR REFLECTIONS ON A CRISIS

Congar's concern with the Church's self-reform did not cease with the Second Vatican Council, when many of the changes he had wanted received formulation in Church documents of various kinds, including those inspired by the great Dogmatic Constitutions, notably the new liturgical books and the revised Codex of the Latin Church, itself an essay in applied ecclesiology. He continued to comment on Church affairs as one who, though living in a book-filled friar's cell, was no mere *livresque* academic, but rather someone passionately concerned with all that affected the lives of the Church's members.

However, within a decade of the Council's ending, the direction of Congar's criticism as a Church reformer shifted markedly. He noted with stress a new phenomenon: the boredom which mention of the Church's name aroused and the flight from her of so many of her erstwhile members, and especially of the young (see *Eglise catholique et France moderne*). The reforms for which he had worked, coinciding as these had with a further massive draining away of Christian consciousness in Western culture, had not secured the desired fruits. Although Congar's expressions of dismay were circumspect, and mainly private, the undertone is that of the lament in Jeremiah 14:19:

> Expectavimus pacem, et non est bonum;
>   et tempus curationis, et ecce turbatio.

We expected peace, but good was it not;
a time of healing, but there came disturbance.

True, many of the criticisms levelled at the Church by lapsing Catholics were criticisms of her failure to live up to her own principles. Yet Congar felt that the Church's historic failures and retardations were being given exclusive attention, to the exclusion of her divine constituent, which itself had been shown to be so humanly productive in her saints.

> This same Church whose human tares they condemn is from Jesus Christ, from the living and holy God. The Church is not a mere human creation. As the concrete form of Christianity she is *given* prior to Christians, namely in Christ. Her dogma and her theologies are radically given in the Word of God whose witness is the Scriptures. There exists in the Church an element of transcendent purity. (ECFM, pp. 13–14)

And Congar cited Georges Bernanos (1888–1948), a Christian writer who, he remarked, had known as well as any humanist how to denounce crimes against humanity: 'Our Church is a Church of saints'.[3] Without awareness of the only Holy One at the source of the Church's existence, her divine roots, one would naturally fail to notice the 'sap which gave her life and still gives life', in the movement of the present and the possibilities of the future. Addressing himself particularly to young people, Congar echoed some words of Pope John XXIII:

> The Catholic Church is not an archaeological museum. She is the ancient village fountain which gives water to the generations of today as she has to those of the past.[4]

Congar showed himself well aware that much of the difficulty which Catholicism is currently encountering both in the fundamental proclamation of the faith and of its pastoral development derives from the fact that an abyss separates its theological anthropology and consequently its ethics from the version of what it is to be human, and so a moral agent, commonly found in contemporary society in the West and wherever the West's influence is at work. The resulting 'credibility gap' has, alas, done much to neutralize and weaken the very self-reform which Congar had argued for so persuasively in his writings before 1962, and then seen vindicated at the Second Vatican Council. Rather than attempting to tailor the Church's vision of man and human behaviour to the expectations of secular society, he opts decisively for an attempt to make it speak again with power to move minds and hearts.

An 'anthropology for God', as Congar calls it, must begin, he tells us, from the fundamental affirmation of all anthropology: namely, that man is something different from nature, though he is also in solidarity with nature. Spirit transcends the feeling, instinctual animal life to which it is united. In unmistakably Thomist language, Congar speaks of the feeling mind as 'open, of itself, to all that is intelligible': on the basis of this 'openness', it forms critically, in the judgement, the notion of truth. It judges man's own situation and acts; going beyond calculative thought, man has a 'meditating activity which scrutinizes the meaning of his own existence'. In the Bible and Christian tradition, this primordial *donné* of all anthropology worth the name is expressed in the affirmation that man is 'in the image of God'. Subordinate, dependent though he is, he is nevertheless God's 'counterpart', his *partenaire*. This implies, in the first place, that man can be called by God, can receive a word from God; in the second place it means that he has the quality of being a person. Here Congar shows himself influenced by Vladimir Soloviev's idea of Godmanhood; citing Soloviev (1853–1900), he writes

> In man nature transcends itself and passes, by way of awareness, into the sphere of the Absolute.[5]

In man, being, the analogous 'stuff' of the universe, is concentrated in the mode of *personal* existence: it becomes hypostatic. Despite their extraordinary individualization, a tree, a raindrop have no absolute value in themselves, whereas every human being is a subject in his own right and bears in his free will the determination of an existence which is his own. Historically, Congar believes, leaning here on the work of such students of the history of thought as Claude Tresmontant, the idea of personhood is a gift of Christianity to the world.

Today, instrumental reason, which effaces man if only by omitting to consider the meaning of the goals of the human being thus summarily described, is king. Yet its reign is not, Congar notes, undisturbed. The success of Herbert Marcuse's analysis of 'one-dimensional man'; the renewed interest in the religions of Asia; the attraction of Orthodox spirituality: all these are witnesses to a 'search for an interiority open to transcendence' (ECFM, p. 165). In this situation, what has the Catholic Church to offer? Only the *pulchritudo tam antiqua quam nova* of which Augustine spoke, an old tune, but one that is never played out:

> If man is openness, desire, appeal, the response comes from God, from beyond the world and history. It is called God's intention or design; election, revelation, Jesus Christ, salvation. Its treasure is confided to the Church so that she may communicate it to the world. She offers it for the free acceptance of men. (ECFM, p. 165)

If this is the theological anthropology which the Church must ceaselessly proclaim on pain of self-destruction, what is its corresponding ethics? As Congar envisages the matter, the Catholic tradition affirms with equal force *both* the reality of human freedom, in the sense of man's capacity to orient and determine his life, *and* the primacy of the good or of objectively defined values. What Congar particularly stresses is that these two things cannot be played off against each other. Freedom is conceived with reference to the Good: free will, as the possibility of choosing this or that, derives from the fact that our mind does not coincide fully with the absolute plenitude of the true, nor our will with that of the good.

Free will is the 'magnificent condition of our conversion to the good'. Indeed, it is in its ordering to the absolute God that free will is founded, precisely as *free*. As Congar's fellow Frenchman the Oratorian philosopher Nicolas Malebranche (1638–1715), put it:

> When the soul is actually enjoying a partial good, it still has the momentum to go further.[6]

The call of God in revelation is, Congar insists, demandingly concrete. Christian tradition preaches the need to emancipate oneself from the slavery of the passions and from egoism—however little popular this message may be today. The life it offers is at once *disponibilité* to human joys, and the capacity to detach oneself from them. Congar reminds his readers of the mediaeval iconography which shows free will climbing up the ladder of the Cross. In this connexion, he stresses that law—when ordered to the good—is not a constraint on freedom, but its helpmate. Referring once again to Thomas: so long as our freedom does not coincide with the good, it needs this external aid. It is true that one can abuse this notion, and moralists in the Church have done so, separating rules and commandments from spiritual experience, sundering obligation from joy. But *abusus non tollit usum*. The freedoms offered by the permissive society are too often formal freedoms: self-styled 'liberations' which are not real 'liberties' since they remain external, and do not assist in the coming-to-be of free personalities. Congar, then, at once recalls us to the primordial idea of a nature of things, founded on an all-creative will, yet also insists that the positive norms which such objectivity indicates be mediated in any given human conjuncture—such as that of the Catholic Church in the West after the Council—by human 'prudence', Thomas's word for the virtue of applying means well.

Christian moral truth will always be hard, Congar warns, since it cannot be true to itself unless it is, as he puts it, 'total'. The totality involved lies on two planes: that of anthropology at large and that, more specifically, of the Gospel. The general anthropological ideal of totality Congar borrows from the Catholic lay moralist Alexis Carrel and, more specifically, his *L'Homme, cet inconnu*.[7] Man is not himself save when all the levels of his being, all the elements of his 'structure'—spiritual and moral, physical and sensuous—are taken into consideration. As for Christianity itself, it offers an ethic so high, a balance so difficult, that it cannot be achieved except through such means as prayer, asceticism, the help of example and community support, the sacraments, communion with Christ and his Holy Spirit. For, as Congar explains, the specificity of Christian ethics consists

> in a formula repeated a hundred times in the Scriptures, in doing in our turn what God has done for us, and, supremely, what Jesus has done. (ECFM, p. 170)

And this is impossible without a 'coherent ensemble [of Christian doctrine, worship and spirituality] which renders its demands possible' (ECFM, p. 182)

More widely, then, the renaissance of Christian anthropology and ethics which is needed if the conciliar self-reform is not to be baulked of its fruits forms part of an imperative need for a Christian maximalism which will do justice to revelation and salvation in their totality. Specifically, there is a need, Congar believes, to transcend a certain 'horizontalism' which has invaded many Catholic milieux since the Council. Such horizontalism, he explains:

> is a matter of a certain way of feeling or translating Christianity where the preponderant weight, the accent, and in a way the self-evident quality of the thing falls not on the transcendent and vertical moment of the positive supernatural fact, but on what it signifies for our human behaviour in the human world. (STPT, p. 63)

In the affirmation that Christianity must be lived in a way of solidarity with human reality at large—no stranger to the author of *Vraie et fausse réforme dans l'Eglise*—people are sliding all too easily from 'That is true' to 'Only that is true'. And Congar traces the features of such horizontalism in the deportment of many priests and religious, in preaching, in the Catholic press, and in the practice of the liturgy. Congar suggests that the question for many today is not, as it was for Luther, 'How may I obtain a favourable God?' but 'How may I obtain a favourable neighbour?' (STPT, p. 65)! Thus in the film by the Spaniard Luis Buñuel (1900–83) entitled *Nazarín* (1960), a priest who finds the institutional Church distasteful is converted to a quasi-literal imitation of Christ only to find that what he loves and is seeking is not so much Christ as humanity. Congar does not deny that the preaching of justice is an aspect of the preaching of the Gospel; but he most strenuously denies that those two ideas are identical or interchangeable (*Un peuple messianique*, pp. 145–95).

Such horizontalism can only be overcome, to Congar's mind, by a new reflection of a properly *theo*-logical kind on what the relation between man and God is at the level of the intimate being of God. It is the fruitfulness of the inner divine mystery, displayed to us in the Trinitarian initiatives of revelation and salvation, which provides the only permanent conditions for the human attaining of this world's goal. In terms of the debate over the Conciliar reform, intensified as that has been in modern Catholicism by the (almost simultaneous) personal intervention of Cardinal Joseph Ratzinger, and the papal decision to call a special Synod of Bishops for its evaluation in the autumn of 1985, Congar's position is clear. If the Council flung open the doors of the Church to dialogue with the world, ending its own sessions by the promulgation of the pastoral constitution *Gaudium et Spes* which proclaimed the offer of aid to the world in its own problems, this is only because the Council had already assured the *en-soi*, the intrinsic identity, of Catholicism in its three 'classical chapters': *Dei Verbum* for the Church's faith; *Sacrosanctum Concilium* for its cultic and liturgical life; *Lumen Gentium* for its corporate life devoted as that must be to service and witness (STPT, pp. 67–8). It is by fidelity to this pattern, which was the Council's own, that its reform will be in the end 'true', not 'false'.

'The crisis', Congar declares, 'is a real one' (CC, p. 50). Though its profoundest causes lie in shifts of sensibility in culture and problems in 'world society', those extra-ecclesial factors have been exacerbated by inner-ecclesial malpractice, notably in three areas:

the liturgy; theology and catechesis; and what Congar terms 'politicization': a synonym for his earlier 'horizontalism'. He does not scruple to call for a greater rigour in the conformity of catechetics, preaching and teaching in terms of that 'norm' which is the faith of the Church.[8] But he adds also that one of the things most lacking is a knowledge of history, that 'great school of intelligence and wisdom', which enables one to distinguish the absolute from the relative and to put all things in their proper place (CC, pp. 70–1). It is to Congar's own work as an historian of theology that we must finally turn.

Notes

1 Congar mentions three manifestos of such 'reformism': in France, Cardinal Suhard's letter 'Essor ou déclin de l'Eglise?'; in Italy, G. Papini, *Lettere agli uomini del Papa Celestino Sesto* (Florence, 1946); and in Germany, I. F. Görres, 'Briefe über die Kirche' in *Frankfurter Hefte* (1946), pp. 715–33.

2 *Summa Theologiae* IIIa, q. 82, a. 5, c: 'This pertains to the excellence of Christ'.

3 G. Bernanos, *Jeanne relapse et sainte* (Paris, 1934), p. 61. Cf. Congar's 'L'Eglise selon M. Georges Bernanos', *La Vie intellectuelle* 43 (1936), pp. 387–90.

4 Cited in ECFM, p. 18.

5 Cited ibid., p. 163, from J. Rupp, *Le Message ecclésial de Soloviev* (Paris/Brussels, 1975), p. 157.

6 N. Malebranche, *Traité de la Nature et de la grâce*, III, 1. 7.

7 A. Carrel, *L'Homme, cet inconnu* (Paris, 1935).

8 In the second edition of VFRE, p. 518, he had already proposed guidelines for the limiting of public contestation in the Church, fearful of the polarization of Catholicism into a 'High Church' right and 'Low Church' left (the comparison with Anglicanism is his own), and even of an eventual cutting of the Church into two.

11

Congar as historian of theology

As well as making a notable contribution to the particular history of one theological discipline, ecclesiology, Congar has bravely essayed a history of the development of theology as a whole. He has also worked out a concept of what theology should be, and, in the aftermath of the Second Vatican Council, offered some animadversions on the state of Catholic theology and its possible future. First of all, then, how does Congar, speaking *in propria persona*, understand the term 'theology'?

THE CONCEPT OF THEOLOGY

Congar's reflections on what theology is are inseparable from his understanding of revelation, so it is from there that we must take our point of departure. The content of revelation, as we saw in Chapter 2, is, in Congar's eyes, the mystery of communion between God and man. As such, revelation carries with itself its own justification. However, at the same time, it also offers to the mind of man quite inexhaustible possibilities of reflection. And this is the proper task of theology which must bind itself to seek (without ever fully comprehending) the totality of revelation in its internal coherence. Attempting to unite the characteristic emphases of the two mediaeval mendicant masters Bonaventure and Thomas, Congar insists that theology must show a continuous reference both to revelation's centre, Jesus Christ (hence Bonaventurian 'Christocentrism'), and to revelation's term, God himself (hence Thomist 'Theofinality') (FT, pp. 25–6).[1]

> Though the life of the Blessed Trinity is only revealed and accessible to us in Christ, theology is obliged to state these things separately, which gives rise to the pseudo-problem of an alternative between Theocentrism and Christocentrism. But what meaning could we attach to a Christocentrism which was not for the sake of Theocentrism, or to a Theocentrism which was not 'Christomorphous'? (DC, p. 60)

With regard to the essential structure of theology Congar's starting-point is the observation that, in the original language of revelation, the eternal divine *being* has clothed itself with human expressions which themselves belong to the realm of historical and cultural *becoming*. This, for Congar, is the ultimate foundation of the need to integrate positive or historical and systematic or speculative theology: 'One can only grasp the thought of the Absolute by way of passing through this relativity' (FT, p. 27). Though the theologian's aim is to translate the meaning entertained by the believing Church into precise conceptual terms, this must not be at the expense of the richness and subtlety found in the original metaphors of revelation. Although Thomists have here failed by frequent insensitivity to the texture of biblical language, they have been entirely right to see as a transcendental condition of possibility for revelation the analogical value of our language about the divinity, and the fundamental aptitude of our mind to grasp his self-disclosure. Here, for all his stress on the sovereignty of the Word of God, Congar underlines his separateness from the school of Barth. At the level of natural theology, Congar happily espouses the common Scholastic notion of the 'pure perfections' as a basic language for speaking about the divine. In a movement that includes both affirmation and negation the concepts of being, unity, goodness, beauty, can be ascribed 'by analogy' to God himself, thanks to the trace of self that the all-creative Logos has left in things. Congar emphasizes, however, that when God takes the initiative in addressing man, he proposes further analogies that could not have occurred to the unaided human being. So even the essential attributes of God, such as his power and justice, are qualified through revelation in a new way. Theology, therefore, has a first foundation in the creation, where the divine Wisdom has become to a certain degree immanent to the world. But more deeply still, it is based on the Word, the 'humanization of the Thought of God', which, having spoken to our fathers fragmentarily and in various ways, has spoken to us in these latter days through his Son.

The research which theology prosecutes is born of love for this divine truth. In theology, man:

> opens his human intelligence, containing as this does a need for logic which is a reflection of the Logos, and rich with human culture, to contemplate and express as fully and rigorously as may be, the content of the divine communication insofar as that is intelligible to us. (FT, p. 128)

Theology is a human project, but one whose cognitive resources are made available by divine generosity: it is, then, a necessarily *ecclesial* undertaking. Not only is it impossible without some kind of corporate collaboration, but also it depends on that transformation of faith into knowledge, *gnōsis*, which our membership of Christ's mystical Body alone makes possible.

> The condition of an orthodox knowledge of the objects of faith is communion in the Church, for the correct view of these objects is given by the Holy Spirit, who unveils the truth only to those who live in the communion of love. [Indeed] the last and finally only efficacious criterion of this orthodox knowledge is the teaching Church. For the Church cannot live as a body and ecclesiastically in the unity of truth, except thanks to an ecclesiastical criterion of unity and belief. (HT, p. 270)

Within this unity of faith, there is also room, and spacious room, for the theologian's liberty. The creativity of theology consists in its taking further the affirmations of doctrine; attempting syntheses where doctrine provides only elements; and tackling problems for which doctrine furnishes only a point of departure. Within the unity of faith of which the *magisterium* is the guardian and judge, the theologian will conduct his research on his own responsibility, in accordance with the maxim *in necessariis unitas, in dubiis libertas*.

With his Thomist background, Congar stresses the interrelated factors of unity and order in the theological mind's penetration of its materials. Yet the manner in which such unity and order are sought can vary enormously, and that for three reasons. Firstly, the 'given' of faith is so rich that it

> authorizes different manners of approach and, according to the intellectual orientation of each one, different manners of posing the problems themselves. (HT, p. 258)

An initial orientation of the individual theologian suggests a certain angle of vision on the totality of Christian revelation. Secondly, the intellectual climate of theology may be as diversified as the cultural worlds of Alexandria and Carthage were in the ancient church.

> If theology is the elaboration of faith by human reason using its own resources, it is clear that the content and inspiration of a *milieu* . . . of a tradition of religious life and of philosophical thought will determine in large measure the theological work and the rational construction of faith. (HT, pp. 258–9)

Thirdly and finally, the multiplicity of theologies may be caused by a deliberate choice of particular conceptual instruments.

> The Church, indeed, imposes on all the same datum of faith, but, by reason of its very transcendence, this datum supports, in its rational organization as theology, the service of a diversified philosophical apparatus. (HT, p. 259)

Yet, despite this generosity of judgement in regard to the many theologies of the *Catholica*, Congar always returns to lauding the merits of the Thomism of Le Saulchoir: capable of 'assuming and ordering a multitude of particular aspects' which elsewhere lie side by side like the pieces of a half-finished mosaic, the Thomist 'system' has, in Congar's eyes, a value which none of its competitors can rival.

THE HISTORY OF THEOLOGY

Still, given his ample view of the nature of *ecclesial* tradition, Congar could hardly take so narrow a view of *theological* tradition as to be satisfied with a straightforward repristination of classical Thomism. He quarried the theological past at all points following the imperative, 'Return to the sources'. His concept of *ressourcement* was indebted to Péguy, who had used the self-same term in the context of social reform, for 'a summons to leave a more superficial tradition for a more profound one . . . a going beyond in depth'. In his poetry, moreover, Péguy had glimpsed the distinctively Christian bearings of this idea, imaged in the faithful entering a church building where 'they bless themselves with holy water, passed on from hand to hand'.[2] To Congar's mind, as all Christian ages lie open to the Son and the Spirit, there should be theological riches to glean in them all. He has given evidence of the rightness of this conviction, not simply in his own *History of Theology* or in his tracing the history of ecclesiology, but throughout his work.

Moreover, history provides not only inspiration but also, more soberly, enlightenment. If, in the post-conciliar crisis which he felt Catholicism was facing, history could be a 'school of wisdom', this was not a special case, but a special application of a universal case.

> Knowledge of history makes possible a healthy relativism, which is quite different from scepticism. Relativism is, on the contrary, a way of being and seeing oneself more truly, and by perceiving the relativity of that which is really relative, it is a way of attributing absoluteness only to what is really absolute. Thanks to history we take proper stock of things, we avoid the mistake of taking for 'tradition' that which is only recent and which has altered more than once in the course of time.[3]

Here we shall highlight some of the more notable judgements which his survey of theological history suggested.

For Congar, the practice of theology is essentially a creation of the patristic period. The Apologists, and notably Justin, Tatian (*c.* 160) Athenagoras (second century) and Minucius Felix (second or third century) win their laurels as, in Congar's eyes, the first ever theologians, because they set out to re-express the apostolic tradition in categories drawn from pagan culture. This does not mean, however, that Congar neglects the role of factors internal to Christian faith in the development of theological culture. In the Alexandrian school the philosophy of religion was invoked not only, or even mainly, for apologetic and controversial purposes, but in the service of Christianity's own self-understanding. Thus for Clement of Alexandria (*c.* 150–*c.* 215):

> the act of faith itself becomes a form of intellectual contemplation which superlatively develops its intelligibility and virtualities. (HT, p. 41)

The systematic element missing in Clement was supplied by Origen, for whom Congar has considerable respect. The rationality exercised in so thoroughgoing a way on the texts of Scripture in the *Peri Archōn* provided the groundwork on which those more central figures of the dogmatic tradition, Athanasius and the Cappadocians, could build.

From Christian Hellenism Congar turns to consider the theological method of Augustine. In the voluminous pages left behind by a complex man both humanists and anti-intellectuals in the later Church would find sustenance. If the *De Doctrina Christiana*, with its message of the practical usefulness of profane studies for the understanding of Scripture, gave the Latin Middle Ages their theological programme and 'encyclopaedic spirit', the Augustinian *intellectus*, believing and loving, refuses to separate knowledge from its moral value—its relation to man's last end, his beatitude.

The patristic tradition bequeathed to writers of the early Middle Ages their concern with the biblical text and many of the hermeneutical tools with which to appropriate that *sacra pagina*, from grammar to allegory. Moreover, the Augustinian programme of despoiling the Egyptians would have a great future in the 'liberal arts', an educational ideal renewed in Cassiodorus's (*c.* 485–*c.* 580) *Institutiones Divinarum et Saecularium Litterarum*, Isidore's *Etymologiae* and the work of Alcuin of York (*c.* 735–804).

> More generally, the helpful, propedeutic value of profane knowledge was a structural concept of the culture of the Middle Ages, itself characterized by the subordination of all the elements of knowledge to the sacred science, which latter was essentially conceived as the explanation, the penetration and the illustration of one text, the Bible. (HT, p. 53)

Congar, remembering perhaps the attempt of his own masters at Le Saulchoir to instil a text-centred approach in preference to a manualist pedagogy of theses, stresses that mediaeval theological work was essentially the assimilation of a text, *lectio*, its teachers *lectores*. When the texts of the Fathers are placed just below those of Scripture, a 'theological jurisprudence of textual interpretation' arises, thus pushing into prominence such gracious conciliators of authorities as Peter Lombard.

The other presiding spirit of Western theology in the pre-Scholastic period, alongside Augustine, is Boethius (d. 525). That late Roman intellectual in the service of the Ostrogothic kings represents for Congar the continued rôle in theology of the philosophical heritage of the ancient world. While Aristotelean philosophical method influenced pagan Neo-Platonism well before it had any effect on patristic Platonism, its entry onto the Eastern theological stage with Leontius of Byzantium (sixth century) and John Damascene is paralleled, and eventually overtaken in significance in the West by a three-pronged advance. Through Boethius the mediaevals received Aristotle's *logica vetus*, a tool-box of technical instruments for the textual analysis of statements; in the twelfth century other Aristotelean writings were added, enabling the making of a theory of knowledge and demonstration; finally, at the turn of the twelfth and thirteenth centuries the arrival of Aristotle's metaphysics, psychology and ethics caused a major crisis in theological practice, inspiring in some a new Christian naturalism, in others a return by reaction to Augustine and the Fathers.

Even before this point, Congar insists, dialecticians and anti-dialecticians struggled for mastery in the theological life of the Church. They may be summed up in such contrasting portraits as those of Berengar of Tours (*c.* 1010–88) and Peter Damian (1007–72), Abelard (1079–1142) and Bernard. Congar shows sympathy for both sides, trying to do justice to the philosophical current and to its monastic and sapiential alternative. He finds the two provisionally united in Anselm, definitively in Thomas. The attempt to construe theology as a science in Gilbert de la Porrée (*c.* 1084–1154), and especially Alain of Lille (d. 1202), comes into its own with the brilliant intuition of William of Auxerre (d. 1231) that the part played by the natural light of self-evident principles in natural knowledge is played in theology by faith. Congar regards this as the most important piece of background to Thomas's concept of theology as laid out in, above all, his *Commentary on the Sentences*, on Boethius's *De Trinitate*, q. 2, and in the *Summa Theologiae* Ia, q. 1. The truths of revelation received by the light of faith are derived from the absolutely certain and transparent knowledge which is God's understanding of himself. As inhabiting the human mind they may be further penetrated either by that connaturality which charity brings about between God and the saints with its attendant *Einfühlung* or sympathetic awareness, or by a properly intellectual mode of activity, namely theology.

> By this intellectual effort, *sacra doctrina* will reproduce, as far as it can, God's *science*, that is to say, the order according to which God, in his wisdom, links all things together, each according to its degree of intelligibility and being, and finally brings all things to himself. We are here at the heart of the Thomist notion of theology. (HT, p. 95)

Congar stresses the distinction, central to the 'Albertino-Thomist revolution', between the supernatural light of faith and the natural light of human understanding: at the cost of a certain loss of theology's religious warmth, a warmth palpable in the mediaeval Augustinianism of Bonaventure and others, by no means all Franciscans, the distinction was vital in permitting the created order its own consistency.

At the same time, however, the legitimacy of using our created concepts and terms in relation to the uncreated God became, by the same token, more problematic. The position of an account of the divine Names, and, more widely, of theological discourse at large, was unsettled and could be pressed in the directions either of agnosticism or of rationalism. The beauty of Thomas's position, in Congar's eyes, is that it surmounted these dangers. As he writes on the topic of Thomas's method:

> The process which consists in abstracting something 'formal' and disengaging this from its modes and then applying this 'formality' to the mysteries of faith by the use of analogy, rests entirely on the distinction between a *ratio* and its mode, and on the conviction that a *ratio* does not change its essential laws when it is expressed under these different modes. In short, a rational theology rests entirely on the conviction that in the transposition of an idea to the level of transcendental realities, which positive mode escapes us, the *eminenter* does not destroy the *formaliter*. (HT, p. 110)

Thus, while Thomas accepts, for instance, that the manner in which Christ influences human beings is something unique, and that—to take a second example—the procession of the Word of God from the Father is not only unique but inaccessible to the human mind, he nevertheless also holds that a metaphysics of causality can usefully be invoked in exploring the nature of Christ's action, and a philosophy of 'intellectual generation' brought into play *vis-à-vis* the mystery of the Word—so long as these ideas have been suitably purified, and acquire thereby the quality of purely formal *rationes*.

Basically, Congar describes the further development of mediaeval theology among Scotists and Nominalists in terms of this overriding concern with theological epistemology. As the Middle Ages melt into Renaissance, he presents theology as pursuing a zig-zag course of reactions and counter-reactions. Although Ockham's Nominalism was, in part, an apophaticism before the sovereignly free God, the excessively dialectical character of much Nominalist theology stimulated people to seek, by reaction, a more immediate, spiritual, evangelical variety of thinking, which culminated in the *devotio moderna* of the Netherlands. However, the intellectual weaknesses of such an approach suggested to yet others, such as Nicholas of Cusa, the desirability of a return to the sources as the only possible remedy for a theological culture in decline. The development of philosophy and textual criticism made possible such a movement of *ressourcement*, beginning with such Italian humanist figures as Pico della Mirandola (1463–94) and Marsilio Ficino (1433–99), but soon spreading north of the Alps to England, France and Germany, finally to culminate in the work of Erasmus of Rotterdam (1469–1536).

The disdain of many of the new humanists for mediaeval Scholasticism arouses ambivalent feelings in Congar. On the one hand, the Scholastics by no means neglected the Bible or the Fathers: what else did the humanists print but collations of mediaeval texts? On the other, Congar considers that the development of the *quaestio* method, whereby 'questions' originally attached to a text slipped anchor and began to sail away on their own, did predispose the later Scholastics to privilege commentaries over the texts themselves. Scholasticism had, also, a feeble sense for history; it could be needlessly subtle, as John of Salisbury had already pointed out in the twelfth century; above all, in the setting of the 'Schools', it lost vital contact with the wider life of the Church. Congar's criticism of Scholasticism is not only of that movement in its decadence, for, as he remarks, the decay of an institution shows the mortality of some element within it. He holds that, nevertheless, the 'problem of Scholasticism' is nothing other than the 'problem of theology' as such: how to promote reason in the service of faith without eviscerating the realities of faith it would serve.

Like other students of theological method, Congar was much struck by the disintegration, or 'disaggregation' as he termed it, which Catholic theology underwent between the end of the fifteenth century and the start of the nineteenth. Around 1800, thanks in part to the impetus provided by Romanticism, Catholic theology started to seek the 'remaking of its former unity' (FT, pp. 180–2).

Following the approximate order of events, Congar describes the stages of this disaggregation as follows. The first pair to split up were Scholasticism and Christian mysticism, something which Congar ascribes, as we have just seen, to the unhealthy inflation of debate in the Schools, and of the rational techniques used in the latter. 'Ascetical and mystical theology' from the later Middle Ages onwards will stand not for the work of dogmaticians but for that of spiritual authors writing to nourish the lives of fervent souls. Congar notes that their identification of spiritual experience as a *locus theologicus* in its own right was of somewhat ambiguous value. The danger here was that Christian mysticism would cease to be a 'mysticism of the mysteries', nourished by Scripture, liturgy and theology itself.

The next unity to go was that of dogmatics and moral theology. Whilst in the high Scholastic period practical manuals for the use of confessors had flourished, the novel element surfacing in the late sixteenth century is the wholly self-sufficient moral manual, composed of a discussion of casuistic problems (like the mediaeval manuals) together with a lengthy preamble offering the reader a conspectus of the entire corpus of moral theology, which thus found itself severed from the rest of dogmatics. This carried with it the danger that people would forget the *theo*-logical character of Christian moral reflection, which is always reflection of the God who communicates himself to us in Christ, sanctifying us and requiring from us behaviour fitting to his Covenant.

Lastly, apologetics also took its birth from a rupture within the once unitary theological culture. Established as a separate discipline towards the middle of the seventeenth century, it soon came to invade theology itself in an improper way, rendering theology excessively polemical, and giving the question of rational credibility a disproportionate influence in the the act of faith.

Now Congar does not wish to deny that, at one level, theology is rightly said to have 'parts'. Positive theology is the *hearing* of faith in its scientific condition; systematic theology (Congar terms it 'theory', *la théorie*) is the *understanding* of faith at that same pitch of exactness. Looking at the same composite quality of theology from the standpoint of its content, rather than mode, the various treatises that have come to be the classical 'parts' of theology each deal with a subject matter in a way that makes sense, granted that one writer cannot be expert on everything. Again, theology can hardly help making use of a plurality of disciplines. Apart from philosophy which has been the preferred handmaid of Catholic theology, there are such disciplines as philology, exegesis and the history of doctrine, vital to positive theology, and again, in theology's apologetic cast of mind, such disciplines too as the history of thought and culture, and the philosophy of religion; and in relation to the 'practical' or 'applied' subdivisions of theology a host of auxiliary sciences or arts almost beyond number in relation to morals, pastoralia, missiology and ecumenism.

However, Congar insists with even greater force on the necessary unity which must contain the centripetal tendencies of theology, and finds in much of the theological activity of the eighteenth and nineteenth centuries an implicit search for the lost unity of the subject. Whether by way of the theological 'encyclopaedias' favoured in late eighteenth-century Germany, or the pursuit of the organic whole of revelation in later efforts, inspired by the Idealist and Romantic movements, in that same culture, or again in the papally-sponsored revival of Christian Scholasticism whose manifesto was the encyclical letter *Aeterni Patris* of Leo XIII, a common thread binds together an otherwise disparate variety of enterprises. It was an irony of fate that, just at the moment when the re-creation of the unity of theology seemed, albeit in very different conceptual and literary styles, to be once again within grasp, the flowering of historical criticism made the task of integrating positive and speculative theology that much more complicated. At the same time, the ugly offspring of the historical revival, historicism, entered the walled garden of Catholic intellectual life in the shape of Modernism (HT, pp. 180–92).

In the years before the Second Vatican Council Congar maintained that the pre-eminent task of his generation was to continue the overcoming of the theological disassociations already charted; the atmosphere in which this must be done is one of return to the sources, at once biblical, patristic and liturgical; in this, theology must not be scared by the spectre of Modernism into neglecting a long overdue incorporation of the data of the historical sciences 'without detracting from its unity of the laws of its work' (HT, p. 199).

THEOLOGY IN PRESENT AND FUTURE

How, then, does Congar see the *present* tasks of theology? Writing from the troubled standpoint of the immediately post-conciliar period, Congar does not hesitate to affirm his continued conviction of theology's value to the Church:

> As reflection on faith, theology is a scientific function indispensable for a full life of faith in the Church, indispensable for assuring the normal human possibility of communicating the faith, of faith's radiating out, faith's defence, faith's illustration. (STPT, p. 58)

At the same time, theology is necessarily bound up with the general situation of the Church at a given time, a situation which itself can rarely be wholly disentangled from the wider human world in which the Church is placed. And there's the rub. At the present time 'everything seems to be called into question or about to be': whether it be in encounter with modern philosophical currents, questions of biblical hermeneutics, or the problems posed by the sciences, and especially the human sciences. At the same time, among the people (to whom theologians might look for an inspirational *sensus fidelium*), a feeling for the Church itself is, it seems, being displaced in favour of the demands of personal awareness, an awareness which, if it remains Christian at all, does so in an existentialist mood more concerned with being in the human world than in the world of grace. Without wishing to minimize the seriousness of this situation, Congar invites us to consider its historic analogues: the menace of a full-blooded Aristotelean naturalism in the Middle Ages; the challenges of humanism and the Reformation in the Renaissance era; the replacement of the ancient *imago mundi* by the infinite, homogeneous, non-hierarchical universe of early modern science; the rise of critical historiography in the nineteenth century; the Modernist crisis. If the Church, its doctrine and its theological culture have survived these mighty onslaughts, then why not this last?

Congar's own modest proposals are divided into two: what he has to say about the problems that arise for Christian reflection at the level of the *donné* of revelation, in positive theology; and those which are posed in the course of the theological elaboration of that *donné* in systematic theology, termed by Congar *le construit*, since it is 'built' by thought from out of the deposit of the Word of God. With regard to the original 'given', Congar agrees that

> faith, aided by a serious historical culture, must appreciate the historicity of its own religious tradition and exercise a critical function *vis-à-vis* 'received ideas' in the Catholic world, which should be distinguished from the deep Tradition. (STPT, p. 73)

But, he warns, this must be done 'without haste and with prudence', because the historic forms, relative though they may be, are nevertheless

> the concrete forms in which the absolute values themselves have been lived out and transmitted. Moreover, faith has its own critical function to exercise in relation to what the world has to offer today's believer. Not to realize this is to lay oneself open to accepting as established facts, 'givens' which are potent only by 'the prestige of being current', and which, once incorporated into the work of theological construction, would behave there as foreign bodies. Too marked a reaction to the 'closed Catholicism' of the past will lead theology to adore what it once burned. In this connexion, the warning voices of

conservative Catholics can help theologians to achieve a 'more vigilant criticism'. (STPT, p. 73)

At the level of 'construction' Congar envisages the future of theology as lying in a union of theology with anthropology—but carried out in a non-reductionist way. Citing the Jewish philosopher Abraham Heschel, Congar remarks, 'The Bible is not man's vision of God but God's vision of man'.[4] Revelation concerns the human situation, yet it does so by way of a gracious initiative of God. Congar senses that a future theological anthropology will be written with the assistance of a 'method of immanence', showing how, sociologically and psychologically, humanity's own condition has its healing resolution in

> the historic fact announced by the Christian proclamation, because Jesus is self-identically the creative Word. (HT, p. 79)

Yet if Congar shows himself thoroughly familiar with the current state, and prospects, of Catholic fundamental and dogmatic theology, there is a curious disjunction between his theoretical approval, even enthusiasm for its speculative tasks, and his own theological practice which remains stubbornly an exercise in historical, and above all patristic, remembering. The contrast appears sometimes on the same page. Thus, in his triptych on the Holy Spirit, Congar offers an exceedingly 'open' definition of theology as

> the cultivation of faith by the honest use of the cultural means available at the time. (IBHS III, p. xiii)

But at the same time, he confesses to being himself something of a revelational 'positivist', a lover of facts, who has offered his own theology in the form of *dossiers* of documentation, perhaps, he writes, 'too much'. Such self-description should not be regarded, however, as a statement of penitence for a life devoted to theology as an activity of remembering. For Congar closes his preface to the final volume of his pneumatological trilogy with a resolute defence of neo-patristicism, a defence which should provide the context for understanding what his own definition of theology means. The criticism that he should speak not the language of the Fathers but 'that of today'

> raises the immediate question: Which language of today? And would it be more easily understood? All language is related to man and to whatever relationships he has, and that of the

Fathers of the Church is related to God and his mystery. It not only calls for a great intellectual effort to move into the country inhabited by the Fathers—it even requires a religious conversion. And is their language really so remote from the language of today? Their writings are certainly being widely read, questioned and heeded again today. (IBHS III, pp. xiii-xiv)

Notes

1 Cf. 'Le moment économique et le moment ontologique de la *sacra doctrina'*, *Mélanges offerts à M.-D. Chenu, maître en théologie* (Paris, 1967), pp. 135–87.

2 C. Péguy, *Le Porche du mystère de la seconde vertu* (Paris, 1929), p. 116.

3 'Church history as a branch of theology', *Concilium* (Eng. ed.) 57 (VIII.6; 1970), p. 88.

4 A. Heschel, *Man Is Not Alone* (New York, 1951), p. 129.

Conclusion

Congar's achievement is primarily that of a theologically gifted, historically-minded preacher and pastor, rather than a speculative or systematic theologian. The Russian Orthodox layman Leo Zander, in an encomium of Congar, called him 'the icon of Saint Dominic', another 'evangelical man' whose concerns were wholly enfolded in the Church's life.[1] In evaluating Congar in terms of Dominic of Calaruega rather than of Thomas Aquinas, Zander was surely correct. For whereas Thomas's theology in the *Summa contra Gentiles* is pastoral and missionary in its concern to address different categories of religious man at the points where they are, the *Summa Theologiae* marks a decisive shift to a systematic theology concerned with the rationale of faith in the interconnexion of its various aspects.[2] As Marie-Jean Le Guillou has fairly noted, Congar's philosophical equipment as a theologian was inadequate to take him far along the path of a speculative reconstruction of Christian tradition.[3]

Congar concentrates on an evocation of the divine economy in its richness, rather than an account of its foundation in what both the Greek Fathers and the early Scholastics would have called *theologia*. At the same time, he is fully aware that *someone* must produce a renewed theological ontology suitable to Catholic Christianity, since a purely phenomenological description, taken by itself, will not suffice (TT, p. 259).

Congar's religious impact has been as a reformer who meets conditions he himself laid down for authentic reformation: prophetic yet traditional. His monument is to be seen in the shifts of sensibility he has helped to bring about in the Roman Catholic Church and beyond: in a return to the sources at once biblical, liturgical and doctrinal, manifested in ecumenical generosity and a juster sense of the Church's communion as a complex of 'ministries', both lay and ordained.[4] Yet the means whereby he achieved all this can themselves only be termed theological. Probably Jean-Pierre Jossua is right to see Congar as recreating by his practice a more ancient model of what it is to be a theologian than that found, ever since the thirteenth century, in the world of the Western universities.[5] Like many patristic divines, his theology consists in the service of the Church's peace and welfare, and of the spiritual life and mission of all its members.

For the future, two questions suggest themselves. First, is not the desire of the human mind, thinking theologically, for intellectual coherence itself a genuine Christian need which it would be pastoral for a shepherd to meet? (Congar's own Bonaventurian–Thomist account of the aim of theology, cited above, implicitly admits this.) Hence the desirability of a more *synthetic* presentation of the multitudinous material Congar has salvaged from the tradition, material present in the form of an embarrassment of riches in much of his writing. Secondly, in an age marked by philosophical, and especially epistemological sophistication in the academy, and by ideological competition in the market-place, can Congar's consciously naïve reliance on the language of the Fathers suffice to ground the Trinitarian vision of a world moving, as the Church, to its eschatological completion? Is there not a need here for a Christian *ontology*, itself in close touch both with philosophical rationality and with revelation, to ground the synthetic presentation which may emerge from the students of Congar's work? Such an ontology, to be a suitable partner for Congar's theology, would have to be relational, like the Church 'of the Trinity'; Chalcedonian, with the finite and the Infinite in unconfused union, like the Church 'from Christ'; and marked by the dynamic integration of an ever richer diversity into an ever more complete unity, like the Church 'taken from amongst men' on its way to the Kingdom.

But no theology can properly aspire to be the last word on divine revelation: to do so would be, as Karl Rahner has written, to blaspheme. The voice of Congar is a contribution to what has been termed the 'symphony' of the theological life of the Church.[6] Congar's words belong to that great collaborative enterprise which is Catholic theology down the centuries. What will linger of his intellectual personality is the tireless and fruitful dedication to the salvaging of the historic culture in which Christian truth has come down to us, as well as to the invitations which the God of truth may be issuing to the Church of today.

> I've consecrated my life to the service of truth. I've loved it and still love it in the way one loves a person. I've been like that from my very childhood, as if by some instinct and interior need. When I was a young Dominican, I took over the motto of St Hilary which St Thomas Aquinas had first made his own, and which was reproduced on his statue at the house of studies at Le Saulchoir:
>
> Ego hoc vel praecipuum vitae meae officium debere me Deo conscius sum, at eum omnis sermo meus et sensus loquitur.
>
> I am aware that I owe this to God as the chief duty of my life, that my every word and sense may speak of him.[7]

A man whose personality is in some ways dry and dour, yet with a radiant love for Christian truth; a critic of Catholicism frank and even acerbic, yet filial in his devotion to the Church, Congar has been described by a fellow-prisoner of Colditz as rather like that not only 'mellifluous' but sometimes acid doctor, Bernard of Clairvaux.[8] Is not Bernard called 'the last of the Fathers'? The stream of patristic inspiration has evidently not run dry.

Notes

1 J.-P. Jossua OP, *Le Père Congar. La théologie au service du Peuple de Dieu* (Paris, 1967), p. 102.

2 Q. Turiel OP, 'La intención de Santo Tomás en la *Summa contra Gentiles*', *Studium* XIV (1974), pp. 371–401.

3 M.-J. Le Guillou OP, 'Yves Congar' in R. Vander Gucht and H. Vorgrimler (eds), *Bilan de la théologie du XXe siècle* (Tournai/Paris, 1970) II, p. 805. Congar admits as much himself in his 'Reflections on being a theologian', *New Blackfriars* 62.736 (1981), p. 409.

4 That is, these things at their best. For Congar's balance sheet of the post-conciliar period, see especially CC, pp. 37–49; EC, pp. 43–71; 'A last look at the Council' in A. Stacpoole OSB (ed.), *Vatican II by Those Who Were There* (London, 1986)/*Vatican II Revisited* (Minneapolis, 1986), pp. 337–58.

5 J.-P. Jossua OP, *op. cit.*, p. 53.

6 H. U. von Balthasar, *Die Wahrheit ist symphonisch. Aspekte des*

christlichen Pluralismus (Einsiedeln, 1972); J. Ratzinger, 'Le pluralisme: problème posé à l'Eglise et à la théologie', *Studia Moralia* XXIV, 2 (1986), pp. 299–318.

7 'Reflections on being a theologian', *art. cit.*, p. 406; cf. Thomas, *Summa contra Gentiles* I, 2; Hilary of Poitiers, *De Trinitate* I, 37 (PL 10, 48C).

8 Conversation of the author with the Rt Rev Denis Huerre, Abbot-President of the Benedictine Congregation of Subiaco on 26 March 1988.